The Story of
Charlotte's Web

The Penguin Book of Victorian Women in Crime (editor)
Dracula's Guest: A Connoisseur's Collection of
Victorian Vampire Stories (editor)
In the Womb: Animals (companion to a National Geographic
Channel series)
The Penguin Book of Gaslight Crime (editor)
Apollo's Fire: A Day on Earth in Nature and Imagination
Arsène Lupin, Gentleman-Thief (editor)
The Annotated Archy and Mehitabel (editor)
Adam's Navel: A Natural and Cultural History of the Human Form
Darwin's Orchestra: An Almanac of Nature in History and the Arts

The Story of
Charlotte's Web

E. B. White and the Birth of a Children's Classic

Michael Sims

BLOOMSBURY

LONDON • BERLIN • NEW YORK • SYDNEY

First published in Great Britain 2011

Copyright © 2011 by Michael Sims

The moral right of the author has been asserted

Quotations from E. B. White's unpublished manuscripts in the E. B. White
Papers, as well as photographs and drawings in the E. B. White Papers
(Collection #4619, Division of Rare and Manuscript Collections, Cornell
University Library), are used by permission of Cornell University Library and
the executors of the E. B. White Estate.

Bloomsbury Publishing, London, Berlin, New York and Sydney

36 Soho Square, London W1D 3QY

A CIP catalogue record for this book is available from the British Library

ISBN 978 1 4088 2305 7
10 9 8 7 6 5 4 3 2 1

Typeset by Westchester Book Group

Printed in Great Britain by Clays Limited, St Ives plc, Bungay, Suffolk

www.bloomsbury.com/michaelsims

To the amazing Dr. Patterson

CONTENTS

Introduction: Translating Yourself   I

PART I: ELWYN

Chapter 1: Enchanted   9

Chapter 2: Fear   19

Chapter 3: Trustworthy   33

Chapter 4: A Writing Fool   42

Chapter 5: Liebesträum   55

PART II: ANDY

Chapter 6: Olympus   69

Chapter 7: Interview with a Sparrow   86

Chapter 8: Crazy   96

Chapter 9: As Spiders Do   106

PART III: CHARLOTTE

Chapter 10: Dream Farm   127

Chapter 11: The Mouse of Thought   143

Chapter 12: Foreknowledge   157

Chapter 13: Zuckerman's Barn   169

Chapter 14: Spinningwork   175

Chapter 15: Paean   189

Chapter 16: Some Book   208

Chapter 17: Completion   226

Coda: After *Charlotte*   236

Acknowledgments   245

Abbreviations for Frequent Sources   249

Notes   251

Selected Bibliography and Further Reading   289

Index   297

Every unattributed quotation that appears before a chapter or between chapter sections is a comment by E. B. White on his own life. Because of house style at the *New Yorker*, where the first person plural resulted in such royal phrasing as "we saw it ourself," and because of White's habit of reminiscing about his childhood in third person ("I knew a boy"), these remarks appear in a number of voices, but they are all E. B. White's.

But real life is only one kind of life—
there is also the life of the imagination.

Introduction

TRANSLATING YOURSELF

M Y WIFE AND I were in Maine, standing in the barn that had belonged to E. B. White and chatting with the current owners, when I backed up to get a better view for a photograph and hit my head on something. Turning around, I saw a heavy old rope dangling in front of me, and I glanced up to where it was looped through a ring attached to a beam over the barn doors. Then I realized what I was staring at.

I turned to the South Carolina couple who had bought the White farm after his death in 1985. "Is this—"

Mary and Robert Gallant smiled and nodded. "Fern and Avery's rope? Yes."

"So it was real too."

I was in the barn that had inspired *Charlotte's Web* because, a few years earlier, I had been reading E. B. White's collected letters when I ran across his reply to a letter from schoolchildren: "I didn't like spiders at first, but then I began watching one of them, and soon saw what a wonderful creature she was and what a skillful weaver. I named her Charlotte."

"Wait a minute," I said aloud to the empty room. "There was a real Charlotte?"

This question was my first step toward discovering the story behind *Charlotte's Web*. Was there a real Charlotte, I wanted to know, or was White merely performing in this letter? As I traced the inspirations, discoveries, and research that White brought to one of the most acclaimed children's books of the twentieth century, I soon learned that there had been numerous Charlottes and Wilburs and Templetons in his life—but that there was indeed a particular clever spider who helped inspire the book.

Robert and Mary Gallant showed us the barn cellar, where White kept the pigs that inspired Wilbur. We saw the stalls for sheep and cattle, the doorway that had held the webs of countless orb weavers, the path through the woods, the rocky pasture with its view of Allen Cove and misty Cadillac Mountain on Mount Desert Island. We stayed for a while in the boathouse down by the water. As I sat at the plank table White had built, I noticed that a patterned brown spider hung motionless in a web to my right.

Many novelists admit that their characters are inspired by real individuals, but it seldom occurs to us that the authors of children's fantasy might make the same confession. Yet examples abound. Brave and levelheaded Alice was based upon the young Miss Liddell. The name of the Dodo in Wonderland reflects Lewis Carroll's stuttering trouble in pronouncing his true surname, Dodgson. Christopher Robin was not only a real boy but actually often played inside a large hollow tree on the Milne property—and Eeyore is gloomy because a broken wire in Christopher's toy donkey made its head hang low. Most of the characters in Beatrix Potter's stories she drew from life as well, because she spent her days with rabbits and ducks on Hill Top Farm in the Lake District.

So perhaps it isn't surprising to learn that, while composing his most popular book, E. B. White was obeying a cherished maxim: *Write about what you know.* He knew his characters from the barns and stables where he spent much of his childhood and adulthood. He knew a barn's earthy smells and sounds, the variety of its animal population. *Charlotte's Web* was hardly a simple report from the barn, as White claimed, but it grew from his experiences there with many animals. His return to a barn in adulthood ignited smoldering memories of the stable in his childhood home in Mount Vernon, New York. By creating a fictional hybrid of the most enchanted settings from both childhood and adulthood, White became one of the rare authors who solve what the American critic and essayist Clifton Fadiman once called "the standing problem of the juvenile-fantasy writer: how to find, not another Alice, but another rabbit hole."

White's attitude toward nature, with its unblinking response to the inevitability of death, strikes me as realistically hardheaded despite being wrapped in anthropomorphism. A farmer who wrote children's fantasies needed both ways of thinking. During my research I became fascinated by other aspects of White's personality as well. From childhood to old age, he was painfully shy, terrified of speaking in public or before a microphone—yet hugely ambitious and willing to try almost anything when no one was looking. Afraid of commitment and romance and confrontation, he hid behind animals even in his early love poems and letters to his wife.

Charlotte's Web is about animals because throughout his long life animals were E. B. White's favorite acquaintances. He had plenty of friends; he got along well with editors and other colleagues; he was happily married and a proud father, stepfather, and eventually grandfather. But he liked to spend as much time as possible around nonhuman creatures. "This boy," wrote White about himself as a child, "felt for animals a kinship he never felt for people." It's all the more impressive, therefore, how many people have felt a kinship with E. B. White.

The book for which most people cherish him fits into a long-standing tradition in literature—tales of animals who think and speak like human beings. From Aesop's ungrateful eagle through the trickster fox Reynard in the Middle Ages, from the autobiography of Black Beauty in the nineteenth century to the quest of Despereaux in the twenty-first, talking animals have accompanied us throughout history. Folklore around the world laments our loss of innocence in the golden age of humanity, when we could speak with our fellow creatures. In *Charlotte's Web* this lost era is childhood.

"Remember that writing is translation," White wrote to a student while composing this tale about the animals in his barn, "and the opus to be translated is yourself." *The Story of Charlotte's Web* explores how White translated his own passions and contradictions, delights and fears, into a book that has had astonishingly broad appeal across age groups and national boundaries. He knew that empathy is a creative act, an entering into another's reality. Empathy and curiosity happily coexisted in his spacious imagination. He studied the lives of spiders for a year before writing his novel. "I discovered, quite by accident," he explained, "that reality and fantasy make good bedfellows."

White himself emphasized that biographical writing is always a matter of interpretation—and he was wary of it. As I wrote this book, I became aware that, although I was determined to portray Elwyn Brooks White as accurately as possible, he was also becoming a character in a particular story I wanted to tell. I invented nothing; to the best of my ability, I misrepresented nothing. But by focusing on particular aspects of his career, such as his interest in natural history and farming, I have produced an account inevitably biased toward this facet of his life. His writings about government and civil rights, for example, find little room here, and beyond his childhood I don't explore his relationship with his family in depth. I hesitated over presuming to refer to White by his first name, but this is a personal book about his intimate daily life, so in childhood I call him Elwyn and in adulthood Andy—the latter a nickname he acquired at Cornell and kept for the rest of his life. This book is a biographical narrative distilled from hundreds of sources, but at every stage I tried to keep in mind that these people did not know what was going to happen next.

More than a quarter century after his death, E. B. White lives in our cultural dialogue. Some of his personal essays are canonized anthology standards, and to the connoisseur of the genre he stands beside Montaigne. Students underline every axiom in *The Elements of Style*. *Charlotte's Web* is better known than *Moby-Dick* or *Huckleberry Finn* and usually described as "beloved." How beloved? *Charlotte's Web* has already sold many millions of copies; in annual summaries of bestselling children's books in the United States, often it still outsells even *Winnie-the-Pooh*. For *Publishers Weekly*, a poll of librarians, teachers, publishers, and authors, asked to list the best children's books ever published in the United States, set *Charlotte's Web* firmly in first place. A 2000 survey listed *Charlotte's Web* as the bestselling children's book in U.S. history, with *Stuart Little* and *The Trumpet of the Swan* both following in the top one hundred. As of

2010, *Charlotte's Web* has been translated into thirty-five foreign languages. Thus every day somewhere in the world, countless children and adults are opening the book and turning to the first page and reading in English or Norwegian or Chinese or braille:

"Where's Papa going with that ax?" said Fern to her mother as they were setting the table for breakfast. . . .

Part I

ELWYN

Our rich experiences, as a child, were secret, unexpected, and unreported.

Chapter 1

ENCHANTED

He lived a life of enchantment; virtually everything
he saw and heard was being seen and heard by him
for the first time, so he gave it his whole attention.

THE COACHMAN SAID the eggs would never hatch. They were infertile, he insisted, as he tossed them onto the manure pile outside the stable. Elwyn's indulgent father had bought his children an incubator with fifty eggs and only these three failed to hatch. Barely more than a toddler, skinny big-eared Elwyn had stretched on tiptoe to peer over the edge of a workbench and excitedly witness the primordial ritual of chicks' tapping inside their shells as they prepared to emerge into the world. He didn't want to give up on the remaining eggs—and later he was the first to hear a cheeping sound outdoors. He ran outside, thrilled to find that the chicks had hatched by themselves, rejected by human beings and incubated by nothing more than the manure pile's own natural warmth. The birds were scurrying around, tiny and wet and rumpled, squawking hungrily.

The stable was behind the family's spacious home in Mount Vernon, New York. During his childhood in the first decade of the twentieth century, it was one of Elwyn White's favorite places. Painted pale gray, matching their big, handsome house even to the gables in the loft, it had a square towerlike peak that sported a weather vane as high as the domed turret on the front of the house. Elwyn loved the pungent scent of hay in the stable's loft above his head and of the dusty oats in their bin with its chute that carried grain down to the three stalls below. He liked to walk into the dark stable, through the coach doorway created when the main door slid left into its wall pocket, and find himself surrounded by the exciting wild scent of the horses themselves. In front the barn was lit by a small, four-paned window to the right of the sliding door, as well as by a couple of similar windows in the loft, on each side of the high door that opened downward for loading or unloading wagons. Still the corners inside were always enticingly dark, the light angling down and splashing on hay to turn it golden. Outside, to the left of the big door, stood a lattice-walled stall, and nearby was the fragrant manure pit whose warmth rescued the chicks. Sometimes the coachman, Jimmy Bridges—whom Elwyn admiringly followed around—smelled more horsey than human, mixed with the aroma of liniment and harness dressing. Bridges had his own private room upstairs among the hay bales. Most of the coachmen in the neighborhood were Irish immigrants, friendly to Elwyn and his pals; often he knew a friend's stable well without ever having entered his home.

Young Elwyn tended various animals in the stable, especially birds; he kept pigeons, chickens, a turkey, ducks, geese. He helped with the horses as much as he was allowed, and a hutch housed his soft-furred, big-eyed rabbits. But not every animal there belonged to the White family. Elwyn enjoyed watching the predatory antics of a stray cat that sometimes camped out under the stable. And sneaking around the stalls, as well as nesting under them, were thieves who added a frisson of villainy to the happy scene—rats. Elwyn saw no contradiction in loving mice and hating rats.

From early childhood, Elwyn found the dark and pungent stable intoxicatingly rich in romantic associations of life and death and adventure. But it was also a refuge where a thoughtful young boy could spend time by himself. From infancy, he saw barns and stables and farms in a symbolic light. The White family owned a toy farm that had belonged to Elwyn's mother in her own childhood—an entire nighttime scene with moon and stars in a dark blue sky over a bucolic farm with toy sheep and cows. "My dream farm," she called it. Every December she placed this peaceful miniature world at the foot of the Christmas tree, where its barn and duck pond were at Elwyn's eye level as he sprawled on the rug and wondered what was inside the colorfully wrapped Christmas gifts behind it.

Much of the year in New York, the stable was too cold for animals less hardy than the rats. Because his mother wouldn't allow a dog in her handsome and well-kept home, Elwyn kept his first of a long parade of canines, a bright-eyed collie named Mac, in the always dank cellar. The dog's bed was near the nineteenth-century servants' toilet that Elwyn sometimes sneaked down to use, although now and then he walked past it to secretly pee into the coal bin instead. Keeping Mac in the cold and dark left Elwyn racked with guilt. Whenever he opened the big door, the dog was already at the top of the stairs, waiting with barely leashed affection and smelling of ashes and darkness. In better weather, Mac was assigned a sheepskin-lined bed in the barn. He accompanied Elwyn on neighborhood explorations, panting happily and looking back over his shoulder to keep an eye on his young master. For years, as Elwyn returned from school in his beret and tweedy knickers and high-button shoes, he found Mac waiting at the same rendezvous to escort him home. Sometimes Elwyn would sneak Mac into the public library, where the dog would lie on the wooden floor nearby as Elwyn tried to decipher Virgil or worked on other schoolwork or simply prowled the shelves. The drowsy quiet of one spring evening at the library was shattered when Mac heard the high-pitched yap of a poodle outdoors and bounded to the window to reply in deep barks that resounded throughout the building—startling a white-haired old man nearby out of his browse through a magazine.

There were secretive animals in Elwyn's life as well. His many childhood illnesses included severe hay fever and other allergies. Once, while he was sick in bed, a fearless young house mouse not only visited him in his bedroom but proved interested enough in this large but quiet neighbor to gradually become a tamed pet. Elwyn supplied him with a house and watched rapt as the mouse explored with its tiny paws and turned its dark eyes to look up at him. He even taught it several tricks. He also kept an array of less cuddly pets—frogs and turtles, caterpillars and lizards, canaries and snakes—but they didn't come alive in his imagination the same way that mice did, with their fellow-mammal warmth and air of miniature humanity.

The basement and stable were havens for even smaller animals that caught the boy's eye. In every corner of the stable, from stall planks near the ground to roof beams above the hay-loft, different kinds of spiders spun their webs and waited for manna to fall into them. Some of the spiders were anonymous gray smudges in cobwebby corners, others elegantly patterned and displayed in the center of their web like a cameo in a neck-lace. All of the webs were wonderfully engineered and many were beautiful. The stable's sweaty animals and fresh dung at-tracted countless flies and other insects that ended their brief lives struggling in a spiderweb. Nearby, chicks were hatched and foals born. A scurry and squawk in the eaves might mean a snake or a rat had invaded the barn swallow's nest and eaten eggs. For a sheltered middle-class suburban child, the stable provided a memorable everyday glimpse of a world that managed to be both beautiful and cruel.

> *My first and greatest love affair was with this thing we call freedom . . . It began with the haunting inti-mation (which I presume every child receives) of his mystical inner life; of God in man; of nature publish-ing herself through the "I." . . . To be free, in a planetary sense, is to feel that you belong to earth.*

AT THE BEGINNING of the twentieth century, during Theodore Roosevelt's first term as president after the assassination of Wil-liam McKinley, Mount Vernon was already a popular bedroom community for New Yorkers. In Westchester County, border-ing the Bronx, it rose west of New Rochelle, perched high on shady, rolling hills. The three-story White family home, which they had built eight years before Elwyn's birth, was atop Ches-ter Hill, in a street inevitably named Summit Avenue, half an

hour's train commute from the center of Manhattan to the southwest. The hill was high enough that, on quiet days, a good wind
would carry to the house the somber foghorn of the lighthouse
that guarded the reef called Execution Rocks, on Sands Point to
the southeast across Long Island Sound. Gabled Queen Anne
houses with large wraparound porches lined Summit Avenue.
In this calm and leafy neighborhood, the scent of honeysuckle
and lilac drifted in at their windows, where the maid lowered
shades halfway on bright days but raised the window so that
filmy sheers fluttered in the breeze. The Whites' lawn at 101
Summit, on the corner of East Sidney, was bright with iris, pan-
sies, and showy-blossomed crabapple and pear trees, in delicate
contrast to the black cast-iron urn; in the spring, jonquils and
multicolored tulips outlined the property boundary along the
sidewalk, beyond the privet hedge. A sprinkling cart still pa-
trolled the streets to keep down the dust. Automobiles were just
beginning to be seen chugging by; their backfiring still brought
children and adults running to get a closer look at the newfan-
gled contraptions.

The house faced Summit, but the stable—that essential building and status symbol—faced Sidney. In Elwyn's early childhood,
the family traveled mostly in carriages. A subset of Whites could
get about in a simple buggy whose roof, in good weather, folded
back behind the single seat. Elwyn would come out of the house
onto the roofed porch above the carriageway and race down the
stairs to where a dark gelding stood hitched to a buggy, his eyes
watchful, his tail switching flies. But for Elwyn's parents to take
the whole family out required a surrey, with three wide seats
under a flat roof whose fringe never stopped wiggling during the
ride. As the well-dressed family filed down the stairs on special

occasions, the surrey looked elegant waiting in dappled shade
at the corner of the big gray house.

Elwyn thought of this house as his fortress. The ogee dome
on the octagonal turret inspired medieval daydreams. From one
of the tall windows on the third floor of the turret, above the
screened porch, he imagined himself watching enemies sneak up
from behind neighborhood trees or lurk around the privet
hedge that surrounded the yard. In his mind a brace of cannon
guarded the long second-floor porches. On hot, sticky summer
nights he slept alone in a hammock on the screened porch and
anxiously listened to nighttime noises in the yard. Why were
those leaves rustling? Was that a twig snapping? In the dawn he
woke to scuffing horse hooves and the creak of a wagon, followed by the glassy music of milk bottles being set down by back
doors. It sounded like home and safety to him. Weekend and
summer mornings, the rising sun found him going out to brave
the uncertain world, knowing that when he encountered trouble he could always return home to the safe family castle.

He was the last of seven children, but one before him had
left the world so quickly that her death in infancy was seldom
mentioned. Apparently Elwyn was unexpected. His father was
forty-five and his mother forty-one when Elwyn Brooks (soon
nicknamed En) was born on the eleventh of July 1899. Two of
his sisters were already in their mid- and late teens, and his
brothers Stanley and Albert were eight and eleven. By the time
he was three, his oldest sister, Marion, was already getting married. Elwyn's earliest faint memory was of the parlor roped off
to form aisles for Marion's wedding, which occurred shortly
before he turned three. The closest sibling to his own age was
his five-years-older redheaded sister, Lillian.

For the first several years of his life, Elwyn's Victorian parents dressed him in clothes as girlish as Lillian's. In 1902, when Elwyn was three, Buster Brown first appeared as a comic strip character—an angelic-looking prankster accompanied by his pit-bull terrier named Tige, who talked to Buster but to no one else. Soon Buster's sailor suit took children's fashion by storm. Just as Albert had worn a Little Lord Fauntleroy suit several years earlier, Elwyn spent much of his childhood in a white suit precisely like Buster's, its wide collar square in the back and coming to a point in front below the anchor on his shirt. The jacket was like an abbreviated dress over baggy short pants; black buckled shoes and an exaggerated wide-brim hat finished the costume. He wore this striking ensemble even while exploring the woods around Mount Vernon, and the comical hat would sometimes top off a different outfit.

Elwyn was surrounded by the usual household chaos of a large family—kids running up and down stairs, screen doors slamming, a talkative crowd at every meal. Albert and Stanley were always busy; they even built a boat in the barn. Stan, who was as skinny as Elwyn but taller, was nicknamed Bunny (further shortened to Bun) because he twitched his nose for comic effect. A born teacher who already wore professorial spectacles, he tutored his younger brother in arcane rituals such as handling a pocketknife without cutting himself or paddling a canoe in a straight direction. In clowning demonstrations, Stan also taught Elwyn about such physics concepts as inertia and momentum and introduced him to the mysteries of the harmonic circle on their pianoforte. To demonstrate centrifugal force, Stan cried, "Now watch this!" and twirled a bucket of water until it swung horizontally around him. Even tilted sideways, the water didn't run out. "You see?" Stan called to Elwyn. "Centrifugal force!"

In 1910, when he was eleven, Elwyn stood outdoors on a warm April night and peered up at the pale streak of Comet Halley in the sky—a celestial migrant on its way back from the other side of the solar system. The bushy-tailed comet was easily visible and a favorite topic of conversation. Many people, including the Whites' cook and maid, worried that it was a bad omen. A few scientists speculated that it might at least cause contagion as Earth passed through its tail. The newspapers reported that, as he had predicted, Mark Twain died during the weeks while the comet was at its brightest in the sky, just as he had been born during its nineteenth-century visit. The time-traveling comet had last been seen from Earth seventy-five and a half years earlier, when Elwyn's now deceased grandfather was about the age that Elwyn was now. The papers emphasized that the comet wouldn't be back again to visit Earth until 1986.

On summer nights Elwyn liked to sit on the front steps after dark. His was a quiet and safe neighborhood where each family knew the others on the block, and as the heat of the day faded, many people could be found strolling along the street or sitting on a porch and chatting. Elwyn would let his mind wander and his senses fill up with the sounds and smells of the safe, domesticated darkness around him. He could hear the clip-clop of carriage horses on their way to unknown destinations, the frenzied and exciting roar of an automobile a few blocks away, and feel the breeze that rustled the trees and hedge, where birds and squirrels and other animals lived lives so different from his own.

Gradually, in early childhood, Elwyn became aware that animals were actors themselves, living their own busy lives, not merely background characters in his own little drama. The song of the crickets rose and fell like a symphony. He realized that countless tiny musicians were out there in the grass, hidden but just as real as human beings, as alive as himself, playing music on their own legs like animated violins. He was a part of nature like every other creature. Yet he was very much an *individual* creature, which meant that they were too. Like his friend Freddie, whose voice he could often hear from the Schuler house across the street, like Miss Kirby with chalk on her hands at school, like his mother in her lace and bun chatting indoors behind him with his mustached and oratorical father, he was unique. Yes, he was a part of nature, but somehow he was the only Elwyn Brooks White.

Chapter 2

FEAR

I don't know whether a passionate love of the natural world can be transmitted or not, but like the love of beauty it is a thing one likes to associate with the scheme of inheritance.

WHILE HIS SIBLINGS were too far away in age to provide ideal playmates, Elwyn was born at the right time to get more attention from his father than had any of his brothers and sisters. Slender, dapper Samuel White, whose big gray mustache couldn't hide his affectionate smile, was a thrifty, formal, teetotaling businessman who came downstairs on week-day mornings in starched cuffs and wing collars. In his youth he had found time to write and publish a handful of songs, including one called "Sweet Dreams of Childhood." Starting at the age of fifteen, doing office chores, he had worked his way up through the successful New York–based piano manufacturer Horace Waters & Company, from clerk to branch manager and then officer of the company. By the time of his youngest son's birth, he was scrawling *Sam'l White* above the titles "General

Manager and Vice President." Now a prosperous man, Samuel appreciated his family and enjoyed his leisure hours with them. He could also spare more time now because he was employing other staff at home besides the coachman. As a baby, Elwyn was tended by an English nanny, a girl named Kezzie Simpson, who was so fond of her infant charge that she later named her own firstborn son after him.

Elwyn's maternal grandfather, Scottish-born William Hart, had been a successful landscape painter, a member—as was his brother James McDougal Hart—of the loose affiliation called the Hudson River School. William Hart's legacy to the family was about nature as much as art. Starting out as an eight-year-old apprentice to a coachmaker, decorating door panels, he later painted portraits until he built up enough of a career to concentrate on portraying nothing but his true love in life—landscapes. He found, wrote a contemporary journalist, "that there was an inexhaustible fund of subjects among our hills and beside our streams." Famed for his uncanny ability to remember minute details of a scene long after he observed it, Hart painted luminous panoramas of New England mountains and rolling hillsides in golden late-afternoon sunlight, such as his lovingly detailed portrait of Mount Madison rising behind the placid Androscoggin River in New Hampshire. He was also known for his skill in painting animals, especially the cows that, despite their careful breeding toward a one-sided goal beyond their control, became a popular symbol of harmonious nature among Hudson River artists. Hart became a fellow of various academies. Elwyn's mother referred to him as an Academician. His work sold for impressive sums; a painting might fetch five thousand dollars even in the 1870s. He was so well-known that his death in 1894, five years before Elwyn was born, prompted long obituaries in the New York papers. "He refused," declared the *Register*, "to be an imitator." Elwyn's brother Stanley was the only child to receive their grandfather's surname as a middle name. Tall and skinny and red-haired, he also resembled Hart and enjoyed painting and drawing.

Elwyn's mother, Jessie, cherished the family heritage. She may have married a businessman, she seemed to imply at times, but while Samuel was the son of a carpenter, she in contrast was the daughter of a famous artist. (Samuel's own parents had lived out a similar dynamic, his English mother losing access to her family estate because she married a mere tradesman.) Elwyn absorbed respect for artistic achievement from the very air he breathed at home on quiet Summit Avenue—and perhaps also inherited impatience with social conventions that didn't rate this kind of accomplishment highly. He browsed through his grandfather's sketchbooks, slowly turning the oversize pages and admiring details of animal figures laboriously worked out in charcoal before they made it into a painting—especially the cows, their tilted horns and split hooves, their milk-heavy udders and sad, dark eyes. The former home of William Hart was just across the street on Sidney Avenue. Jessie's stories about him made it easy for Elwyn to imagine his grandfather standing on the porch or sitting in his studio, finishing up a painting of hillsides bathed in the kind of slanting, moody light that his grandson also loved. In Jessie's photos, her father had the beard of a Civil War general but the faraway gaze of a poet.

Jessie Hart White was much older than the mothers of Elwyn's friends. Each morning she perched round metal glasses high on her nose and pulled her silvery white hair back and up to form an elegant bun. A gracious and kindhearted woman, she loved order and comfort, privacy and family. For a formal portrait with her youngest son, she wore a crisp white scalloped lace collar over a dark brocade dress and a large bow around the high waist. Jessie seldom appeared energetic; even her smile looked almost sad. By the time of Elwyn's birth, his mother was already experiencing the diminished vigor that would mark the rest of her life. Elwyn once found her in the seldom-used reception room, across the hall from the parlor, lying stretched out on the sofa. Always expecting the worse, Elwyn immediately thought she was dead, but she turned out to be recovering from a harrowing ride on a runaway horse. In household administration she managed the cook and maid but tired quickly. Yet her temperament was mostly optimistic and uncomplaining, like that of the man she married. She was plainspoken in contrast to his grandiloquence, but they enjoyed each other's company. Together they traveled often in the United States and once even crossed the Atlantic via steamship to visit Europe.

Elwyn was closer to his father. "All hail!" wrote Samuel White to his son on his twelfth birthday, "with joy and gladness we salute you on your natal day." Elwyn and Lillian rolled their eyes at their father's rhetorical flourishes but basked in his pride. Father and son spent many daytime hours exploring the world together. Samuel once wrote to Albert, who was attending Cornell, about recent adventures with Elwyn: "Oh, the joy, the joy of my little boy; we have lots of good times together." After dinner Samuel and Elwyn engaged in wide-ranging conversations. Samuel was interested in the outdoors and the strange workings of nature. On warm mornings he liked to ride his bike around the reservoir east of town, before catching the train to work, and admire the sunlight and birdsong.

Sometimes, after Sunday lunch, he would herd the family onto a succession of rattling trolley cars for a trip to the New York Zoological Park, which had opened the year Elwyn was born. (It was later renamed the Bronx Zoo.) They would happily file past fat wrinkled elephants and monkeys like caricatures of people, or stand peering up at the foreshortened, oddly patterned necks of giraffes. The family took young Elwyn along to see the hugely popular Broadway extravaganza *The Wizard of Oz*. It bore little resemblance to L. Frank Baum's children's book from 1900. In place of feisty Toto was Imogene, a cow whose vaguely bovine frame was inhabited by an actor. But these discrepancies didn't stop Elwyn from admiring the cyclone, the marching chorus girls, and the wonderful snowstorm that buried in white all the actors and even the chorus dressed as poppy blossoms.

Samuel also took them to the circus in Madison Square Garden. Several times they attended spectacles at the colossal Hippodrome Theater on Sixth Avenue between Forty-third and Forty-fourth. Built by the architects who had conjured Luna Park at Coney Island, the Hippodrome had a stage literally a dozen times larger than an average Broadway theater. Circus acts might entertain between an opera and a drama. An entire circus could stomp the boards at once—hundreds of costumed people and animals cavorting. Once at the Hippodrome Elwyn thrilled to the ranks of beautiful, scantily clad women marching down a flight of stairs into a pool and somehow remaining underwater for several minutes before walking back up to rapturous applause.

When he asked his father how this miracle was accomplished, however, Samuel's hemming and hawing left Elwyn doubtful about what he had formerly considered paternal omniscience.

Naturally the children of a piano manufacturer were kept supplied with musical instruments. Besides a grand piano, the house held at various times a reed organ and even a high-backed Waters player piano called an Autola. Stan played violin and Elwyn himself tried mandolin and piano and even took cello lessons. In 1908, at the age of nine, he informed Albert, who was already at Cornell, that their father had given him a new book of sheet music. "I know eight pieces out of it already," he bragged, and added, "I am also composing pieces too." Other siblings could turn to a banjo or a guitar or even a set of drums. Elwyn would visit his father's Manhattan office and hear somewhere in the building the distant melancholy sound of a piano being tuned.

Every Christmas Eve, a local German band would stand in the yellow glow of the gas lamp at the corner of Summit Avenue and play their uncertain way through "Heilige Nacht." Then the musicians would appoint an envoy to venture onto the porch and ring the front doorbell. Inside his cozy home, intoxicated with the nearness of Christmas, Elwyn always waited for the ring as if watching a familiar play. It was traditional that Samuel would open the door himself to reveal the grinning, pink-cheeked, and snow-frosted musician, who had tucked his shiny horn under his arm to ring the bell, because Samuel already had in his pocket a holiday token with which to thank the band. Soon the carolers could be heard launching into a new chorus down the block, at the home of Elwyn's friend Billy Denman. Going up to bed, Elwyn would pause at the top of the stairs, looking down at the wrapped parcels hanging on the hat rack in the hall. They held candy that was expected to last until New Year's Day. It never did.

> *I suffered nothing except the routine terrors of child-hood.*

WITH THEIR INCOME and family legacy, Samuel and Jessie White would have been able to join Mount Vernon's influential moneyed class with its own narrow definition of Society. They simply didn't want to. Both paid far more attention to their family than to the world beyond Summit Avenue. Few outsiders entered their home; they seldom invited a guest for dinner. This limited social circle was one reason why, as his older siblings drifted away from home into college and jobs and marriage, quiet Elwyn depended more and more upon his own imagination for entertainment.

Unfortunately his imagination naturally led him toward a brooding anxiety about almost everything. How easily the human body can be harmed, he thought; how dark the attic is. Once he woke from a nightmare to find moonlight pouring across his face from the open window, its light so bright he thought for a terrified moment that a prowler was shining a flashlight into his eyes. He stopped leaving the window uncovered at night. Instead he carefully pulled its shade down to keep the moonlight out, but for years he felt anxious during every full moon.

His daylight hours were haunted in different ways. Elwyn loved weather. He found rain exciting. He basked in sunshine and cavorted in snow. But for him the unpredictable variety of the elements meant an equally capricious internal weather.

Practically from birth, he was prone to sudden wild shifts in mood—spiking and flat, ecstatic and melancholy—and many a mood swing was brought on by even a slight change in weather. A sudden cloud over the sun could mean despair. A change of wind might turn him toward melancholy as if he had scented grief. Weather wasn't the only source of such changes; anything might leave him disconsolate, especially something the obsessively visual child saw out in the world. Riding on a train, he could happily enjoy the silent, scrolling movielike panorama of strangers and houses and streets until a chance glimpse of a lonely backyard seemed to tug him down into depression. A late-winter thaw, melting the snow off his favorite sledding hill, might spiral him into a yearning nostalgia for the exquisite pleasures that would now be lost.

He was often on the edge of sadness or fear. The thought of school especially frightened him. As a small child, he threw screaming tantrums, begging to stay home in his beloved family castle instead of entering kindergarten. This battle he naturally lost. Soon he found himself sitting in a circle of tiny chairs at the Lincoln School, P.S. 2, with other children his own age, listening to Miss Green read aloud and dodging the hand-holding ambitions of a pudgy girl he didn't like. While Elwyn was still in kindergarten, Stanley taught him to read, beginning by handing him a copy of the *New York Times* and demonstrating how to sound out the syllables. All too soon his mother was dressing him in a white linen suit and taking him to enter the first grade. Thanks to Stan's early tutoring, Miss Hackett and his fellow students discovered that he was already a skilled reader.

Then came a parade of other teachers—the Misses Kirby, Crosby, Douglas, Ihlefeldt, Bourne, and Sheridan, and espe-

cially pretty Mrs. Schuyler, his favorite in the elementary years
and for a while the unwitting focus of a crush. Schooldays began with assembly in the auditorium. First the students rose
and, accompanied by shuffling feet and clearing throats, faced
the American flag. It had forty-five stars until 1908, when an
extra star was added a week before Elwyn's ninth birthday, because Oklahoma had become a state. Four years later two more
stars were added, for New Mexico and Arizona. The students
held their right arms out at an angle toward the flag, beginning
with the palm facing downward in a military-looking salute but
gradually turning their hand over during the brief patriotic oath.
Written by Christian Socialist minister Francis Bellamy with the
goal of publicizing the utopian socialism in the novels of his
cousin Edward Bellamy, it was published in the popular children's magazine *The Youth's Companion* only seven years before
Elwyn's birth. It had since become established in public schools:
"I pledge allegiance to my Flag and to the Republic for which
it stands, one nation indivisible, with liberty and justice for all."
Then the principal read a Bible passage and a student recited a
brief poem or other bit of inspirational literature. Elwyn kept his
gaze on pretty Mrs. Schuyler, who at the end of each day's assembly played the piano piece that accompanied students as they
marched out of the auditorium together.

The school was a squarish, two-story brick building with
huge chimneys and a dome in the center of the roof. In warm
weather, the shades were drawn halfway down and the lower
window raised, just like at home. White curtains fluttered around
terra-cotta pots on the windowsills, where flowers provided a
welcome splash of color that drew Elwyn's eye away from the
dusty blackboards and rows of desks. He stared longingly out

the window until recess, when he could rush outdoors with classmates and stand in the shade of big-armed oaks. Then some of the boys would squat in their short-pants suits, with berets tilted above bare knees, and draw a ring in the sand and shoot marbles. The girls giggled and chased each other and stood chatting in their light blouses and dark skirts and even darker stockings, some of them in hooded cloaks that made them look like Red Riding Hood.

Although he enjoyed learning, Elwyn never really liked the straightforward and disciplined classes in reading, spelling, arithmetic, and geography. The school's raucous, foot-tramping, elbow-nudging crowds frightened him. Slight and shy, a natural target for bullies, he hated the unwelcome intimacy of the bathrooms, with their slate urinals and masculine bluster. Before he even reached his teens, he was worrying about how to make a living after he graduated from high school into the scary world of adulthood, marriage, and profession. Worry haunted his days. He was never abused but always anxious, never deprived but somehow always nostalgic. And he was miserable when more than two people at a time looked at him. A crowd of any kind could overwhelm him—even a glimpse of too many faces on a trolley car—without its members being aware of their collective power. He lived with a paralyzing fear of having to speak in front of the school during each morning's assembly. Every day, as he walked or biked to school, he agonized that he would have to face this ordeal. Because his surname began with one of the last letters in the alphabet, however, and because most speaking occasions began over again at *A*, he was spared—except for a single, terrifying occasion.

Elwyn was not a particularly bookish child. He enjoyed

reading, but it was seldom the first activity he chose. On rainy days he would turn to his Meccano set, to its endlessly reusable metal gears, wheels, and plates that could be built into a train or an auto or a fort. Invented during his infancy, Meccano had soon taken the toy world by storm, and Elwyn seldom tired of its infinite recombinations. Once a blizzard closed school— announced early in the morning by a particular blast of the fire department's siren, magically transforming an ordinary day into a sudden holiday. Elwyn delightedly climbed up to the attic and hid out from the white-covered world, alone, inventing his own world with Meccano. The attic also housed a cabinet exhibiting a beautiful collection of birds' eggs, a family legacy from the Victorian era's passion for natural history. The eggs were arranged in order of size, from a hummingbird's white pearl to an ostrich's six-inch egg looking like a roc's from the *Arabian Nights*. Through watching chicks hatch in the barn and admiring the elegant simplicity of the collection in the attic, Elwyn began to think of eggs as the symbol of life and versatility, the almost divine source of mystery.

Whenever possible, though, he preferred adventuring outdoors. Sometimes he joined friends at the Stratton family's barn, where the coachman would let the boys climb up into the loft and swing wildly down on a rope. He loved the wild sense of freedom as he fell toward the ground and then flew up into the sky. He didn't care much for team sports, but he played games at twilight in the neighborhood alleys with a few friends, especially with Freddie Schuler across the street and Billy Denman next door. When a boy in the neighborhood needed a football inflated, he would call upon Freddie, who was legendary for his lung capacity. Inflating the ball was a chore that might require half an hour or longer. First they had to find a lacing needle, which usually required a search through the harness closet in the barn. Then they had to loosen the football's laces, working them free with fingernails or the thick end of the needle, and wiggle off the rubber band that sealed the air bladder. The remaining air would whoosh out cool and stinky. Finally Freddie would blow up the bladder far beyond anyone else's abilities. Then every task had to be done in reverse. Always the bladder bulged a little through the lacing as the boys began to throw the ball to each other on the quiet streets and lawns.

Elwyn also played with an older boy named Kenny Mendel, whose menagerie of pets—including a monkey and a raccoon in cages—he envied. One dusty September day, Kenny told Elwyn that turtles lay eggs. This theory shocked him, but then he began to wonder how turtles would reproduce if they *didn't* lay eggs. The parade of ever-shifting but disturbing mental images haunted him. Where exactly did baby turtles come from? He found the thought of sexual reproduction confusing and frightening. Why did Kenny laugh when he talked about how rabbits behaved in their hutch when no one else was around? Was it like what bucks must somehow do with does to make fawns? To Elwyn this hypnotic enigma felt shameful, even tragic.

He wanted to ask someone about this problem, but he had learned that he couldn't discuss such a topic with his father. When a cute mongrel pup had followed Elwyn home from school, he was allowed to keep it only one night. The next morning his father said in a low, awkward tone, "My son, I don't know whether you realize it, but that dog is a female. It'll have to go."

"But why does it have to?"

"They're a nuisance." His father was clearly embarrassed. "We'd have all the other dogs in the neighborhood around here all the time."

To Elwyn such a scenario sounded like heaven. But his father was adamant, leaving Elwyn with an inarticulate suspicion that there was something shameful and unclean about being female. And now he was afraid that Kenny would laugh at him. So Elwyn kept his late-night worries to himself.

Meanwhile the boys roller-skated and climbed trees. After Christmas 1908, Elwyn proudly sailed down the sidewalks astride the first kid-size bike in his neighborhood. In the snowbound New York winters, he sometimes hitched a ride on a horse-drawn sleigh down the hill by their house, to visit the post office and look for letters from Albert and Stanley. When Elwyn turned eleven in the summer of 1910, his parents gave him his own canoe, an elegant dark green invitation to freedom and adventure. And every winter he waited for the first day cold enough to freeze the pond in the Dell at the foot of the hill, so he could play hockey or skate across its silvery frozen surface. He loved sledding even more. With other kids who gathered near the hilltop White home, Elwyn coasted his Flexible Flyer sled downhill on Sidney Avenue, gaining speed on its S curve and swooping down into the Dell. Sometimes Lillian rode on board behind him while he lay on his stomach and steered the movable forward runners. He enjoyed sledding so much that now and then, whenever he had to go to bed before the older kids, he would take off his striped stocking cap and tall, lined boots and glumly trudge upstairs and sit at the window in his room, gazing enviously down at the fortunate few who were still out there sledding in the darkness.

As he grew older, he spent a great deal of time outdoors alone, especially during warm weather. He prowled the pond's shore. He lifted damp masses of leaves to look for salamanders, frogs, and garter snakes. He watched shoals of minnows and their darting shadows and raised his eyes to follow the zigzag flight of swallows. He walked east several blocks to Wilson's Woods, down by the Hutchinson River, which formed the unofficial eastern boundary of Mount Vernon, where he waded through anemones and jack-in-the-pulpit to capture lizards to take home as pets.

Many of his explorations took place at night, when he wandered farther afield than his parents realized. Sometimes he biked across the bridge from Pelham to Hunters Island on the Sound, then walked the rest of the way, setting off alone in the dark, on the uneven trail along the shore and then across a hill. Behind some large rocks was a hideaway where during the day boys occasionally sunbathed in the nude. Elwyn crept through the dark and aromatic marsh, past croaking frogs and unexplained scurries, to the boulders, beyond which distant lights shone on the water. There this short and slight boy, who would run blocks to avoid a bully but who felt safe in the natural world when no other people were around, would shed his clothes and slip into the black water. Quietly, so as not to attract attention, he swam in the darkness, floating under the stars, unafraid.

Chapter 3

TRUSTWORTHY

This seemed an utterly enchanted sea, this lake you could leave to its own devices for a few hours and come back to, and find that it had not stirred, this constant and trustworthy body of water.

SUNDAY-AFTERNOON RAMBLES IN the surrey led to the family's first realization that Elwyn had severe hay fever. Every time he rode behind a horse, his eyes itched and burned and he had terrible sneezing fits. In the spring of 1905, when he was not yet six, he speculated to his father that it was the smell of the horse itself that bothered him. Samuel looked skeptical but, unable to deny his son's persistent symptoms, consulted a doctor. He came to their house, climbed the steps to Elwyn's room, sat down in the rocker, and asked both him and his mother a number of questions. Afterward he sat rocking and thinking, while Elwyn and Jessie waited for the verdict. Suddenly the doctor stopped rocking, rose, said to her, "Douse his head in cold water every morning before breakfast," and walked out. They adopted this alleged treatment immediately and kept at it for almost two years. Every morning a rubber sprayer baptized Elwyn with chilly water. Though it was a cold and messy way to start the morning, he finally decided it helped him wake up quickly and made him eager to jump into the day instead of lie in bed daydreaming. At times he seemed to be allergic to the lawn, the cat, and the dog, but he didn't let inflammation deter him from enjoying their company. The companionship of animals was more important than anything else he could think of.

Another treatment had a better impact on his life. By the turn of the century, physicians already considered the still wooded northeast a healthier environment for respiratory illnesses than sooty suburban New York. Many doctors prescribed country getaways for stressed city folk. Inland freshwater lakes offered tempting lures that were unavailable on coasts, including lazy waves and a generally safer environment. Parents liked being free of threats—real or imagined—from sharks and undertow, and even Maine seldom had a problem with bears. Tree-surrounded calm water tended to warm up quickly in the morning and treat swimmers well. A seasonal migration to lake country had become a staple of upper-middle-class life, with camping also available, especially for the poorer. Elwyn was also born during a widespread back-to-nature movement, its many ecclesiastical and secular apostles preaching the physical and moral virtues of fresh air, camping, and outdoor sports, as well as the inspirational camaraderie of skinks, orioles, and cinnamon ferns.

In July 1905, around the time of Elwyn's sixth birthday, Stanley and Albert journeyed to the lake country of Maine to visit friends. For some reason, Samuel followed them—and the beauty and quiet of the region was a revelation to him. By the time he returned to Mount Vernon, he had an exciting announcement to make: immediately, he was going to treat the entire family to four weeks at a rustic lakeside camp on Great Pond, the largest of many lakes surrounding Belgrade, a village ten miles northwest of the capital in Augusta. Rich in waterways, Maine could offhandedly call a nine-mile-long lake a pond; Belgrade had once been called Pond Town. Messalonskee Stream powered the Cascade Woolen Mill in nearby Oakland, helping the town maintain its title as "axehead capital of the world."

As a result, Elwyn discovered a world far beyond Mount Vernon, because this adventure-filled, pollen-fleeing northern trek became an annual tradition. The trip began when the usually frugal Samuel—who normally rode the dusty commuter train to work every day—purchased eight decadent first-class round-trip Pullman tickets. With bulging trunks in tow, the excited family began the journey by riding the local train into the smoky clamor of Grand Central Station (later Terminal), at Park Avenue and Forty-second Street. Out front a statue of Mercury, with winged hat and strategically girded loins, peered down at streets crowded with trolley cars and horse-drawn ice wagons. Already one of the larger and busier train stations in the world, the thirty-four-year-old Grand Central was undergoing reconstruction as the Whites began their first trip in 1905. They sat on giant pewlike benches in the already renovated passenger waiting area. From there they boarded the Bar Harbor Express, a seasonal night train that had begun its passengers-only service three years earlier, with Grand Central as its southern terminus and Belgrade as one of its last stops before Bar Harbor. It was a popular holiday train for those fortunate souls who could afford an escape to the resorts of the north.

The family boarded the Express at eight in the evening and slept all night; to be ready for the next morning, Jessie White slept fully dressed. Elwyn was dazzled by this first big journey. He loved the luxurious green walls of the Pullman car and the shiny ladders to the upper berths and the clever way a sort of hammock was strung nearby to hold his clothes. He couldn't stop playing with the controls of the three-speed electric fan and thought the loud and gloriously shiny toilet worthy of a caliph. And he was impressed when a porter clamped a pillow between his teeth so that he could tug a white pillowcase up around it.

They arrived in Belgrade midmorning the next day, trading the din of the New York station for birdsong and fresh pine-scented woodland. To carry the trunks to camp, a smiling farmer met them at the train station in a horse-drawn buckboard with redolent hay in the back. Samuel seemed to Elwyn calmly authoritative during the commotion about the many heavy trunks. The fresh country air helped keep the mood high during the jostling, buttock-numbing ten-mile ride to the camp.

Soon they caught their first glimpse, through light-trunked birch and dark-boughed spruce, of the beautiful Messalonskee Lake. Their lakeside cabin was only a few steps from the boulders that mediated between land and water. From the first approach along the sandy path between tree roots, under angular pines and softer-looking deciduous trees, the cabin promised freedom from the usual routine back home in swept and white-painted Mount Vernon. Its porch was rakishly supported by stacked stones at each corner; its posts still wore their bark like living trees; and its three plank steps lacked risers, so Elwyn could see through them to the darkness underneath—a region, he soon discovered, visited by skunks and raccoons during the night. A wooden sign above the door prophetically identified the cabin as HAPPY DAYS. Albert and Stanley, seventeen and fourteen, on the first trip, had to themselves a separate small cabin nicknamed within the family "Alstan." Behind the cabin a path led to a wooden outhouse, where a can of chloride of lime was kept near the seat-hole to sprinkle in afterward for reducing the stench. Rustic sapling furniture sat on the porch, but Samuel would sometimes carry a more finished—and thus disappointingly ordinary—rocking chair outside, where he sat in the shade and read, making the porch creak softly as he rocked.

They rented their cabin from a local farmer who also provided meals. Twice a day the family strolled up to the farmhouse, choosing on the dirt road one of its three avenues—the wheel track on each side or the middle path worn down by generations of horses. Elwyn liked strolling along surrounded by the buzz of grasshoppers and sparrows in the fields, amid scattered dark juniper saplings and boy-height shrubs with toothy fernlike leaves (aptly named, he soon learned, sweet fern). In good weather indoor tables and chairs were carried out under the trees and a French-looking alfresco lunch set up, complete with white linen tablecloth and glassware. Laughter and the clink of silverware could be heard a long way off. Even at the camp, at least for meals and other social occasions, men and boys usually wore their ties, and women and girls wore ankle-length dresses. Energetic Albert, now a tanned and handsome young man, occasionally would appear for lunch without tie and even collar. Samuel would sit at the head of the table, smiling, his gray mustache tilted as he surveyed the clan, and Jessie would smile back in her serious way.

Elwyn loved coming indoors at dark and falling into bed upstairs beside the rusty-screened window, gloriously tired in all his muscles after a long day outdoors, then lying there listening to the night sounds, the crickets and frogs, the haunting plaint of a surprisingly nearby owl. He also loved waking up at dawn, ahead of everyone else. He lay in bed smelling the old lumber of the walls and the fresh woodland scent coming in through the screen, hearing a bird chorus start up, the gentle lap of waves nearby, the scutter of a red squirrel on the roof. The cabin walls were partitions that didn't quite reach the ceiling, so he had to step quietly to keep from waking the others. He wanted the new day to himself.

Downstairs, gently closing the door behind him, he would cross the wooden porch and walk softly down the steps and out to where his cherished canoe was moored, with ELWYN in white block letters on the green bow. It was a fine wooden Old Town canoe, built by a company founded around the turn of the century in Maine; bringing it to Belgrade Lakes meant bringing it home, to within a hundred miles of where it had been built. With his skinny, bare knees in the air, he paddled away from shore. Even though he was now too far away to wake his family, the lake's cathedral hush kept him moving as quietly as possible, carefully holding up the paddle so it wouldn't bump the gunwale as he aimed the bow toward the primeval mist rising from the water. Later, when he approached the shore, the cabin looked wonderfully inviting in dappled shade behind the birch whose joined white trunks glowed in the low-angled sunlight.

Elwyn wasn't the only one who loved boats. Sometimes the family fished from silent rowboats—bass were plentiful, as well as perch—while at their feet waited bait worms in tin cans lidded with damp green moss. There were always other canoes as well; once Samuel, fully dressed, capsized his and came home drenched. They plied the lake waters in the small motor launch that Albert and Stanley had built in the stable back home. Samuel had had to call in a boatbuilder to help them finish the job, but the boat was finally lakeworthy. The boys christened it after their mother, and Samuel shipped the *Jessie* northward to await the family's arrival in Maine. As if her name stenciled on the hull wasn't enough, they added a triangular white pennant in the bow that also read JESSIE. With Stanley or Albert commanding the three-horsepower, one-cylinder engine, Jessie rode in her namesake, clutching a stylish parasol to protect her from the sun. Despite her fear of water and inability to swim, she kept smiling her anxious smile. At the stern a yachting flag leaned back, trailing a corner in the water. Sometimes they all traveled together in the boat across the lake to visit Bean's store near the mills on Belgrade Stream. Everyone piled out of the rocking boat for a welcome cold birch beer or Moxie soda, while admiring the prettified postcard scenes and the miniature birchbark canoes. Sometimes Samuel would tempt the gods by loading a heavy case of Moxie into the boat.

Over the years, as the family vacationed at Belgrade throughout Elwyn's childhood, the sound of boat engines grew ever more common in the lake region. The inboard oil engine for small boats had been developed in the last decade of the 1800s, a few years before Elwyn's birth. Both one-cylinder and two-cylinder versions—the stutter and choke of the former, the more reliable purr of the latter—contributed a background sound to Elwyn's drowsy summers. Despite his dreamy air, Elwyn was

practical in a hands-on way. During these family holidays, he
learned the nuances of the one-stroke engine until he could cut
the motor at the right moment for the boat's momentum to carry
it smoothly to dock or shore. He developed this technique only
after humiliating occasions on which the engine sputtered out
and left him adrift or raced the boat ahead to slam the hull into
pilings.

In Maine as in Mount Vernon, Elwyn spent time alone or in
daydreams. Surrounded by his boisterous family but off in his
own world, he would stare down through clear water to where
pebbles and driftwood on the bottom were crossed by the shadows of water bugs and eclipsed by the boat's own shade. He
observed how schools of minnows seem twice as populous as
they really are because of their own darting shadows. He noticed how animals that came down to the shore and fished for
mussels during the night chose the most prominent spot they
could find—the ends of logs jutting out of the water—to leave
their droppings as a territorial signal. He listened to the sound
of a cowbell drifting across the water. And he held the paddle
motionless and let the canoe drift so that he could silently watch
a tall, long-legged great blue heron rise squawking into mist over
the lake.

Often Samuel interrupted the family's leisure to coax them
into posing for a photo. The film's long exposure times required
absolute stillness—not a natural condition for children and teenagers, whose frozen expressions left them looking theatrically
solemn when the photos were printed back home. Such poses
were especially difficult for the dogs, who often wound up a
vaguely canine blur in the final print. In Mount Vernon, mounted
side by side a foot or so from the binocular lenses of a wooden-

handled stereopticon, the pair of arched, duplicate photos achieved the illusion of three-dimensionality. Yet they never quite captured the magic of Maine—days so full and rich they instantly created in Elwyn an aching nostalgia that lasted for the next eleven months, until the family could return the following August. It was an ache he never lost.

Chapter 4

A WRITING FOOL

In those days, my imagination was always immensely stirred by the thought of wildlife, of which I knew absolutely nothing but for which I felt a kind of awe.

ELWYN SPENT AS much time as possible outdoors, and often his mind stayed outside even when his body was in the house. When he read a book, usually he chose one about animals, especially about animals in the wilderness instead of those he saw in the tame streets of Mount Vernon. His own moody, careening mind automatically invested the world around him with personality and character. He was drawn to writers who portray animals, or even the inanimate, with empathy that instills a sympathetic curiosity about the secret peering lives around us.

Around the time of his birth at the end of the nineteenth century, nature writers were lining up on both sides of a controversial issue—how to respond emotionally to nature, especially to animals, while keeping a science-informed reality in mind. The two camps were represented by writers such as John

Burroughs and John Muir, who advocated nature's virtues in a lyrical way but did so within a rigorously factual approach, and William J. Long and Ernest Thompson Seton, who dramatized and fictionalized the natural world while claiming to be meticulously realistic. The question wasn't about the role of personification in literature. No one argued that *Black Beauty* was a bad book because it portrayed animal characters from the inside, imbued with human thoughts and emotions. Such books were avowed fiction, even fantasy. The uproar was over narratives that tried to have it both ways, claiming to be realistic—presenting true-to-life animal behavior—despite their outrageous tales of cunning, vice, and derring-do.

Elwyn gobbled up such tales. He enjoyed books by both Long and Seton. A Connecticut minister, William J. Long spent his summers in what he called "the wilderness" of Maine, until he found it too crowded with tourists—some of whom he may have drawn there with his own writings—and switched his allegiance to Nova Scotia. His first book was published in 1899, the year Elwyn was born. Many more followed, including *Beasts of the Field, Fowls of the Air*, and *Following the Deer*, and Elwyn read all of them. Some were published in the Wood Folk Series. Especially after Maine summers became a part of Elwyn's life and imagination, Long's first book, *Ways of Wood Folk*, could grab his attention even while lying around unopened. On the spine flew three wild ducks. The front of the green cloth cover showed a fox in silhouette on a lakeshore. Alert, its long brush almost touching the ground, it peered from under the low branches of an old pine, watching a canoe on a lake with behind it a sharp-edged northern mountain.

Charles Copeland's black-and-white frontispiece drawing

showed an encounter between fox and man on a snowy woodland path, the fox wary but surprisingly unafraid, the man—
mustached like Elwyn's father—simply standing and watching,
with his hands in his pockets. Clearly this was no hunter. Long
presented himself not as a scientist but as a gentle, admiring
observer who frequently participated in the wild goings-on that
he described. The book's dedication read, "To Plato, the owl,
who looks over my shoulder as I write, and who knows all about
the woods."

Elwyn especially enjoyed Long's book *A Little Brother to the
Bear*. The cover explained the title by showing a bear, in silhouette and facing away from the viewer, looking up at a raccoon
that sprawled across the curve of the cartouche surrounding the
title. The first chapter, "The Point of View," presented Long's
manifesto:

> Two things must be done by the modern nature writer who
> would first understand the animal world and then share his
> discovery with others. He must collect his facts, at first hand
> if possible, and then he must interpret the facts as they appeal
> to his own head and heart in the light of all the circum-
> stances that surround them. The child will be content with
> his animal story, but the man will surely ask the why and the
> how of every fact of animal life that particularly appeals to
> him. For every fact is also a revelation, and is chiefly inter-
> esting, not for itself, but for the law or the life which lies be-
> hind it and which it in some way expresses.

Elwyn loved Long's habit of referring to many animals of
the region by what he described as their Milicete names. The

Algonquin-speaking native people known by European-American settlers as the Milicete or Maliseet originally called themselves the Wolastoqiyik after the Wolastoq (St. John) River in northern Maine, New Brunswick, and Quebec. Using an approximation of their terms, Long called a chickadee Ch'geegee-lokh-sis, a lynx Upweekis, a porcupine Unk Wunk. In Long's vocabulary, a toad was always known by the onomatopoeic name K'dunk. A woodcock was Whitooweek and a bear Mooween. Long called a raccoon Mooweesuk, describing it as "a pocket edition of Mooween in all his habits," a typical sweeping generalization. The animals' names sounded like a North American version of *The Jungle Book*. Their adventures sparked Elwyn's imagination in part because some of them he ran across on his own adventures and others lurked still in the wilderness of the north and of his mind.

Ernest Thompson Seton, a prolific Scottish-Canadian naturalist, author, and illustrator, was even more explicit about his concentration on "the law or the life which lies behind" animal behavior. In his 1901 book *Lives of the Hunted* (dedicated "To the Preservation of Our Wild Creatures"), he wrote that in his stories he tried to "emphasise our kinship with the animals by showing that in them we can find the virtues most admired in Man." A few years earlier, in *Wild Animals I Have Known*, he provided a legend for deciphering his morality plays: "Lobo stands for Dignity and Love-constancy; Silverspot, for Sagacity; Redruff, for Obedience; Bingo, for Fidelity; Vixen and Molly Cottontail for Mother-love; Wahb, for Physical Force; and the Pacing Mustang, for the Love of Liberty." From any scientific point of view, this was bestiary turf. Yet Seton explicitly stated, "The material of the accounts is true," even if he added a telling confession: "The chief liberty taken, is in ascribing to one animal the adventures of several." Seton was a talented illustrator committed to accuracy; during his student days in Paris, he had been notorious for dissecting dog carcasses to better understand their anatomy. He was also an experienced outdoorsman. Yet his allegedly objective stories were steeped in old-fashioned Victorian romanticism.

In 1903, when Elwyn was four, the American nature writer John Burroughs published in the *Atlantic Monthly* an essay, "Real and Sham Natural History," in which he denounced Long, Seton, and their literary kin as "nature fakers." Burroughs was no data-driven lab scientist; he promoted nature appreciation, not just the accumulation of facts. "To absorb a thing is better than to learn it," he insisted, "and we absorb what we enjoy." He believed passionately, however, that falsely dramatized or even unconsciously mythologized nature writing performed a disservice to readers and besmirched a noble calling. He dismissed this subgenre of supposedly fact-based nature fiction as "yellow journalism of the woods" and suggested retitling Seton's best known book as *Wild Animals I* Alone *Have Known.* "Are we to believe," Burroughs asked, "that Mr. Thompson Seton, in his few years of roaming in the West, has penetrated farther into the secrets of animal life than all the observers who have gone before him?" As early as his first book, 1871's bird-oriented essay collection *Wake-Robin*, Burroughs had felt the need to assure his own readers, "I have reaped my harvest more in the woods than in the study; what I have to offer, in fact, is a careful and conscientious record of actual observations and experiences, and is true as it stands written, every word of it."

Over the next few years, while Elwyn was happily reading

Long and Seton and their colleagues such as Charles G. D. Roberts, these authors defended themselves in what the *New York Times* called "the War of the Naturalists." Finally President Theodore Roosevelt entered the fray. Taking time out from declaring Oklahoma the forty-sixth state and inventing the presidential press briefing and posing for photographs advertising his manliness, Roosevelt loudly sided with Burroughs in an essay titled "Nature Fakers" in *Everybody's Magazine*. "We don't in the least mind impossibilities in avowed fairy tales," wrote Roosevelt; "and Bagheera and Baloo and Kaa are simply delightful variants of Prince Charming and Jack the Slayer of Giants. But when such fables are written by a make-believe realist, the matter assumes an entirely different complexion." He called the writings of Jack London and these other authors "unnatural history."

Meanwhile Elwyn reveled in the exploits of Upweekis and Wahb and Bingo and began to create his own stories about nature, not in the least worried about his habit of attributing human emotions to animals.

I was a writing fool when I was eleven years old and have been tapering off ever since.

EVERY FIRST OF September, while the family sat on the southbound train and looked past their own reflected sunburns as Maine's dense dark pines slowly gave way to the softer-looking and more varied deciduous woods of New Hampshire, Elwyn thought about his glorious summer. Back in Mount Vernon, he daydreamed about Maine. As he grew up, he felt an ever stronger urge to preserve the memories. When he was in his midteens, Elwyn designed, handwrote, and illustrated a pamphlet, carefully titled in capitals BELGRADE LAKE AND SNUG HARBOR CAMPS, for his friend Freddie Schuler. Handwritten text surrounded pasted-in photos of the White family members cavorting outdoors—Stanley in the stern of the *Jessie*, Elwyn in his own canoe, Albert with a flock of sheep from a nearby farm.

"Maine," wrote Elwyn ecstatically,

> is one of the most beautiful states in the union, and Belgrade is one of the most beautiful of the lakes of Maine . . . The beauty of the surrounding country makes tramping a pleasure, and the well packed country roads are fine for bicycling or horseback riding. The lake is large enough to make the conditions ideal for all kinds of small boats. The bathing also is a feature, for the days grow very warm at noontime and make a good swim feel fine.

As a result, Freddie came along one summer to the camp. Other writing efforts proved equally encouraging. Elwyn's tribute to Maine was part of an already long-standing tradition in his young life—the conservation of beauty in prose. Early on he began distilling his memories by writing down his response to the world. By the age of eight, he was consciously looking at a blank sheet of paper and thinking, "This is where I belong." Soon afterward he began writing his thoughts in a diary. Many of the entries concerned his questions about the natural world, such as how animals get along in their private lives, how birds hatch already knowing how to build a nest, or what a fox is trying to communicate when it barks in the night. "I wonder," he often wrote to himself, "what I'm going to be when I grow up?"

Often he felt lonely amid the bustle at home, distant from

the noise even while surrounded by it. When he could be persuaded to come indoors, he spent a lot of time by himself, writing down his day or imagining wild adventures, achieving
uneasy accord with life only by laboriously translating his response to it into words on paper. He borrowed the big, heavy
Oliver typewriter from Stan's room to type up his thoughts,
enjoying the labor of carrying it to his own desk, the zipping
sound of the platen rolling until it caught the sheet of paper and
pulled it down, and the bold ruckus of hammering the keys.
When he wondered how to spell a word, he would run down
the hall to Albert's room and consult the fat *Webster's* dictionary
that sprawled on an iron tripod, sagging with the weight of its
knowledge. This was the family source of information to which
Samuel referred all questions about words.

In spring 1909, Elwyn drew upon his experiences with the
secret visitor in his bedroom and wrote a poem, "To a Mouse."
The budding author, not yet ten years old, bravely sent the
poem to *Woman's Home Companion*. To his astonishment and
delight, they accepted it for publication—and even awarded
him a prize for it.

Not surprisingly, he soon took aim at other literary targets.
He was devoted to *St. Nicholas* magazine and waited excitedly
for its monthly arrival in the mailbox—the inviting red-framed
cover, the two-column pages with their sprawling illustrations
of dragons and soldiers, pirates and dogs. Founded in the early
1870s, it was at first edited by Mary Mapes Dodge of *Hans
Brinker* fame. Her original mission statement for the magazine
included the line "To foster a love of country, home, nature,
truth, beauty, and sincerity," and practically from birth Elwyn
tended to think of these virtuous attributes as interrelated. But

Dodge's manifesto began with a goal that broke ranks with the didactic children's literature of earlier decades: "To give clean, genuine fun to children of all ages." The first page of the first issue playfully asked, "Glad to see us? Thank you. The same to you, and many happy returns." Of course, the periodical reflected its era in unsavory ways as well. Nonwhite Americans were subservient helpers at best; the depiction of foreigners changed as Americans became involved in one conflict after another—the Spanish-American War, the Great War—with Spaniards or Germans or Italians turning unsavory or heroic in turn.

By the turn of the century, *St. Nicholas* was unquestionably the foremost periodical for children. It had introduced both Louisa May Alcott's *An Old-Fashioned Girl* and Mark Twain's *Tom Sawyer Abroad*. Mowgli had fled Shere Khan across its columns. Cedric Errol, called Little Lord Fauntleroy, had first appeared in these pages, inspiring an international fad for cutaway velvet jackets and lace collars on little boys. During Elwyn's time the magazine ran stories, poems, and articles of all sorts, from biographical profiles of prominent Americans—one about Lincoln was called "The Matterhorn of Men"—to the ongoing series "Stories of Useful Inventions" ("Next to its usefulness for heating and cooking, the greatest use of fire is to furnish light to drive away darkness. Man is not content, like birds and brutes, to go to sleep at the setting of the sun").

Best of all in Elwyn's eyes, *St. Nicholas* was devoted to animal stories. Besides featuring work by the best-known authors and illustrators of the day, it was gaining a reputation as a cradle for writers. In 1899, the year Elwyn was born, it launched the "St. Nicholas League," a monthly writing competition edited by

Albert Bigelow Paine, author of the charming *Hollow Tree and Deep Woods Book* for children. Three years after the contest's founding, a girl named Vita Sackville-West wrote in about her ancient home of Knole in England. Elwyn read several poems in *St. Nicholas* attributed to a girl in Maine named E. Vincent Millay, until in 1910 she retired (she was almost nineteen, the age limit for contributors) in the same issue that included a prize-winning photograph by a precocious teenager named Scott Fitzgerald. The June 1911 issue included among the honorable mentions for a drawing contest a Mississippi boy named William Faulkner. Others whose prose Elwyn read in its pages included a Massachusetts girl named Katharine Sergeant.

Soon Elwyn joined these august ranks. Two houses up the street lived a slightly older boy named E. Barrett Brady, who was also a reader of *St. Nicholas*. Barrett was the son of a writer for the *Saturday Evening Post*, and with backstage savvy he advised Elwyn to stress in his early writing efforts the evergreen theme of kindness to animals. Elwyn agreed that this was a smart commercial notion as well as an ideal with which he was genuinely sympathetic. He followed Barrett's advice. In June 1911, the month before he turned twelve—just about the time that Lillian, his last older sibling, was leaving home—*St. Nicholas* published his first story.

When the June issue arrived, he would have flipped past the frontispiece, a painting of a Huck Finnish boy with a rakishly torn straw hat, and the photo-illustrated article on "Model Aëroplanes of 1911." The "St. Nicholas League" pages were in the back. There under the elegant logo with its seasonally changing oval illustrations, the first listing under the heading "Prize-Winners,

Competition No. 136" was his name and enough additional information to prove to skeptics that he, not some other Elwyn B. White, was the author to whom they were referring: "PROSE. Silver badges, Elwyn B. White (age 11), Mt. Vernon, N.Y."

On the opposite page was his story, under an ode to June by fifteen-year-old Doris H. Ramsey, and to the left of a hymn to trillium by twelve-year-old Elsie Louise Lustig, on a busy double-column page that also held photographs of a footrace and the roaring falls of Niagara embodying the theme "At Full Speed." Elwyn had given the narrator's dog the name of the dog from William J. Long's *A Little Brother to the Bear.*

A WINTER WALK
BY ELWYN B. WHITE (AGE 11)
(SILVER BADGE)

I awoke one morning in my little shanty to find the ground covered with snow. It had fallen rapidly during the night and was about six inches deep.

I dressed, ate a good breakfast, did some of the camp chores, and set about taking down my snow-shoes and preparing them for wintry weather. Soon I heard a short yelp which reminded me that Don, my pointer, had been left hungry. I gave him some bones and a few biscuits, then, pulling on my heavy overcoat and buckling the snow-shoes on my feet, we started out in the frosty morning air to pay the forest a visit.

Such a morning! There was a frosty nip to the air that gave life to everybody and everything. Don was so overjoyed at the prospect of a walk that he danced and capered about as if he was mad. Jack Frost was busy for fair! My nose and ears were victims of his teeth.

After a small stretch of smooth ground had been covered we entered the forest.

All the trees wore a new fur coat, pure white, and the pines and evergreens were laden with pearl. Every living creature seemed happy. Squirrels frisked among the branches, chattering because we trespassed on their property. Once in a while we caught an occasional glimpse of a little ball of fur among the fern, which meant that br'er rabbit was out on this cold morning. A few struggling quails were heard piping their shrill little notes as they flew overhead.

All these harmless little wood creatures were noticed by Don and he wanted to be after them, but I objected to harming God's innocent little folk when He had given the world such a bright, cheery morning to enjoy.

The issue offered a range of other material. That month's installment in the exciting series "Nature Giants That Man Has Conquered" featured electricity. Motion pictures were all the rage, and so was the collecting of bird eggs; thus there was a cartoon of birds watching a movie called *The Nest Robber*, showing other birds retaliating against an egg-stealing boy. This month Edward F. Bigelow's column, "Nature and Science for Young Folks," was titled "Jewels on a Spider's Web" and featured images by Wilson A. Bentley, who was already famous for his exquisite photographs of snowflakes, taken through a microscope. The article instructed readers in how to photograph dewdrops on a spider's web: "Perhaps the smallest object on which these tiny, pearl-like formations may be observed is a thread of a spider-web. Here the drops are so small that they do not elongate, but keep a beautiful spherical form."

Two years later, the magazine awarded Elwyn one of its half dozen monthly gold prizes for another piece about animals, "A True Dog Story," about the heroic nature of another White family dog—Beppo, an Irish setter. One morning in Maine, as Elwyn and Albert and Stanley walked across a pasture with their father, short-tempered steers left their herd to challenge the trespassers. Instantly Beppo raced to the family's rescue, barking and transforming himself from bird retriever—the breed's traditional job—to a combination guard and herd dog. Not that *St. Nicholas* accepted everything that Elwyn submitted. The October 1914 issue, for example, honorably mentioned but did not publish his drawing "The Love of a Mother Rabbit." Despite this and other setbacks, he kept scribbling and typing. Distilling his experience into words on a page was the only way he could find to prevent his daily life from blowing away like clouds.

Chapter 5

LIEBESTRÄUM

The only sense that is common, in the long run, is the
sense of change—and we all instinctively avoid it, and
object to the passage of time, and would rather have
none of it.

IN THE AUTUMN of 1913 Elwyn found himself at Mount
Vernon High School, where the desks looked very adult to
him with their ink-stained and initial-carved wood, equipped
with inkwell above and book cubby underneath. Each desktop
was attached to the black cast-iron back of the chair in front of
it, creating a solid-looking row where Elwyn sat among his fellow students and drew diagrams of bean plants and scribbled
$a^2 + b^2 = c^2$. He awkwardly translated Caesar and reluctantly dis-
sected frogs. In class, however, he kept getting distracted by the
silk stockings that had recently begun to peek out below
schoolgirls' midcalf skirt hems.

Naturally girls were becoming a big preoccupation, but Elwyn was unable to act upon his growing interest in them.
He was afraid to try. Not once did he take a girl to Proctor's

Theatre on Gramatan Avenue, which from its opening day in his midteens featured vaudeville shows twice a day. He never took a date to the cinema and sat holding her hand before the stylized gestures of a silent film, sneaking a glance at her face in the light from the black-and-white dramas or the blundering big-hatted Keystone Kops, which became popular in his early teens. He didn't once laugh with a girl over Charlie Chaplin. But he permitted himself to daydream. Somewhere out there in this busy world, he would think, is a girl who is going about her daily life, just as I am, and we are unaware as yet of each other's existence, but someday we'll get married and live together.

In the spring of 1916 Albert brought home a Buick that was several years old but still looked shiny and sophisticated to Elwyn, with its running boards, high, round headlights, and flat, squared-off windshield standing as straight as a wall. "To get in right with the girls," Albert explained to his younger brother, but he failed to impress Elwyn with the glamour of dating. Elwyn held a tiny wire in place while Albert cranked the engine, which emitted a consumptive cough and then a death rattle. A cloud of dark smoke rose and a neighbor came running to learn where the fire was. From his first encounter, Elwyn loved cars. So did the boys' father. After selling two of his three carriage horses, Samuel bought a Pope-Tribune runabout, which looked sporty with its long, straight steering shaft and boxy engine bonnet, until he replaced it with a sleek Maxwell roadster whose short running board swooped forward and back to form elegant tire guards like wings. But Samuel never learned how to drive and left that particular twentieth-century excitement to his children.

After school, adventurous stocking-clad girls were drinking a sweet, new import from the south called Coca-Cola instead of Moxie, the bitter yet long-established favorite. Soda shops were a recent innovation but already popular, touting ice cream and soda pop as weapons of temperance. Yet Elwyn never went there to share a Coke with a girl. He looked wistfully around at other boys' impressive accomplishments—dashing down a football field with raucous enemies in pursuit, nonchalantly blowing smoke rings, twirling a girl on a dance floor under romantic lights. He tried his own specialties, such as riding his bike while sitting backward on the handlebars, but no girls seemed to notice. He could play several tunes on the piano, even pieces from *Aïda*, but doing so at home did nothing to attract the opposite sex. Sadly he concluded that he didn't possess any of the talents that girls seemed to admire. He watched amazed as other boys chatted easily with girls at parties or in the school hallways, as if interactions with them were not only less than agonizing but might actually be fun.

Not even his favorite and determined sister Lillian, who was attractive and popular with boys, could persuade him to attend dances or go out with girls. But she didn't stop trying. Anytime they were at home in the parlor together, she might suddenly crank up the Victrola and grab Elwyn's hand and drag him into the middle of the room to dance. As long as she could keep him captured, before he wriggled away, she tried to teach him popular dances such as the one-step, for which the recent hits "The Old Gray Mare" and "Walla-Walla Man" had been written. Soon, however, he would tear himself free and run out of the room.

Only once did Lillian succeed in trapping her brother into

something approaching a date with a girl—and the bait she used was not the girl herself but the *Arabian Nights* allure of Manhattan. Elwyn had visited his father's piano company office downtown and accompanied him into New York's teeming streets on many other excursions, such as the Hippodrome outings or an occasional matinee. The towering buildings and bright lights glowed in Elwyn's imagination, and their memory tempted him into finally accepting one of Lillian's invitations. She asked him to make a fourth member of a party she was putting together to attend a tea dance at the elegant Plaza Hotel. Elwyn went along with her and her boyfriend and another girl. One of the more luxurious hotels in the city, built only the decade before, the Plaza towered nineteen stories above Central Park South, just across Grand Army Plaza from the majestic French Renaissance château that had been built by Cornelius Vanderbilt II but looked worthy of the Sun King. Elwyn was dazzled by the glamour of it all. Dressed up in their best, they sat at a tiny table on the edge of the grand dance floor, so near the action that dancers sometimes brushed against them as the teenagers nibbled sophisticated cinnamon toast and nodded in time with the band.

Lillian must have thought she had wrought a miracle because this stylish outing inspired the most uncharacteristic decision of Elwyn's teenage life. He had long admired a pretty but reserved girl named Eileen Thomas, who lived a few houses up Summit Street. To Elwyn, her older brother J. Parnell, a handsome lad who greeted him cordially on the street, was simply the mortal who had the good fortune to share a house with the enchanting Eileen. Elwyn's secret crush on her forced him to watch her from a distance at every available opportunity and to tremble whenever he passed before her house. But they seldom had occasion to speak to each other. Apparently she was un-aware of his interest until the day he suddenly called her up because he had decided to take her to the Plaza for a tea dance and cinnamon toast.

Waiting until his parents had gone downstairs for dinner, he stepped out of his room and into the telephone closet in the hall. With his heart pounding, he took the earpiece off the wall hook, asked the operator for the Thomas home, and greeted Eileen's mother with the line he had practiced: "Hello. Can I please speak to Eileen?"

"Just a minute. Who is it, please?"

"It's Elwyn."

He stood there trembling in the telephone closet, practicing his next line: "Hello, Eileen. This is Elwyn White. Hello, Ei-leen. This is Elwyn White."

Unfortunately Eileen greeted him with "Hello, Elwyn." He was committed to his script, however, and insisted on begin-ning his side of the conversation by saying, "Hello, Eileen. This is Elwyn White." After a crumb of nervous chat, he got up the nerve to ask, "Would you like to go tea-dancing with me at the Plaza Hotel?" Eileen conferred with her mother and returned to the phone and said yes.

A few afternoons later, dressed in a carefully coordinated and spiffed-up outfit and with money safely tucked into his in-side pockets, he met Eileen at her house and walked her down the street to the train depot. On the journey into the recently rebuilt Grand Central Terminal, they sat side by side, but in-stead of chatting or looking at each other, they both stared awk-wardly at the back of the seat in front of them. Almost prostrate with nervousness, Elwyn kept going only through sheer physical momentum. In the city, they then faced a seemingly hazardous walk across to Fifth Avenue, where they caught a bus up to Fifty-ninth Street and the Plaza. Even when they were seated in the fairy-tale hotel and eating cinnamon toast, things did not turn out quite as Elwyn had planned. He began to sweat terribly. Soon his shirt was clinging to his skin. Gradually overcoming his fear, he summoned a faint memory of the moves his sister had tried to teach him and led Eileen onto the dance floor for a humiliating caricature of a dance. Then, his suit drenched in sweat, he led the slow retracing of their steps and returned her to Summit Avenue. It never occurred to him to suggest dinner.

The next time he fell in love, he kept his feelings to himself. His most romantic experience during his years at Mount Vernon High was skating with a pretty blue-eyed girl on the large and skater-thronged Siwanoy Pond. Her name was Mildred Hesse. She was popular at their school and many boys enjoyed skating with her.

One memorable late afternoon, the red winter sky faded toward twilight behind dark pines as they skated past campfires burning here and there around the shore. With Elwyn and Mildred firmly grasping one end each of a strip of bicycle tape, to hold them together but lend flexibility on the surface, they floated lazily across the ice, sometimes pulling closer together as they explored the iced-over streams that snaked away from the pond and into the woods. Their breath hung in the still air and they skated through it, with the ice creaking beneath the whisper of their skates. Then both took off one glove and he held her hand, which was wonderfully warm.

He never tried to further his acquaintance with Mildred

elsewhere, but his thoughts kept returning to her bright eyes and graceful ankles. One evening after skating with her, a chilled but happy Elwyn rode the trolley home. For some time, the Summit Avenue house had been empty of other children. Quiet Marian had been married for more than a decade to a fun-loving young man about whose fiscal recklessness Samuel often complained, and they had several children. Clara, who acted as carefree in adulthood as she had in childhood, had married a smitten young attorney whose commanding presence promised future accomplishments. Stanley and Albert were at nearby Cornell, and Lillian—one of Elwyn's favorites and the only daughter to attend college—was at Vassar and resisting numerous offers of marriage. Elwyn was on the verge of big changes himself; next fall he would follow his brothers to Cornell. That evening, he carried his skates inside the still house, past the umbrella stand and the big oak hat rack, and for a long time he sprawled on the settee in the front hall, staring up at the ceiling and listening in a blissful romantic haze to Franz Liszt's "Liebesträum [Dream of Love] #3" magically playing itself on the Autola. The popular piano solo's lyrical, rolling chords circled the same melody, returning and dancing away again in melancholy variations, winding down to end on the individual notes of a slow, broken chord. Finally Elwyn climbed the stairs and went to bed.

DURING HIS SENIOR year at Mount Vernon High, Elwyn was assistant editor of the school's literary magazine, which was named with classical flair *The Oracle*. His thoughts turned often to the war that had been cutting a bloody swath across Europe for two years. In one sketch for the magazine, he reimagined

Henry Wadsworth Longfellow's poem *The Song of Hiawatha*, creating a version in which the peacemaking Onondaga chief marries to evade his tribe's military draft. In an editorial, Elwyn abandoned satire and simply argued that the United States should remain out of the conflict. He enjoyed the quick response from readers that he experienced in writing for periodicals.

Most of his literary heroes at the time were newspaper columnists. In nearby New York City alone, every day the groaning presses rolled out hundreds of thousands of copies of the *Tribune*, the *World*, the *American*, the *Times*, the *Globe*, the *Sun*, and many others. In 1913, popular *Evening Mail* columnist Franklin Pierce Adams, known as F.P.A., moved his column, "Always in Good Humor," to the *New York Tribune*, where it became "The Conning Tower." It was a favorite of Elwyn's. Like many other columnists of the era, F.P.A. printed couplets and jokes and newsbreaks by contributors, and Elwyn aspired to become one of them.

Another of his favorites was Don Marquis, whose column "The Sun Dial" appeared in the *New York Sun*. Marquis was one of the liveliest and most literary of the columnists. Poet, satirist, author of stories and novels, Marquis had the kind of professional versatility that the practical but restless Elwyn instinctively admired. His column was regularly visited by an array of outrageous characters, including, by Elwyn's midteens, Hermione and her Little Group of Serious Thinkers, a series of free verse parodies featuring a naive young woman whose balloon-like brain wafted about on every faddish wind, especially the current popularity of Arthur Conan Doyle's favorite hobby, spiritualism. In spring 1916 Marquis introduced a new character who immediately caught Elwyn's attention. On March 29,

Marquis opened "The Sun Dial" with gibes at contemporary news stories. Former associate Supreme Court justice Charles Evans Hughes was running against Woodrow Wilson, who was seeking a second term as president. Pancho Villa, a Mexican revolutionary, had just crossed the border and led a murderous attack on Columbus, New Mexico. There was a new outbreak of scarlet fever. Then Marquis—or rather the often fictional first-person narrator of Marquis's column—described something he witnessed in his office:

> We came into our room earlier than usual in the morning, and discovered a gigantic cockroach jumping about on the keys. He did not see us, and we watched him. He would climb painfully upon the framework of the machine and cast himself with all his force upon a key, head downward, and his weight and the impact of the blow were just sufficient to operate the machine, one slow letter after another . . . Congratulating ourself that we had left a sheet of paper in the machine the night before so that all this work had not been in vain, we made an examination, and this is what we found:

> *expression is the need of my soul*
> *i was once a vers libre bard*
> *but i died and my soul went into the body of a cockroach*
> *it has given me a new outlook upon life*
> *i see things from the under side now . . .*

The cockroach, named Archy, went on to narrate the story of Freddy, a rat who had been a rival poet in their previous life. He was still jealous of Archy's talent and was one of many

enemies that Archy now had to evade. Then Archy instructed
Marquis, ". . . leave a piece of paper in your machine / every
night you can call me archy." Elwyn admired the literate cockroach, who began to appear regularly with dispatches from the
poverty-stricken and overlooked underside of urban life in the
land of plenty. He embodied both Elwyn's ambitions as a writer
and his sense of being small and insignificant, as well as his
need to hide from people. And Elwyn joined Archy in hating
rats. Elwyn liked most animals but he had always thought of
rats as greedy, thieving villains. The first column mentioned a
cat who, soon named Mehitabel, became Archy's foil and part-
ner in literary crime. Claiming to be a reincarnation of Cleopatra, Mehitabel was everything that Elwyn was not—free, wild,
uninhibited, brave, reckless, promiscuous. Marquis had taken
the most common and disdained creatures of the city and had
turned them into an urban Huck and Jim, casually working in
Latin epigrams, critiques of capitalism, mockery of police, and
asides such as Archy's remark that theology was his favorite
sport. Elwyn watched and admired and longed to emulate.

He graduated from high school in January 1917 but didn't
leave for Cornell until fall. With a thousand dollars' worth of
scholarships—ten times Cornell's annual tuition—he had no
financial worries. But the future did not look rosy. The month
after Elwyn graduated, President Woodrow Wilson announced
that the United States had severed diplomatic relations with
Germany, and by April the nation was at war—with, as Wilson
proclaimed, "civilization itself seeming to be in the balance."
The war was everywhere Elwyn turned. Two years before, one
of the most popular songs in America had been the antiwar
anthem "I Didn't Raise My Boy to Be a Soldier," the sheet mu-

sic for which portrayed a young man kneeling at his mother's feet to hug her. Times had changed so much, however, that the career of the singer Morton Harvey had been ruined. Always blustering, former president Theodore Roosevelt had publicly declared that the best place for mothers who opposed the war was China or some other country far beyond the borders of the patriotic United States. Elwyn couldn't browse sheet music for something to play at home for his parents without bumping into "America, Here's My Boy" and George M. Cohan's Broadway hit "Over There." On Palm Sunday, sitting at home with a severe cold, he looked out the window and noticed that neighborhood lawns were sporting so many flags they looked like red, white, and blue spring flowers.

Contributing to his summer anxieties was the family's sale of the big Summit Avenue house and a move to a smaller, far less distinguished-looking home, now that their youngest child was preparing to leave the nest. The setting for his childhood suddenly went away. During his last summer before college, Elwyn read sporting-goods catalogs and looked around for a job. He filled a few pages of his journal with a twenty-four-line poem about skating with Mildred Hesse. Naturally, as he came of age, Elwyn kept thinking about the bloody conflicts in Europe. One friend had already enlisted in the war and was now operating a wireless on a mosquito boat, as the low, fast attack boats (patrol torpedo or PT boats) were called. Another had joined the Naval Reserve. "I don't know what to do this summer," Elwyn confided to his journal in May. The month before, however, New York state's Military Training Commission had created a Farm Cadet Corps at the behest of Governor Charles Whitman, urging boys between the ages of sixteen and eighteen to "enlist" for farmwork. The boys' efforts would be recognized as a commitment to the war effort and honored by chevrons that they could wear on their sleeves. Elwyn worked for a short time on a farm in Hempstead, Long Island. But he thought the farmers were less enthusiastic about the patriotic contributions of their unskilled teenage helpers than they might have been.

He looked into the possibility of other farm jobs—but he was worried that they would aggravate his hay fever. He felt desperately patriotic and wanted to contribute to the war effort—but he simply didn't weigh enough to enlist and wasn't officially an adult yet. He dreamed about joining the American Ambulance Corps and dying a hero's death on the French battlefields—but he had never driven a car and his mother argued against his going to France. On July 11 he exclaimed in his journal, "My birthday! Eighteen, and still no future! I'd be more contented in prison, for there at least I would know precisely what I had to look forward to."

That fall, when he left home for his freshman year at Cornell, among his shirts and winter socks and new pencils he carefully packed the strip of bicycle tape that he and Mildred Hesse had clung to as they skated together across the winter pond.

Part II

ANDY

All writing is both a mask and an unveiling.

Chapter 6

OLYMPUS

*A blank sheet of paper holds the greatest excitement
there is for me . . . What is this terrible infatuation,
anyway?*

WHEN THE YOUNGEST child of Samuel and Jessie
White left home for Cornell University in 1917, he left
Elwyn behind on the screened porch at Mount Vernon and at
the summer lake in Maine. He metamorphosed into Andy.
One of the minor legacies of the college's cofounder, Andrew
Dickson White—whose white-bearded emeritus figure could
be seen haunting the campus until his death in 1918—was that
many male freshmen with the surname White wound up nicknamed Andy. Most let the name slip away over time. Elwyn,
however, embraced the new identity, because he had never
liked his given names. In the family he continued to be nicknamed En, but he began to introduce himself as Andy.

He loved the hilly green Cornell campus, the boathouse at
Beebe Lake, the stained-glass of beautiful old Sage Chapel, the

nearby gorges and woods of upstate New York. From high atop East Hill, he could gaze across the rooftops of Ithaca to a narrow blue stretch of forty-mile-long Cayuga Lake, one of the glacial Finger Lakes. He had never before been around such a diverse group of people as his fellow students, whom he described in a fanciful list: "two men from Hawaii, a girl from Johannesburg, a Cuban, a Turk, an Englishman from India, a Negro from New York, two farmers, three Swedes, a Quaker, five Southerners, a reindeer butcher, a second lieutenant, a Christian Scientist, a retired dancer, a motorcyclist, a man who had known Theda Bara, three gnomes, and a lutist."

When he was invited to join the Phi Gamma Delta fraternity, he wrote to ask his trusty sister Lillian's advice, telling her that he worried he would have to pretend to be someone he wasn't. "For Heaven's sake," she replied, "*don't be scared . . . .* You are just like everyone else underneath only you haven't had enough practice in bringing it out to the surface." She admonished him to take hot baths because cold water wouldn't get him clean, to wear good clothes, and to stop calling a fraternity a frat because it sounded small-town. "You know that you have a much-to-be-desired brain, that you have fine instincts, that you have a sense of humor and a million other things that most boys want." Soon he was wearing the owl tiepin adapted from the fraternity's coat of arms, and in his senior year he was elected fraternity president. But his insecurities remained. On October 13, 1917, he wrote in his journal, "My English prof said the other day that bashfulness was a form of vanity, the only difference being that vanity is the tendency to overestimate your worth, and bashfulness to underestimate it; both arising from the overindulgence of self-consciousness." Eventually he served on several Cornell committees, from the Manuscript Club to the Sophomore Cotillion, and sang in the secular choir.

Cornell was awash in military training. A member of the first class to enter during the war, and unable to enlist because of his low weight and slight build, Andy wrote a poem on the last day of August in which he imagined getting killed in action. He registered for the draft in mid-September 1918, but two months later the armistice was signed by the Allies and Germany— famously on the eleventh hour of the eleventh day of the eleventh month.

His urge to write showed up everywhere. In a playful letter home to his mother as a sophomore, he wrote in paragraphs that hid internal rhymes: "This error corrected, I gracefully turn to the topics of interest, and first you should learn that in spite of the Ithaca weather's contortions (this topic alone might assume large proportions), I now—this is really a subject for prose—am entirely rid of my cold in the nose." He remained preoccupied with his health. Once he confided to his journal that he had been sick for a week: "I think I must have consumption. If I have, I will leave college and travel for my health."

As a junior he took English 8 with William Strunk Jr., a friendly and amusing professor who parted his hair down the middle and blinked owlishly behind steel-rimmed glasses. Strunk was a forceful teacher who had strong ideas about grammar, diction, and other aspects of reading and writing. He enforced his point of view with his own forty-three-page pamphlet—available at the bookstore for a quarter—entitled *The Elements of Style,* which he referred to as "the *little* book." It was full of rules such as "In summaries, keep to one tense" and "Do not join independent clauses with a comma." Strunk had

colorful classroom habits such as repeating himself while recit-
ing a rule about concision, grasping his coat lapels and declaim-
ing, "Omit needless words! Omit needless words! Omit needless
words!"

Every Monday night a few students gathered at the Fall
Creek Drive home of Professor Bristow Adams, where he and
his wife hosted an evening of smoking and chat. Sometimes
students lingered before the fireplace, which had Balinese and
Navajo artifacts on the mantel and walrus tusks on the wall
above, and talked until two in the morning. Andy would walk
back home to the fraternity house in silent darkness, feeling as
if his spiritual wrinkles had been smoothed out. He confided to
his journal an affectionate comment about Bristow: "Sympathetic, kindly, and apparently without a care in the world, he is
a fine balm for a frenzied spirit."

Andy also found that his spirit was calmed by hard work. He
gravitated to the college newspaper, the *Cornell Daily Sun*. One
of only two dailies published by an American university—and
also Ithaca's only morning paper—its eight pages even carried
national and international news, complete with an Associated
Press feed that came in every night via the telephone line. It
seemed sophisticated. Andy's long-running connection with
the paper raised his status until by his last year he walked across
campus with unprecedented confidence. The paper carried a
catchall column modeled after those of Don Marquis and F.P.A.,
to which Andy contributed. In his senior year, he wound up
editor in chief of the *Daily Sun* and graduated with a passionate
conviction that responsible, writerly journalism was a noble calling. He sometimes wrapped up an issue in the wee hours of
the morning and then, before going to class, would nap for a

couple of hours in the office, sprawled across the flatbed press like Archy sleeping under the typewriter keys.

At Cornell Andy experienced his first serious romance. Alice Burchfield, nicknamed Burch, was an intelligent, charming, and beautiful theater fanatic and chemistry major. Although wary of commitment, broadcasting a static of mixed signals, Andy dated Burch for the last half of his college years. Soon he began writing poems to her, publishing them in the *Sun* (without identifying her by name) under the pseudonym D'Annunzio. Even in this situation White thought in terms of animals. His first poem to Burch compared her eyes to the deepest and most appealing eyes he had ever before known—those of his dog Mutt, who lived with him in the fraternity house. For two years Andy and Burch rambled in the woods and watched boat races and meteor showers. But Andy hesitated to pursue the romance to a level of serious commitment. After graduation they wrote now and then, but soon they faded out of each other's life.

All beginnings are wonderful.

IN 1923 ANDY moved to Manhattan and began submitting light verse and humorous paragraphs to columnists. Twenty-nine-year-old Lillian was commuting from the house in Mount Vernon, where she still lived with her parents, to work as a secretary in New York, and Andy proudly squired his beautiful redheaded sister around town. On the bustling streets, as he dodged leg-flashing flappers in cloche hats and bootleggers in overcoats and fedoras, he kept thinking that many gods in his literary pantheon walked the same island: Christopher Morley, Alexander Woollcott, Stephen Vincent Benét, Dorothy Parker, Ring Lardner.

Ever since the *St. Nicholas* days in his childhood and the F.P.A.
and Don Marquis columns of his teen years, he had enjoyed
daily, weekly, and monthly updates from his favorite periodicals. His omnivorous taste led him to read the news from Russia in the *Times* and the news from Yankee Stadium in the *Post*,
the classified ads in *The Nation* and the celebrity gossip in *Vanity
Fair*. He particularly enjoyed Heywood Broun's "It Seems to
Me" column in the *World*, which was so popular the newspaper
promoted it on giant billboards. A humorist and activist and essayist, Broun wrote about social injustice in the new prosperity
following the war. American business seemed like a train that
couldn't be bothered to stop at the local stations; columnists
such as Broun kept pointing out that many little people were
being left behind or run over. Broun defended labor unions and
often took up the cause of an underdog who had been vilified
in the more government-fawning media.

Most of all Andy still enjoyed Don Marquis. Sometimes he
would linger at the corner of Broadway and Chambers Street,
looking up at the gray Italianate marble façade of the *Sun*
building, home of Archy the cockroach. The building had Corinthian columns on the first floor and pediments above some
of the windows on the second. At the north and south corners
a square metal clock with three faces projected out from the
wall, far enough that Andy could walk directly under it and
look up at its underside. Its copper casing was already greening
with age, although the newspaper had only moved there in 1919,
after A. T. Stewart, the city's first department store, moved up-
town and left the space available. On the clock, the words *The
Sun* stood above the octagonal, white face, and *it shines for all* was

written below. Somewhere in that building, Andy would think as he loitered on his way home from work, Don Marquis types up his "Sun Dial" column and then goes out to a speakeasy for a drink or three before heading home. Meanwhile Archy would be crawling out of a stack of paper to type up his report from the underside—throwing his whole body at the keys, hammering out one letter at a time—and Mehitabel, his scruffy feline comrade, would show up to brag about her past life as Cleopatra. Andy also enjoyed some of Marquis's more serious poetry, although much of it was replete with apostrophizing and archaisms. Andy liked the simplicity of a favorite line—which he almost adopted as his own motto—from Marquis's 1915 collection *Dreams & Dust*, in his poem "The Name":

My heart has followed all my days
Something I cannot name.

Animal characters often struck a chord with Andy, as did Archy's melancholy view of life and his skepticism about the hypocrisy and cruelty in the world. Marquis's saga featured such guest stars as a hornet addicted to eating beer-dazzled bar flies and a spider whose maternal lament took the form of a ballad denouncing flyswatters for killing the primary source of food for her children. Over the last few years, Archy had also become one of many voices crying out about the evils and inequalities of Prohibition, and Marquis had created another character, the Old Soak, for whom the difficulty in obtaining alcohol was a running theme. The tragic muddle of Prohibition had been in effect for five years. An Eighteenth Amendment had been proposed

late in 1917, the year Andy started at Cornell, but it wasn't rati-
fied by enough states until more than a year later, and it took
another year to go into effect.

Just as in childhood his anticipation of the monthly issue of
St. Nicholas had been greatly enhanced by the suspense of con-
tributing to it, so had his trips to the newsstand gained in importance as he sent out light verse and small stories to newspaper
columnists. Christopher Morley ran Andy's sonnet about a rooster
in his column "The Bowling Green" in the *Evening Post*. Franklin Pierce Adams (F.P.A.) published a couple of Andy's poems in
"The Conning Tower," the famous column that in 1922 Adams
had moved from the *Tribune* to the *World*. Adams especially was
considered a columnist who could lift other writers' careers into
a new level of fame. Andy dreamed of such a career boost coming his way.

This kind of writing paid little when it paid anything, so Andy
supported himself with jobs at advertising agencies. First he
worked in production for Frank Seaman, Inc., a bustling Fourth
Avenue company whose founder had become a well-known
advertising guru for both domestic and foreign markets. Occasionally Andy got to write copy, but for most of the first year he
ran an electrotype machine, which produced duplicate plates
for printing. The job allowed him to glimpse much of what
came through the office. After the war, American marketing
had become a carnival of pious boosterism, composed half of
imperialistic imagery and half of the kind of joshing platitudes
that Sinclair Lewis had recently pilloried in his novel *Babbitt*. A
1916 article had said about Seaman, "He is one of the men who
saw early . . . that advertising is away bigger than smart description, pictures, and typography—that it is the heavy artillery of

sales management, and that sales management employing the heavy artillery is generalship requiring the solidest grasp of fundamental business principles plus a generous appreciation of the intricacies of just common human nature." Andy found such writing pompous and ridiculous. He disliked advertising and felt he ought to be doing more respectable work. He couldn't bring himself to care whether one particular kind of window-shade material outsold another.

ONE DAY IN late February 1925, Andy strode the crowded, noisy floor of Grand Central Terminal, checking at newsstands for the debut issue of a humor magazine that he had been told was about to appear. The terminal's latest incarnation was twelve years old, an elegant replacement for the Grand Central Station of Andy's childhood, from which he and his parents had departed every summer for Maine. As he scurried past the four faces of the round-headed clock above the main information terminal, cigarette smoke eddied upward in light slanting down from giant windows that gave the echoing space its cathedral air despite the lack of stained glass.

He stopped to survey a newsstand. The *New York Times* happily reported robins and daffodils in New Jersey, a month ahead of the equinox. *Film Fun* had a color portrait of a laughing young woman in an eye-catching red swimsuit; a closer look revealed her to be Kathryn McGuire, Buster Keaton's costar in his recent movies *The Navigator* and *Sherlock, Jr.* In deliberate contrast to the flashy mags, two-year-old *Time*'s stark white covers always showed a plain black-and-white drawing of a prominent public figure. This week it was Harry New, the postmaster general, who had been appointed by Warren Harding and then reappointed a couple of years ago, when Harding suddenly died and skinny little Calvin Coolidge became president.

Finally Andy found the new magazine. Its cover was in color but drawn in a calligraphic black brush line, showing a high-collared and top-hatted Regency dandy peering through a monocle at a hovering modernist butterfly. The magazine looked resolutely frivolous, a pose that Andy himself was known to adopt occasionally. In the pink clouds over this Beau Brummell's head was a title in a sans-serif font that looked both modern and lighthearted: THE NEW YORKER. The first issue arrived on newsstands a few days ahead of its cover date of Saturday, February 21, 1925. *Liberty* and *Collier's* cost a nickle, *Photoplay* and *Good Housekeeping* a quarter; Andy plunked down fifteen cents for this premier issue and hurried to catch his train.

The first issue of *The New Yorker* looked much like *Judge* and *Life*, neither of which was as limber in old age as it had been in youth. A cartoon showing an elegantly dressed man and woman strolling past a revival of the Victorian melodrama *The Wages of Sin* bore underneath it the kind of two-line overkill dialogue that had been standard-issue since *Punch* was in diapers, complete with scriptlike identification of the speakers:

UNCLE: Poor girls, so few get their wages!
FLAPPER: So few get their sin, darn it!

Later there was a similar setup, without a drawing, but this time it was inverted in what at first seemed like a mistake:

POP: A man who thinks he can make it in a par.
JOHNNY: What is an optimist, Pop?

On the first page, under the heading *The New Yorker* and an illustration showing the monocled dandy working at a desk with a feather quill, was a section entitled "Of All Things," a gossipy tour of Manhattan, signed at the end "The New Yorker." It included an apologetic note: *"The New Yorker* asks consideration for its first number. It recognizes certain shortcomings and realizes that it is impossible for a magazine fully to establish its character in one number." This first slim issue reviewed a few books and plays, even some moving pictures. A two-page column called "Profiles," whose heading bore a literal-minded illustration of people seen from the side, covered the Metropolitan Opera's Italian-born impresario, Giulio Gatti-Casazza. The text wrapped around a caricature of sleepy-eyed Gatti-Casazza's wedge-shaped beard and waxed mustaches and rakishly tilted fedora.

Andy liked that most items in the magazine were brief and amusing. He decided to submit a few paragraphs, perhaps some light verse, and see if they might be interested.

They were. During 1925 the magazine bought several brief pieces. His early contributions included a parody of advertising writing, one section of which also managed to include a favorite bird and a favorite time of year. Under the title "New Beauty of Tone in 1925 Song Sparrow" was the description "Into every one of this season's song sparrows has been built the famous VERNAL tone. Look for the distinguishing white mark on the breast." Another piece was about the travails of commuting. After a long trip out West with a college buddy, he had moved back in with his parents for a couple of years. Like many other families, they found this arrangement less than satisfying, and Andy also tired of the daily train commute to the advertising agency in Manhattan.

In November 1925 he moved into the city, settling into his first apartment, in Greenwich Village at 112 West Thirteenth Street, a four-story brick walk-up around the corner from Sixth Avenue. He roomed with three other Cornell alumni, in a two-bedroom apartment on the third floor, a sitting room and a single bedroom that held two dormitory-style bunk beds. Bob Adams and Gus Lobrano worked for Cunard, the shipping company; Mike Galbreath worked for the publisher McGraw-Hill. Rent on the two-room apartment was $110 per month, with Andy's quarter coming only to $27.50, manageable even on the budget of an electrotype operator. His bank balance was also slightly raised by the small checks that trickled in from *The New Yorker* and elsewhere.

Although his first contributions were amusing and achieved their modest goals, late in the year he wrote up a real-life experience in a more distinctive tone of dry wit. He described a lunchtime encounter in a Childs restaurant. Starting out with a single family-owned location on Cortlandt Street in the 1880s, Childs had grown into the first major restaurant chain, a hugely profitable enterprise now serving dozens of cities with more than 100 locations. Instantly recognizable by their white marble tabletops on gleaming nickel legs and their white tile floors— they were sparkling clean, catering not only to economy-minded locals who didn't have time for a leisurely lunch, but also to a populace newly afraid of old-fashioned germs. The waitresses— themselves an innovation when they were introduced around the turn of the century, when most restaurants hired only waiters— wore starched white uniforms and could be seen at a griddle in the windows, flipping pancakes.

When Andy sat down to lunch he was wearing a dark blue

serge suit that looked good until a waitress spilled a glass of buttermilk on it. He hid his embarrassment behind performance. He gazed stoically down at the wreck of his clothing, thinking that so few dark spots showing through his now yellow-white coat made him resemble a fire-hall dalmatian. Reassured by his lack of anger, the waitress gave him a handful of paper napkins, with which he began to dab ineffectually. A woman at the next table issued unwelcome advice. Reassuring the crying waitress, Andy felt heroic. Aware that everyone was watching him, he rose, pulled on his overcoat, and, with theatrical nobility, slipped a dime tip under the edge of his plate. Then he went to pay his check, which came to seventy-five cents. He waved away the change, saying, "Let that take care of the buttermilk."

Soon he wrote up the incident in a tone of placid virtue and sent it to the new magazine. In the story he even had himself think, "Perhaps this is one of those 'smart backgrounds' *The New Yorker* is always talking about." His surprise Christmas gift was a check for the piece, which appeared in the last issue of the year, with its cover montage of holiday festivities—a champagne bottle in a bucket, opera glasses and tickets, a glittering diamond necklace. Apparently the magazine was doing well; the Christmas issue had been the largest yet, at fifty-six pages, and this one was also healthy-looking, including advertisements for Old King Cole cigars and a profile of Cornelius Vanderbilt Jr. Andy's story was tucked between a caricature of Harry Houdini, who was drawing crowds over at the spacious Forty-fourth Street Theatre—with its speakeasy, the Little Club, in the basement—and a caricature of the Russian actress Olga Baclanova, who was starring in the Moscow Art Theatre Musical Studio's production of *Lysistrata*, which *The New Yorker*'s columnist described as "the naughtiest, most hilarious, most timely and by far the most entertaining play in town." Andy's story was on page 17, titled "Child's Play" (incorrectly, because the name of the restaurant family was Childs, not Child). Under the title was the line "In Which the Author Turns a Glass of Buttermilk into a Personal Triumph." The story covered almost the entire right page, opposite a piece called "Sex Is Out," by none other than Robert Benchley. It was heady company for a young writer.

"ARE YOU ELWYN Brooks White?"

The woman striding purposefully toward him across *The New Yorker's* reception area was in her midthirties, about seven years older than Andy. She had a straight and rather patrician nose, beautiful dark eyes under dramatic brows, and long, dark hair pulled into an elegant bun on the back of her head. She wore a stylish, expensive-looking dress and a string of pearls. With a slightly reserved but still charming smile, she introduced herself as Katharine Angell, and her voice, while warm and friendly, had an educated refinement to it.

It was late 1926. Angell was the editor who had bought a dozen or so of Andy's light verse and brief humorous prose items over the previous year. She had invited him to drop by their small suite of offices at 25 West Forty-third Street and go to lunch with her and the magazine's maestro, Harold Ross. Fourth in her 1914 graduating class at Bryn Mawr, Angell had majored in English literature and philosophy. Only a few months after founding the magazine, Andy soon learned, Ross had hired the sharp, well-educated, and witty young woman to read manuscripts for a couple of hours each day. Soon she became indispensable. The first head of the Fiction Department, she also participated in almost every other decision, from poetry and layout to cartoons and advertising.

Soon her boss joined them and they went out to a restaurant. At thirty-four, Harold Ross was gaunt and angular and pale, with small, intense gray eyes. He brushed his hair into a pompadour worthy of a cockatoo, and his nervous habit of running his big-knuckled hands through it didn't calm it down. Even at first glance, Ross was a mass of contradictions. His chiseled, austere upper lip rested uneasily on a full, sensuous lower lip. Like his other features, they were constantly in motion, bouncing from a disapproving purse to a sudden good-humored smile showing a prominent gap between the incisors. His voice varied just as much, from a doglike growl to a higher-pitched Western twang. As if to make himself invisible, Ross wore a plain dark suit and tie. Despite his air of youthful distraction, he was already an experienced newspaperman, having worked for two dozen papers in his eighteen-year career, and having managed *Stars and Stripes* during the Great War. He had a distracting way of gesturing by flailing his arms about, and because of his ulcers, he ordered lunch only after a careful perusal of the menu. Beside Ross, the beautiful Mrs. Angell seemed an oasis of calm. Together, over the meal, Angell and Ross invited Andy to come to work for them part-time as a staffer at *The New Yorker.*

Despite his longtime daydreams of a successful writing career, Andy resisted, hesitating as usual over commitment. But Angell and Ross persisted. Especially after talking with Andy at lunch, Ross—who trusted his instincts and was always looking for new talent—decided he wanted Andy on board the ship of which he himself was the profane and restless captain. Over several lunches, they expressed their admiration for his writing and extolled the virtues of working for a burgeoning enterprise such as *The New Yorker.*

In the year and a half since its debut, the magazine had matured at a breakneck pace. Ross's friends among the Algonquin Round Table—Robert Benchley, Arthur Kober, Marc Connelly, Dorothy Parker—were finally coming aboard, at least occasionally. (Few had taken the magazine venture seriously at first and most were still skeptical.) Ring Lardner had submitted one small piece. Ross was hoping to get Alexander Woollcott interested. The quality of the material was rising, although not quickly enough to suit Ross. He still quested after the perfect crew to staff his quixotic venture. He kept saying he was searching for the right "formula." Although he yearned for the magazine to develop a unique persona, at first it was very much of its era. The brief paragraphs, usually humorous, that comprised the front departments of the magazine—"The Talk of the Town," starting out with "Notes & Comment"—followed the popular catchall format of Andy's own favorite columnists: Morley, Marquis, F.P.A. Each owed a debt to nineteenth-century forebears such as Eugene Field's "Sharps and Flats" in the late 1800s. Unpredictable, even anarchic, the format permitted almost anything and in its honed brevity built up a kind of narrative momentum. He wanted Andy to take charge of this department.

Finally, in January 1927, Andy agreed to contribute new work every week and to show up every weekday, at least for a few hours, at a small office that was assigned to him. In return Harold Ross agreed to pay him $30 per week. Andy had left Frank Seaman and was now working part-time at a different advertising agency, J. H. Newmark, where he earned the same amount. Surely a frugal young man could live on $60 a week, especially while still rooming with three others. More important than the money, about which Andy had an almost cavalier attitude, was that at twenty-seven he had suddenly become a salaried professional writer.

Chapter 7

INTERVIEW WITH A SPARROW

New York is part of the natural world. I love the city,
I love the country, and for the same reasons. The city
is part of the country . . . People are animals, and
the city is full of people in strange plumage, defending
their territorial rights, digging for their supper.

ANDY SOON EVOLVED into a professional chronicler of everyday life. Finally he had a venue for airing his observations of the city's miniature dramas, its sparkling elevators and dustbin alleys, its quiet and largely unnoticed wildlife. The mental snapshots that he had portioned out in letters to friends and family he now wrote up for a larger audience. Over the next few months Andy indulged his zest for observation and his bent for rambling. Any experience or observation, no matter how small, might be distilled from his daily life in staccato bursts of typing at his heavy iron typewriter, the smudged carbons and X-d out errors soon to metamorphose on the pages of the magazine that quickly became the center of his city life. Now in his late twenties, he was ready for his first big intellectual romance. It was invigorating, practicing a craft that demanded weekly production but also welcomed a dynamic writing style not permitted to journalists on daily newspapers.

As he had been in Mount Vernon and Maine, in Ithaca and out West, Andy remained preoccupied with nature. He could not step outdoors without noticing and identifying the birds calling and fluttering around him—the raucous jay in the sidewalk-trapped lindens, a kinglet on a hedge, the brown thrasher and white-throated sparrow on the lawn. Nor did he stop responding emotionally to changes in the weather. Walking along in a remarkably peaceful snowfall one February day, he happily admired the way that the world grew still and quiet. The cabs' usual roar was muted to a whisper, and the elevated subway seemed like a ghost train in the white sky. Then snowplows began roaring and scraping to keep the streets clean—a sudden intrusion into his childlike fancy that Andy found annoying. In early spring he wrote an ode to the humble city garden, "its skinny ailanthus tree, its vagrant cat, its indomitable privet hedge."

One balmy April day he explored Bronx Park, not just the botanical garden and zoo but the wandering paths along the river. Two miles of the Bronx River fell within park boundaries. For a quarter of a mile, beginning on the footpath near the rose garden, where tall, sunlit hemlocks stood almost in the water's edge, Andy was gloriously alone—a state difficult to achieve in New York City. The city seemed impossibly far away; even the sound of a train was too distant to be real. A duck honked overhead. A couple stood on a bridge, leaning against the railing, staring down at sunshine sparkling on the rushing water. The man was talking and the woman crying. At this

point Andy fled the suddenly tense scene and soon found himself on the subway, already composing a casual about an idyllic
glimpse of nature and its off note of soured romance.

February 1928 found him braving the crowds flocking to see
the newly opened Reptile and Amphibian Hall at the American Museum of Natural History. Overhead were double rows of
chandeliers, and on each side large windows rose up to the ceiling. Looking into display cases past these many reflected lights,
Andy peered at stuffed specimens and at dioramas of habitats.
He especially admired a nine-foot-long monster nicknamed
the "dragon lizard," which had been brought back, during a museum expedition the year before, from Indonesian islands such as
Komodo. It looked no less dinosaur-like for also seeming fat and
lazy, its wrinkled, loose skin looking as impenetrable as a medieval coat of mail. Andy enjoyed learning the natural history behind Kipling's story "Rikki-Tikki-Tavi" and about the Russell's
viper, a dramatically patterned Indian snake thought to have
inspired the Sherlock Holmes story "The Adventure of the
Speckled Band." The fat, green-and-black-patterned heads of
the Brazilian horned frogs made him think of Tweedledum and
Tweedledee, and one lizard reminded him instantly of the actor
William Boyd as he had looked in the finale of the recent play
What Price Glory. As usual when he dropped in at the museum,
Andy also revisited favorite exhibits. He was always impressed
by the stuffed, oversize black-and-white "raccoon bear" that had
been captured in China in 1916 by the German zoologist Hugo
Weigold. It looked like a giant version of a child's teddy bear.
Although the museum's display stated that Weigold had seen the
animals live and had even purchased a cub (which didn't live

long), every time Andy saw the stuffed exhibit of this creature he speculated whimsically that perhaps it was merely a master-piece of taxidermy.

MOST OF THESE rambles and flights of fancy made it into *The New Yorker*. Its pages offered a nourishing environment for Andy's kind of thinking, for lushly textured observations and playing with language, for his ability to recount a passing expe-rience and overlay it with both thoughtful irony and a kind of uncluttered clear-sightedness. He noticed more than nature, of course. In his first years, he commented on everything from a Shriners convention to the trial of Sacco and Vanzetti, from an orchid show to the pauper cemetery on an island in Long Island Sound. In one casual he might complain about the hubbub of lunch hour in the city, but later in the same issue he would be off to a larger view of the world. "A lot has been done by novelists and playwrights to discredit war," he observed, "but occasion-ally it becomes clear that most men seem to like it quite well: middle-aged veterans who get drunk and recall old glories, young men who stay sober and hear drums four thousand miles away." In August 1928 he ironically surveyed the newspaper re-ports of Coolidge's secretary of state, Frank B. Kellogg, who the month before—with Aristide Briand, the French minister of foreign affairs—had led the signing of the General Treaty for the Renunciation of War. Nicknamed the Kellogg-Briand Pact, it claimed (with numerous caveats) to prohibit aggressive war for any purpose other than self-defense. Signatories included Ger-many, Japan, France, and Britain. "While the pacific ink was still fresh on the peace treaty," Andy wrote with skeptically raised eyebrows, Kellogg boarded a warship and made a cannon-bristling tour of France, Ireland, and elsewhere, always surrounded by a demonstration of military power, usually America's.

The next month, Andy was back to writing about nature, in his usual oblique way. In a newspaper he ran across a long article about the mysterious chemistry that goes on inside a living cell. As he read, he thought for a moment that perhaps scientists were really going to decipher some golden secret of life. Shortly after finishing the article, however, he bent down to peer into his goldfish tank. Frisky, the solitary snail he had placed in the tank, had been preoccupied with its own chemistry. Andy was surprised to find a baby snail creeping wetly along the lower glass of the tank wall, turning its cartoon head this way and that, extending and retracting its knobby antennae. This glimpse—a reminder of the secret lives around him—seemed to ensure mysteries enough to keep him and all of science occupied for the immediate future, he decided, as he threw out the paper with the article.

He observed that New Yorkers, as they step up to a curb, instinctively know which way the traffic is coming from, no matter how many one-way streets they've just crossed. "They glance in the right direction," he wrote, "as naturally as a deer sniffs upwind." He speculated that Ziegfeld Follies maintained a field corps of "Follies girls," because they seemed to show up anywhere a newspaper photographer happened to be—including when an injured wild duck landed to rest on the roof of a new hotel. One sunny mid-October he pointed out that autumn's colorful chemistry was not lost even on the citybound:

Down in the Village the people whose houses look out on the garden between Sullivan and MacDougal have seen autumn in the visitation of the brown thrasher and the veery. One drifting yellow leaf on a windowsill can be a city dweller's fall, pungent and melancholy as any hillside in New England.

He was still plagued by wild anxieties and indefinable nostalgia. "As we grow older," he wrote in one casual in early 1929, "we find ourself groping toward things that give us a sense of security." He was twenty-nine. He worried constantly, for example, when riding the subway and commuter trains. Even on the familiar Sixth Avenue el, swaying with one hand in a monkey grip on the strap, he feared that the train's momentum alongside too close buildings and above too busy streets was reckless. Andy invented a new name for this fear. Freud had used the term *locomotor phobia*, which was sometimes written as *locomotophobia*, for agoraphobia, but Andy casually revised Freud. He redefined *locomotophobia* as "fear that the engineer is dead," and that as a consequence any moment now you will die in a train wreck.

To counter his anxiety, Andy looked for rhythms and unity everywhere. Now and then he peered into the cosmic paradoxes of Einstein's theories. He enjoyed the dizzying revelations of astronomy and found that they cleared his mind and enlarged his perspective on everyday life in a visceral rather than an abstract way. At times the Einsteinian cosmos seemed to Andy as varied but sporadically comprehensible as New York City, which appeared to alter with every change in lighting or vantage point, every evocative glimpse up a side street. Such a universe inspired "the moods of an open-and-shut day," he wrote, using a Northeastern term for a day of alternating clouds and sun. In early 1931, *The New Yorker* published Andy's ode to Einstein's cosmic visions, which included his remark, "We trot along with Einstein from one cosmology to another, holding tight to his trousers-leg like a child." As Andy wrote this piece, the surreal ironies of relativity called to mind Lewis Carroll, so he suggested that perhaps Einstein had been reading Carroll more than he had been looking through telescopes. A particular image occurred to him and he flipped through a copy of *Through the Looking-Glass* until he found it. It was from the scene in chapter 5, "Wool and Water," in which, after Alice helps the White Queen brush her hair and in return gets offered a job as maid ("Twopence a week and jam every other day"), the Queen explains to Alice the paradoxes of living backward. Andy added the passage to his casual about Einstein:

"It's a poor sort of memory that works only backwards," the Queen remarked.

"What sort of things do *you* remember best?" Alice ventured to ask.

"Oh, things that happened the week after next," the Queen replied in a careless tone.

Then Andy went back to describing more mundane topics, such as the police officer who accosted him outside the public library. Andy was sitting on a step, leaning back and basking in the early June sunshine, lulled by the arterial flow of cars down Fifth Avenue, the rush of people on the sidewalks, the strutting pigeons that clustered and cooed in their primordial social dance.

Suddenly a cop interrupted his sunlit daydream by walking up and snapping, "No sitting, standing, or lounging on the stoop."

Andy was offended. He replied that the steps were there *for* people to sit on in the sun—and besides, he argued, sitting in the sun was really all there was to life anyway.

The cop wasn't interested in a philosophical discussion. "Well, it was pretty bad here, when we let 'em sit on the steps. Women used to loll here and fellers would parade around in front of them."

Andy pointed out that in this respect people were much like pigeons.

HE ENJOYED THE company of other street birds as well and thought of them as interesting neighbors. Naturally he noticed the countless English sparrows that flocked around every scrap on the sidewalks and clustered under park benches, with their bright dark eyes watching every move around them. The male was an elegant brown, black, and gray, with russet temples and a dramatic black bib, but the female so drab by comparison as to be invisibly street-colored. Actually neither a sparrow nor particularly English, but a weaver finch that occurs naturally in Europe and Asia, this bird had been deliberately introduced into the United States—fifty pairs released in Brooklyn in the mid-nineteenth century. They had multiplied wildly and adapted to almost every kind of habitat, especially urban.

One day shortly after joining *The New Yorker*, Andy wrote a piece about how the birds seemed to experience early nesting urges before either spring or their own hormones were quite ready. He noticed one particular bird in Madison Square, where Broadway and Fifth Avenue met at Twenty-third Street. The sparrow picked up a straw and carried it in its beak with an air of importance and impending decision, as it hopped along near the restless traffic. By then the traffic hubbub featured mostly automobiles. Few horses were in sight, and those mostly in the parks—a long way from the trolley cars and horse-drawn wagons that had filled these streets during Andy's childhood. An admirer of many aspects of both nature and civilization, Andy cast an experienced eye on the many honking cars jostling down Manhattan's streets—Chevrolet's Series F Superior and other recent competition, but still mostly Fords, even the old Model T's, from the apparently ageless roadster of his childhood to boxy black Tudor sedans with red wheel spokes, from wooden-bedded pickups to the buslike Woody wagon. Despite only a couple of decades of experience, the street birds navigated these perils with ease. The straw-carrying sparrow he was watching peered around and up—perhaps at the towering wedge of the Flatiron Building nearby—and industriously hopped about for a moment, tilting the straw this way and that. Then it suddenly dropped the straw, as if postponing its nest dreams until later.

In this piece Andy imagined interviewing the bird about a topic that often preoccupied the writer himself: the relative merits of rural and urban living. Why, he asks the bird, forage in the city when the countryside offers more easily available food? The sparrow indicates a nearby park bench and the candy wrappers and other trash beneath it, mentioning the sizable percentage of peanuts that fall to ground uneaten, the nutrient value of Runkel's chocolate wrappers, the spillage of Cracker Jacks, the amount of oats that trickle out of the park horses' feed bags and fall like manna. "Here in town," the bird adds, "I can get everything that the country offers, plus the drama, books, the museums, the stimulus of interesting contacts. I took space on a ledge of the

Metropolitan two years ago; it afforded an extraordinary out-look on Greek statuary, and influenced my viewpoint."

Naturally Andy saw various aspects of himself in these avian street urchins. "At this season," he wrote, "the sparrows are particularly conspicuous because they are in love—and love addles any creature and makes him noisy." The bird explains that any night he wants to he can fly over to Bryant Park and join the hundreds of birds that roost in the tree overlooking the newsstand. "It is a rowdy bunch (characteristic of Sixth Avenue) but no questions are asked and the next morning I tell my wife I was unavoidably locked in a loft where I had been looking for bits of plaster. Males need to get out of themselves once in a while."

Chapter 8

CRAZY

The whole scheme of my existence
is based on concealment.

IN ADULTHOOD AS in high school and college, romance
was not Andy's strong suit. In 1926, the year he became a staff
writer for *The New Yorker*, he began occasionally seeing a young
woman named Mary Osborn, but the poems he wrote during
this time indicate a typically halting and unrealized relationship. In a sonnet entitled "To the Bronze Bust of Holley in
Washington Square," he apologized for his awkwardness
during a romantic moment and explained why he failed to
kiss her:

> *I could not then unbend to claim my prize*
> *Simply because you would not close your eyes!*

In a later poem he made the odd claim that he had "Too
small a heart, too large a pen." But he was candid about his anxious response to the stirrings of his own yearning for love:

And if I have not said it well,
  Or even loud enough to hear it,
That is because I cannot tell
  How much I like, how much I fear it.

By 1927 Mary was gone and Andy was flirting with a nineteen-year-old named Rosanne Magdol, who had recently come to work at *The New Yorker* as a secretary. She had deliberately chosen the hip new magazine as a road that would lead her out of what she considered the suffocating culture of her family, who were recent Jewish immigrants from Russia. Rosanne was petite, attractive, lively, and—by Andy's standards, anyway—distractingly uninhibited. Unlike him, she simply was not shy. Once she caused a stir during a staff beer party by walking up to Gene Tunney, who was awkwardly standing by himself and looking self-conscious, and casually engaging him in conversation. At thirty, Tunney was a two-time world heavyweight boxing champion, having pummeled Jack Dempsey both this year and last; he towered over Rosanne and smiled down at her. Andy watched from across the room.

Rosanne's relationship with Andy never progressed to an actual three-dimensional romance. As usual, rather than taking a woman out on a date, he invited Rosanne for long walks, during which he tried to amuse her with stories such as the adventures of his pet canary, Baby. Once Rosanne invited him to a lecture on yoga, an occasion he soon mocked in a casual; he also parodied in writing her desire to, as she said, "rub shoulders with the famous." Once he showed up at her apartment at night, unannounced, only to find a man there—an older friend who, she explained, needed a sofa to sleep on for a couple of nights.

Despite having never actually expressed his feelings to Rosanne, Andy was upset.

Eventually he described himself—safely costumed in third person—in a self-conscious sonnet called "Portrait." It was as self-aggrandizing as a Romantic poet striding across the Lake District a century earlier, but candid about his crippling second-guessing and his melancholy bent.

> *He goes his way with a too cautious stride*
> *That checks him safe just short of every goal;*
> *Seeks not conclusions lest they try his pride,*
> *Claims not fair booty lest it glut his soul.*
> *If it be love, he finds it unrequited,*
> *And seasons it with sadness to the taste;*
> *If it be fame, he finds his name is slighted,*
> *And turns his luck aside in conscious haste.*
> *Frustration tickles his most plaintive strings*
> *And satisfies his bent for somber living;*
> *He daubs with mystery the obvious things,*
> *And holds fulfillment off—always contriving*
> *From life (held very gingerly) to press*
> *The fine musk odor of unhappiness.*

About the time he wrote up his interview with the sparrow, during the spring of 1927, Andy used a different bird as mouthpiece for his worries. While working at *The New Yorker* and agonizing as usual over the conflict between his romantic attraction to women and his deep-seated fear that he might lose himself if he committed to love and marriage, Andy wrote up the dilemma as a conversation between himself and the canary Baby, whose exploits he had recounted to Mary. This male caged bird, Andy claimed, thought of himself as an artist. Like the sparrow in Madison Square that Andy had written about, the canary exhibited signs of a nesting urge that made Andy uneasy. One spring night, Andy claimed with Don Marquis chutzpah, he was reading the recently published *Journal of Katherine Mansfield* aloud to Baby, who now and then sang along with the words. But then Andy read an evocative phrase from Mansfield, "the warm soft wind of spring, searching out the heart," the kind of expression of vague longing that he often found moving. Suddenly the bird stopped singing and began fidgeting with a piece of string, finally trying to wrap it around himself and sit down in it.

Andy claimed that he asked the bird about this restless unease.

Baby confessed that he was not entirely happy with his life now that he had been joined in the cage by a "wife," Justa, whose tendency to noble self-sacrifice manifested itself in digging choice bits out of the seed cup and leaving them on top for her husband to find. Baby insisted that he would prefer to find them himself. "Take away an artist's troubles," he complained to Andy, "and what has he?"

In this scenario, Andy pointed out that Baby's love lyrics to Justa during their first few weeks together were his most beautiful music. "That throat-bulging song that ripples my feathers and shakes my frame," Baby replied, "that song of desire and love and conquest—it's life, but it isn't art."

> *"I'm in love, and I'm going crazy."*
> (translation of a Boston terrier's bark)

IN MARCH 1927 a new writer came on board at *The New Yorker*, a tall and nearsighted, bespectacled and mustached thirty-two-year-old named James Thurber. He had considerably more journalistic experience than Andy. He had already worked as a newspaperman in his native Columbus, Ohio, as well as for the *Chicago Tribune* in Paris alongside other expatriates such as William Shirer. Thurber was serious about his career as a writer, but like Andy he couldn't remain solemn for more than an hour at work. In Paris, Thurber liked to sneak in fictional filler paragraphs, including one quoting President Coolidge as having said to a religious convention that a man who does not pray is not a praying man.

Thurber and Andy had met through a mutual acquaintance. Ross got the idea that they were old friends, however, and impressed as he was with Andy, he immediately hired Thurber. Ross was seeking, as always, a managing editor who could orchestrate all the burgeoning departments of the magazine—a "jesus," they called it in the office. Ross himself referred to this elusive messiah as the Hub. Ross didn't quite explain to Thurber that he had nominated him for the role. Completely unsuited, Thurber was miserable, but when offered the job he was having little success as a freelancer. He was so poor he had begun to think of doughnuts and cocktail-party anchovies as sustenance. At *The New Yorker* he wanted to write, not edit, and eventually Ross permitted him to.

Among the early tasks assigned to Andy was writing captions for cartoons, which Ross usually referred to simply as "drawings." Ross was as fanatically attentive to every line of a cartoon as he was to every word in an essay. He tended to ask about characters in them, "Who's talking?" He didn't hesitate to suggest

revisions to a drawing or to apply to it his own passion for narrative lucidity. After spending two long minutes peering at a
drawing of a Model T on a dusty road, he once snapped to his
secretary, "Take this down, Miss Terry. Better dust." Other staff-
ers reported that Ross once examined a cartoon of two elephants
and asked, "Which elephant is talking?"

Thurber was soon involved in this process as well. In November 1928, he and Andy sat in the closet-size office they
shared—it was barely large enough for two desks—and thought
up a caption for a static ink-and-wash scene by a young cartoonist named Carl Rose. The magazine had published Rose's first
drawing during its debut year, and he had become a regular
contributor. But his new drawing was less than inspired. It showed
an elegantly dressed brunette dining in a restaurant with her
young, curly-haired blond daughter. While holding her fork in
midair above her plate, the mother was looking down at her
daughter and speaking. Her expression was neutral and the
daughter barely had any expression at all. The dialogue could go
in any direction. The setting gave no clue to what Rose was
thinking about when he drew it. His own caption had been rejected, but Ross and the others liked the drawing itself.

Although nothing indicated that the child was speaking as
well, Andy wrote under the cartoon an old-fashioned dialogue,
the kind of two-line caption that Ross was trying to get away
from. Ross disliked the antique cartoon that required a script
below with speakers clearly labeled as COUNT and SHOWGIRL.
Andy didn't mind being old-fashioned, especially when he could
amusingly mislead the reader by doing so. In his caption, clearly
the mother speaks first: "It's broccoli, dear." And the daughter
replies, "I say it's spinach, and I say the hell with it."

Not one to chortle over his own humor, and uncertain as always about his work, Andy passed the now captioned drawing to Thurber, who took the sheet of paper and read it without smiling. He said simply, "Yeah, it seems okay to me."

Ross hesitated over it. He wasn't particularly impressed and also worried about the word *hell* because he already felt that there was too much profanity in the magazine. But Katharine Angell, who had become quite fond of Andy and his kind of humor, thought it was hilarious. While Ross was on vacation in Florida, Katharine published it. It appeared in the December 8 issue and soon became the most famous cartoon the magazine had published.

Thurber himself drew, had indeed been drawing compulsively since childhood. In the tiny office with Andy, he filled stray yellow copy paper with graceless flowers, childish lamps and chairs and desks, mournful hounds of dubious ancestry, couples whose rubber arms wrapped around each other like vines and ended in square, three-fingered hands. Because Thurber knew nothing about perspective and never planned a drawing ahead, what had started out as a staircase might be forced to metamorphose into an article of furniture. It was Andy who first appreciated Thurber's skewed, disproportionate, perspectiveless, and yet brilliant talent.

In spring 1929 Thurber quickly scribbled a drawing of a seal—complete with doggish whiskers and deadpan expression— perched on a rock, looking off to its right at two small specks and uttering the boring caption "Hm, explorers." Andy liked the style of the drawing immediately and argued that Thurber ought to send it to the next Tuesday-afternoon art meeting. Thurber already had a tremor in his hands that prevented his inking his own pencil sketches, so Andy carefully drew black India ink lines over Thurber's pencil original to create a reproducible drawing. Then he sent it to the meeting.

Thurber could imagine Ross's and art director Rea Irvin's disdainful responses. Sure enough, the next Tuesday the drawing appeared back on Thurber's desk. On the same yellow paper, beside Thurber's sketch, Irvin had drawn his own more realistic seal portrait and added the note, *This is the way a seal's whiskers go.* Andy attached a note saying, *This is how a Thurber seal's whiskers go,* and sent it to the next weekly meeting. It was rejected without further comment.

Soon Ross was growling at Thurber, "How the hell did you get the idea you could *draw*?"

During the summer of 1929 Andy and Thurber wrote a brief book together entitled *Is Sex Necessary? or, Why You Feel the Way You Do.* A parody of the sex-and-romance advice books that were becoming common, it was a resolutely frothy parade of silliness that read like what it was—a freshman outing by two young men who were only one generation past Victorian. But they also addressed recurring themes in the dance of romance and sexuality.

Just the minute another person is drawn into some one's life, there begin to arise undreamed-of complexities, and from such a simple beginning as sexual desire we find built up such alarming yet familiar phenomena as fêtes, divertissements, telephone conversations, arrangements, plans, sacrifices, train arrivals, meetings, appointments, tardinesses, delays, marriages, dinners, small pets and animals, calumny, children, music lessons, yellow shades for the windows, evasions, lethargy, cigarettes, candies, repetition of stories and anecdotes, infidelity, ineptitude, incompatibility, bronchial trouble . . .

They urged the young to inform their elders about sex, mocked independent working women, and explained to wives how to keep their husbands from feeling claustrophobic. Amid much silliness were some inspired non sequiturs. "There are apartments in New York," they wrote, "in which one must step across an open bathtub in going from the kitchen to the bedroom; any unusual layout like that arouses sexual desire and brings people pouring into New York from other cities."

Three years after Andy's poetic apology for failing to kiss Mary Osborn, *Is Sex Necessary?* featured a chapter entitled "Frigidity in Men," which included a several-page section called "The Declination of the Kiss."

To kiss in dream is wholly pleasant. First, the woman is the one of your selection, not just anyone who happens to be in your arms at the moment. Second, the deed is garnished with a little sprig of glamour which the mind, in exquisite taste, contributes. Third, the lips, imaginatively, are placed just so, the concurrent thoughts arrive, just so. . . . When a kiss becomes actual anything is likely to happen. . . . So you see, frigidity in men has many aspects, many angles.

They submitted the book to Harper & Brothers, which had just published Andy's first book, a small collection of light verse entitled *The Lady Is Cold*. With Andy still championing his artwork, Thurber drew illustrations for it—portraits of the Quiet Type of woman, spineless Thurberfolk gaining no insight at all from contemplating birds and bees and flowers, and a cartoon chart of the North Atlantic including a couple of airplane routes, with a caption explaining that the authors thought it would be more useful than a diagram of the human body. Harper & Brothers expressed interest. When the authors came to meet with three editors, Andy spread out Thurber's sheaf of drawings on the floor. Silence ensued, punctuated by a rustling of paper and a cleared throat. The editors looked at the drawings but didn't say anything. "I gather," one of them asked finally, "these are a rough idea of the kind of illustrations you want some artist to do?"

Andy shook his head. "These are the drawings that go into the book."

The editors conferred, muttering about sales and reader resistance. They protested. Andy held firm. Thurber sat silent. When *Is Sex Necessary?* was published a few months later, Thurber's drawings appeared throughout the text.

Soon after the book was published, Andy was visiting his parents when he overheard them talking about his first book. "I don't know what you think of it," he heard his father say, "but I'm ashamed of it."

In his dealings with parents and editors and publishers, as much as in his writing, Andy was quickly growing and gaining confidence. He was learning to stand his ground, to explore new creative avenues. Only one arena left him as lost and afraid as ever, and it was the one to which he kept returning in his writing—romance, wherein he continued his time-honored habit, when faced with the prospect of love or sex, of hiding behind imaginary animals like a ventriloquist.

Chapter 9

AS SPIDERS DO

What a life I led! How merry! How innocent! How nutty!

DESPITE HIS SATIRICAL gibes at romance and sexuality, even as he and Thurber wrote their book Andy was already in love again. This time the focus of his affection was a highly respected professional woman, a writer and editor who was several years older and decades more mature than he. He had fallen for his co-worker and editor, the woman who had brought him aboard *The New Yorker*—Katharine Angell.

These were tempestuous times at the new magazine. By the time Andy arrived, Harold Ross had weathered a first year of low advertising revenues, low circulation, and low morale. Now he was cautiously thinking that the magazine might become a success, even if it wasn't yet a moneymaker. But there were still days when Ross seemed on the edge of desperation. "God, how I pity me!" he would moan in his theatrical way. Already he had hired and fired—or, whenever possible, had someone else fire—many of his former colleagues and cronies in journalism. Worry exaggerated his personal tics, such as constantly jingling the coins in his pocket. Having once been caught in a cab with nothing smaller than a ten-dollar bill, and having suffered the painful lesson of being forced to overtip, he always carried a few dollars' worth of coins. He flailed his arms as he strode down the hallways, gesturing and complaining. He dropped into offices without knocking, merely announcing "Ross!" as he opened the door. He didn't like to ride with anyone else in an elevator, and when trapped with someone he would try not to speak.

Troubled, not surprisingly, by ulcers, Ross had a long list of foods he couldn't eat, but he loved restaurants and bars. He seemed to know everyone in town and might be seen lunching not only with other members of the Algonquin Round Table but with actors such as Ethel Barrymore or publishers such as Alfred Knopf. He was a close friend of and poker player with the popular young Marx Brothers, whose musical comedies *The Cocoanuts* and *Animal Crackers*—written by another Round Table crony and *New Yorker* contributor, George S. Kaufman— stormed New York during the last half of the 1920s, just in time to be adapted into the hot new format of talking motion pictures. Under his real name, Julius H. Marx, Groucho wrote for *The New Yorker*, beginning in one of the earliest issues with an excerpt from a feeble stage routine between interlocutors dubbed Vaude and Ville.

Andy found Ross a fascinating hybrid of ambition, drive, modesty, prudery, and roughness. Ross seemed to like Andy from the first, but in his cautious way Andy needed time to adapt to Ross's style and approach to life. From early on, however, Ross credited Andy with helping establish the voice he had been seeking for the magazine—sophisticated, ironic, and literary without pretentiousness. Andy also contributed poems and stories that quickly began to establish his reputation as both a humorist and a stylish writer.

Katharine Angell was at the center of all these developments; she had become an essential part of the magazine's daily workings. Despite his frequently professed distrust of women, Ross grew ever more dependent upon Katharine's taste, education, and talent. She participated in meetings about artwork, design, layout, articles, fiction. She championed poetry as an important aspect of the magazine, despite Ross's suspicions of it because he felt more comfortable with light verse. She counseled anxious contributors, persuasively directing their work, listening to their complaints, learning about their personal lives and creating strong friendships with many of them. In the evenings she lugged home an overworked portfolio crammed with stacks of manuscript and page proofs. Katharine was a striking counterpoint to Ross's noisy profanity and restless prowling of the office halls. Patient and calm, a disciplined professional, she was hardworking, interested in a wide variety of topics, amusing when she wanted to be, distant and severe at times but not abusive, and passionately committed to the value of the carefully written word. She was also beautiful, in a reserved and regal way that appealed to Andy. He didn't overlook her beauty. He may have been a fan of sparrows and canaries, but he always had an eye for a pretty woman. So did Ross. When Katharine was about to depart for Paris, Ross handed her a letter of introduction to a friend of his, the famous cartoonist and caricaturist Ralph Barton. Later she found that the letter began, "This is to introduce Mrs. Angell, who is not unattractive."

She was also not unattached. The trip to Paris had been with her husband, Ernest Angell, an attorney she had married a year after graduation from Bryn Mawr in 1914. Angell had himself graduated from Harvard Law School a year before, after only two years in what was normally a three-year program. Passionate about civil rights, famously persistent and hardworking, Ernest had long spent most of his energy on his work, but then so had Katharine. Just after they married, he took Katharine home to his native Cleveland, Ohio, so he could launch his law career near his widowed mother. A long way from friends and family and the entertaining distractions of the Northeast, Katharine spent a few depressing months as an unemployed housewife, then went on to a variety of jobs, including running a hospital survey of handicapped citizens in Cleveland.

When their first child, daughter Nancy, was not quite a year old, Ernest enlisted in the war as a first lieutenant. Soon he was off to France, helping organize the first-ever insurance system for soldiers and winding up doing counterespionage work, for which he was decorated. Lonely and isolated, Katharine would sometimes push Nancy's baby carriage over to the home field of the Cleveland Indians, League Park (which had been renamed Dunn Field after its new owner, but the name didn't last). Growing up in Massachusetts, Katharine had been a fan of the Boston Red Sox. In 1917, the same year she found herself in Cleveland, her favorite Red Sox player, center fielder Tris Speaker, was traded to the Indians, where he was earning the highest baseball salary in history—forty thousand dollars per year. Katharine would push Nancy down the sidewalk alongside the double-decker steel-and-concrete grandstands, listening to the crowd's roar from a distance because women weren't really welcome at ball games. She would think how odd it was that she and her revered Speaker had been traded to Cleveland in the same year. When she talked about these memories later, they merely emphasized the loneliness that had dominated her marriage.

When Ernest returned following his discharge in late 1919, almost a year after the armistice, he had been gone twenty months. He was completely changed—restless, confident, eager to put the Midwest behind him, to achieve something worthwhile. He insisted upon moving to New York City, and Katharine was more than ready to leave Cleveland after the birth of their son, Roger, in 1920. Soon Ernest was working hard and Katharine was working various jobs and selling articles to *The New Republic* and elsewhere. She reviewed for the *Saturday Review of Literature* and *Atlantic Monthly*. When the U.S. Senate launched an investigation of the American occupation of the Dominican Republic and Haiti, an invasion that Woodrow Wilson had authorized in 1915, Ernest was appointed to represent the people of the countries themselves. Katharine went along and wrote two powerful articles for *The New Republic*, in which she not only fearlessly described the racism and injustice of the U.S. occupation, but even condemned President Harding's misguided 1922 appointment of a hated general.

Somewhere during this time Katharine learned that Ernest had returned from France with what she began to think of as French notions of marriage. She never learned how many mistresses he might have had, but he became ever more casual in letting her know about their shadowy presence. Once he was robbed while on a secret date with a lover and never mentioned the incident until Katharine noticed that he was no longer wearing his father's gold pocket watch. Then he told her where he had been at the time of the robbery. For a while he spent his weeknights with another woman and came home to Katharine and the children only on weekends. Thinking she had few options, and worrying that the children needed their father in whatever limited capacity, Katharine tolerated the situation. When she complained, Ernest suggested that she herself have an affair.

Katharine later claimed she was shocked that Ernest would suggest such a thing, but she was already falling in love with the playful, gentle, eccentric young Andy White at the office. Naturally they had learned a great deal about each other during their work. They had a compatible sense of humor and, they gradually realized, had many things in common, from well-educated, upper-middle-class upbringing to youthful interest in writing. Katharine had also been a prizewinner in the *St. Nicholas* league, capturing a silver badge with her entry on trapdoor spiders. Soon they were manufacturing reasons to chat together, and from there the relationship blossomed.

As early as January 1928, *The New Yorker* ran a lighthearted romantic poem, apparently addressed to Katharine, who may also have been the editor who accepted it. Called "Desk Calendar," it hinted at the secret emotions swirling around the magazine's offices. The entry for Monday begins "Now grows my heart unruly / at mention of your name," and each day ends with a variation of "No answer required." It was signed with a pseudonym—Beppo, the name of Andy's childhood Irish setter. But this time Andy's choice of pen name may have been more than his usual hiding behind animals. As widely as Andy read (despite his disclaimers), surely he knew now what he didn't know in childhood, that "Beppo" was the title of a satirical

poem by Lord Byron that contrasted English and Italian atti-
tudes toward adultery, arguing that the intolerant English version was hypocritical, that there was nothing wrong with a
woman having one husband and one lover.

While Katharine and Ernest were in Europe in the early
summer of 1928, Andy was there too, traveling with his room-
mate and old Cornell alum Gus Lobrano. (Andy claimed that
when French prostitutes approached him on the street and asked
if he was lonely and wanted to get a drink, his deadpan reply
"No man is lonely who has Jesus on his side" sent them quickly
away—but actually he didn't speak French.) For a while Katharine and Ernest were apart, perhaps so that he could meet another woman, and Katharine wound up in a brief romantic
rendezvous with Andy, in St.-Tropez and Corsica. They recalled
later the Hôtel des Étrangers, with its aromatic, vine-draped
garden populated with singing birds and scurrying lizards. Then
it was back home to New York City and The New Yorker and her
attempts to make a marriage work and his attempts to avoid
commitment.

There were many other stresses on the Angells' marriage.
They spent well beyond their financial means, sending their
children to expensive schools in New York, employing various
servants, renting a country house year-round, throwing lavish
parties, even ordering all their groceries by telephone. In December 1925, a few months after Harold Ross hired her, Katharine had published a rather desperate-sounding anonymous
article in Harper's describing the financial and social challenges
faced by a working wife and mother. The stresses continued to
build. Ernest was loud and argumentative, with a volatile temper,
and shouting fights sometimes resulted in his slapping Katharine.

The children would awaken in the night, terrified by the screaming and crying. Once, to let his parents know that he could hear
and was afraid, Roger innocently called out that he was just getting up to get a drink of water. Then one day early in 1929 Ernest slapped Katharine hard and knocked her down. She moved
out.

At the time women had little legal recourse, and shared cus-
tody meant that the children would spend most of their time
with their father, having only weekends with Katharine. To tell
eight-year-old Roger about the impending breakup, Katharine
took him for a walk at Sneden's Landing, the Sergeant family's
summer place on the shore of the Hudson River fifteen miles
upriver from New York. They walked down the narrow path
to where a brook rushed down ledges and became a waterfall.
Roger loved this area and was pleased to have a rare opportunity to be alone with his mother. Naturally Katharine had
trouble bringing up the terrible news. They were on their way
back before she led Roger across a neglected lawn and sat him
down on the steps of an unoccupied Victorian house. They sat
side by side facing the lawn; Katharine's family, like Andy's, did
not hug and were awkward in expressing affection. Slowly she
explained that she and Ernest were going to live apart. Then
came the most alarming news of all for Roger: he and Nancy,
who was twelve, would live most of the time with their father.
Katharine assured Roger that she would still see them constantly and be in their lives, and that they would come to stay
with her every weekend and on summer vacation and holidays.
"No, no, I want to stay with you!" Roger exclaimed. "I'll come
too. Nancy can stay with Father—I don't mind." But it didn't
work out that way. Roger kept watching for signs that his parents

still cared for each other, but Nancy became angry at both—particularly, at first, at her mother.

Soon Katharine was spending the requisite three months in Reno, Nevada, to get a divorce. Andy didn't visit her during this time, nor did he promise love or commitment. Already he had long been feeling claustrophobic about his job and his confusing feelings for Katharine. On the first day of January, in fact, in his annual melancholy soul-searching, he had sat on the roof of his apartment building, just outside the window, and gloomily contemplated his life and work as he stared at the heavy fog that made streetlights look like luminous balloons. He walked around the reservoir in the damp and wondered if he ought to leave town suddenly, without telling anyone where he was headed. A couple of days later, Andy found his romantic poem to Katharine, "Rhyme for a Reasonable Lady"—in which he wrote about "the animal alertness to the other's heart"—reprinted in F.P.A.'s column in the *World*. He stayed.

In Nevada, Katharine discovered a renewed sense of vitality and passion for life. She stayed at a dude ranch, rode horses, learned to herd cows, and even bought an old car to use during her time there. As she requested, in her absence Andy sought the perfect lodging for her to return to and found a three-bedroom apartment in Greenwich Village, on the third floor of an East Eighth walk-up. Its many windows looked out onto the quiet private street of Washington Mews, where tall, arching first-floor windows recalled the street's origin as stables. The whole season Katharine was away, Andy proved indecisive and noncommittal about what might lie ahead for them after her return. He didn't visit Nevada. They wrote letters. Once Katharine mailed him a sage blossom and once he clipped to his letter a couple of Baby's tail feathers.

IN NOVEMBER SHE and Andy were married by a justice of the peace, in an impromptu ceremony in a small town north of New York City. "If it lasts only a year," Katharine sighed to a friend, "it will be worth it." She made the mistake of not telling the children beforehand, following so soon after the impact of the divorce. The fallout for these decisions and what she felt as her abandonment of the children haunted her relationship with them. Roger handled it better than Nancy. For one thing, he enjoyed Andy's company. In December, only a month after the wedding, Katharine took children and new husband to visit her sister Rosie and her husband, John Newberry, in Boston. A couple of days before Christmas, Andy took Roger for a ramble—carrying their skates—down Charles Street and to the iced-over lake in the Public Garden, where they found mittened children and overcoated men already skating. There was no stove-heated shack for putting on skates, so they sat on a park bench, and Andy hid their shoes nearby. Both were good skaters, not inhibited by frozen ripples on the surface, which the wind had cleared of snow in many places. Roger laughed in delight as he and Andy bent low and skated together under an arching bridge. Afterward they found that Andy's shoes had been stolen—probably, in those hard days just after the crash on Wall Street, by a hobo. Andy had to hobble back to Myrtle Street in tiptoe on his skates. He would try not to meet the eye of amused passersby, but after they were gone, he would double over in laughter at himself. "The Skater," he said to Roger, as if captioning a satirical *New Yorker* drawing.

Andy wound up moving into the apartment he had found for Katharine. Soon, to double their elbow room as a newly married couple who both did considerable work at home, they rented the apartment above and convinced the landlord to permit them to build an internal stairway to join the two. Having decided to postpone their planned Bermuda honeymoon until spring, they were back at work the day after their wedding. Working together in the *New Yorker* offices after they married, they sent many notes to each other. In November 1929, using an interoffice memo form as he often did, Andy tried to show, in his oblique way, how he felt about his new bride. Recently the magazine had published a Rea Irvin cartoon that beautifully responded to recent news stories about the Einsteinian worldview. It showed people on a city street—an array of Irvin's standard types, from dowager and cop to doorman and working-class immigrant—all looking mournfully thoughtful. Below them ran a quotation from Albert Einstein: "People slowly accustomed themselves to the idea that the physical states of space itself were the final physical reality." In November Andy copied onto a memo form one of the characters from the cartoon: a knickers- and beret-clad boy who, sitting on the curb in the lower left background, looked rather like himself fifteen years earlier. There were a half dozen adult men in the cartoon, but Andy chose the child to represent himself. He sharpened a pencil and wrote underneath the drawing in his neat, simplified cursive, "E. B. White slowly accustomed himself to the idea that he had made the most beautiful decision of his life." Even though Katharine called him

Andy, as did everyone else in the office, he used his authorial name in this caption, as if he might experience a writerly suspense in not knowing when his audience would read these words or how she might respond.

As always, Andy managed to find all sorts of animals—even spiders—not only inspirational but even romantic. On the last day of the month, a lonely Saturday only three weeks after they were married, he was in Toronto to check on his investment in Camp Otter, an Ontario boys camp at which he had served as counselor during college. While staying in the elegant King Edward Hotel downtown, Andy spent a lot of time thinking about Katharine. Finally he wrote a poem to her that united his close-up observation of nature and his growing sense that their marriage was the right antidote to his rootlessness. Over the three decades of his life, he had spent more time watching spiders than he had experiencing romance. Now, with the easy acceptance of anthropomorphism he had learned in childhood, he used one to see the other more clearly. He called the poem "Natural History."

The spider, dropping down from twig,
Unwinds a thread of his devising;
A thin, premeditated rig,
To use in rising.

And all the journey down through space
In cool descent, and loyal-hearted,
He builds a ladder to the place
From which he started.

Thus I, gone forth, as spiders do,
In spider's web a truth discerning,
Attach one silken strand to you
For my returning.

In the spring of 1930, a few months after Andy wrote this poem, he went to the Cort Theatre on West Forty-eighth Street in midtown, which had been in operation since before he was a teenager, to see Jed Harris's revival of Chekhov's play *Uncle Vanya.* Probably seduced in part by the Cort's marble Louis XVI interior and illuminated proscenium, he sat in the darkened auditorium and surrendered to the spotlit charms of Lillian Gish as Elena and Osgood Perkins as Mikhail. The glamorous memory of them stayed with Andy for weeks: Elena in a floor-length fur-trimmed dress with a purse dangling coquettishly on a long strap as she talked with a mustached and shiny-coiffed Michael. Mostly Andy kept remembering Michael's expression of unrequited love.

Andy was thinking a lot about love. He agonized about what it meant and how it had changed his life and how it might change it more in the future. Change always frightened him, even when it was thrilling, and the uneasy blend of fear and excitement was almost overwhelming him now. Katharine had told him that she was pregnant.

So glib in his observations about pigeons and nostalgia and strangers passing on the street, Andy was unable to express to Katharine his response to this predictable but still dumbfounding revelation. Both delighted and terrified, he found himself tongue-tied. Not only could he not get around the logjam of words in his mind, but his throat began to tighten up and twitch.

He kept finding himself staring at Katharine as she moved around the apartment. He worried about how the pregnancy would affect her health, about the baby's future, about his lack of experience in this role. He felt that with her considerable experience as a mother—Roger was nine and Nancy thirteen—he in his ignorance ought to defer to her. Deferring to others, however, was not something that Andy did well. As if afraid he might run out of topics to keep him anxious, he finally worried that Katharine would think he now saw her mostly as mother-to-be rather than already-a-person. Yet he was unable to say any of this aloud.

In trying to convey his confusion, he turned to his usual way of figuring out life: he typed up his thoughts. Fleeing the complexities of adult life, again he hid behind animals. Andy and Katharine had a dog, Daisy, whose mother had been Jeannie, Jim Thurber's Scottish terrier who inspired his 1927 *New Yorker* story "The Thin Red Leash," with its memorable opening: "It takes courage for a tall thin man to lead a tiny Scotch terrier pup on a smart red leash in our neighborhood." Andy called Daisy "an opinionated little bitch," but he was fond of her—as he wound up feeling about most animals he was around. Using Daisy as a shield and a puppet, he groped his way toward intimate communication with his wife.

"Dear Mrs. White," the letter began.

White has been stewing around for two days now, a little bit worried because he is not sure that he has made you realize how glad he is that there is to be what the column writer in the *Mirror* calls a blessed event . . . I know White so well that I always know what is the matter with him, and it always comes to the same thing—he gets thinking that nothing that he writes or says ever quite expresses his feeling, and he worries about his inarticulateness just the same as he does about his bowels, except it is worse, and it makes him either mad, or sick, or with a prickly sensation in the head.

It was signed, "Lovingly, Daisy."

In late December, a few days before Christmas, the real Daisy accompanied a nervous Andy on a quick walk around the block. Dog and man stood together in front of the arch on the north side of Washington Square Park and watched an electric star hoisted into place atop the big Christmas tree. Then Andy took Katharine to the hospital to give birth. It was a horrific experience. Katharine wound up having to have a cesarean section. Their son, Joel, was born healthy, but for a while doctors worried that Katharine might not survive. She lost too much blood. Someone went out on the street and talked a taxi driver into donating for a blood transfusion, and in time she rallied.

At one point a worried nurse bent down to whisper in Katharine's ear, "Do you want to say a little prayer, dearie?"

She snapped back in her Boston accent, "Certainly not," and a terrified Andy was encouraged to think that they might go home as a new family after all.

Katharine and the baby stayed in the hospital for several days, through Christmas and beyond. On New Year's Eve, Daisy again served as ambassador between Andy's emotions and his loved ones. This time the dog wrote a letter to Joel (already nicknamed Joe), wishing him a happy first New Year and encouraging him to come home and see the blossoming narcissus in pots in the apartment. She included a typically Andyesque dollop of melancholy: "White tells me you are already drinking milk diluted with tears—in place of the conventional barley water they used to use in the gay Nineties; so I take it life is real enough for you, tears being a distillation of all melancholy vapors rising from the human heart."

This letter was signed, "Faithfully yrs, Daisy."

IN 1931, WITH six-month-old son Joel in tow, Katharine and Andy went to spend the summer on the coast of Maine. Because they always felt they needed servants to help out, they took along both a nursemaid for Joe and a cook. They found a pleasant little cottage, owned by a woman with the Dickensian name of Miss Nila Slaven, in the village of East Blue Hill, across the beautiful Blue Hill Bay from Mount Desert Island and Acadia National Park to the southeast. The park had received this name only the year before, having formerly been dubbed Lafayette National Park when, in 1919, it became the first national park east of the Mississippi River. The island really did include both mountain and desert, its peaks providing Olympian views of the region's bays and coves. South of Bangor and east of the cherished Belgrade Lakes of Andy's youth, the Blue Hill area was largely undeveloped. Both the people and the landscape were reserved but not unfriendly. Both Andy and Katharine kept working; Andy even went back into New York for some work visits. Maine may first have appeared in the White family's lives in part because of Andy's childhood allergies, but as an adult he had discovered that his hay fever actually bothered him more in rural Maine than in downtown Manhattan, so work trips into the city had their virtues. Also he found the urban world more agreeable during the summer, when many natives were out of town.

But he spent most of the summer weeks in Maine with his family. Andy loved this region—the hard-edged outlines of the pines, the softer birch, the rocky shores. Many days dawned with fog that was slow to burn off but eventually vanished to reveal an afternoon of improbably lucid light. Gulls spun overhead. Ospreys hovered above the bay until they plummeted suddenly into the water like a dropped rock, emerging with a wriggling silver fish—or, if they missed, climbing back into the sky to fall again. The boulder-strewn shores were alive with color. Round spiny green sea urchins looked as tooled as a Fabergé egg until a solemn gull opened one up to reveal the vulnerable orange and purple flesh within. Periwinkles crept across granite boulders sheathed in colonies of white barnacles shaped like tiny volcanoes. Plovers stepped delicately among the flaking shells of blue mussels and purple razor clams, amid the tide-flung brownish orange capes of knotted wrack.

The next summer they returned to the area, this time chartering a sailboat in Blue Hill and exploring the coast and islands. In 1933, having fallen in love with the region's natural beauty and quiet people, they repeated the pattern, and this time they were looking for a place to buy. One day they sailed aboard a thirty-one-foot yacht, anchoring for the night in a small inlet called Allen Cove, around the western curve of the bay and due south of Blue Hill, with Mount Desert looking grand in the east. Next morning, from the water they could see a big, solid-looking barn and some outbuildings, up beyond a decrepit old dock that projected unnaturally straight from the gentle curve of shore. The buildings stood safely back from the water, on a slight rise above the cove. To the left was a gently sloping pasture with a herd of granite boulders.

The next day Katharine and Andy explored the same region by car. Eventually they found the house that was attached, in traditional cold-region fashion, to the barn they had admired from the water. It was near a village called North Brooklin. Painted white under dark roofs, with its tall firm chimneys and dark shutters, its self-sufficient village of clustered outbuildings, the house looked strong and independent. Out by the road, beyond a yard full of fine tall trees, was a sign that read FOR SALE.

Part III

CHARLOTTE

I knew of several barns
where I thought the past might lie.

Chapter 10

DREAM FARM

Animals are a weakness with me, and when I got a place in the country I was quite sure animals would appear, and they did.

IN THE SUMMER of 1933, Andy and Katharine soon learned that the Allen Cove farm belonged to a music professor at Juilliard. He parted with its forty acres—which included three hundred feet of coastline—for eleven thousand dollars. Another immediate expense came from the decision to continue employing the caretaker, Howard Pervear. Both Katharine and Andy had grown up with servants, and Katharine still employed a cook and housekeeper and occasionally other help; adding a caretaker for their country home came naturally to them. In the middle of the worst economic times since before the Civil War, Andy and Katharine were able to buy the farm while maintaining their large, two-floor apartment on Eighth in New York, and later one on Forty-eighth Street in Turtle Bay. With *The New Yorker* flourishing—in 1934 profits passed six hundred thousand dollars—both writer and editor brought home a good income throughout the Depression. Harold Ross wisely decided that both were indispensable and kept raising their salaries. Earning close to thirty thousand dollars together in the mid-1930s between writing and editing and Katharine's small inheritance, they continued for years to live half in New York and half in Maine, with the romanticized freedom of farm life calling from behind the urban world's honking horns and claustrophobic subways.

Exposed above Allen Cove, the house encountered strong winds, but with its thick walls and broad plank floors—it had been built around 1800—it felt secure even in a snowstorm. They set up ground-floor studies across the hall from each other, his in the northwest front room and hers in the southwest, where he continued to write for and she continued to edit for the magazine that had brought them together. Over the years they developed a companionable routine. Late mornings, after farm chores were done and the rural postman had driven up with their daily array of fat envelopes containing books and manuscripts, both settled down to work. Their facing studies were separated only by the narrow space of the front hall, and neither felt the need to close a door for more privacy. His study was one giant map, the room wallpapered corner to corner in connected survey maps of Penobscot Bay, showing blue inlets and narrows and countless irregular tan island shapes from Rockport to Deer Isle and beyond. The wall to Andy's left held cabinets below and bookshelves above—a worn thesaurus, an old set of the *Encyclopaedia Britannica*, eventually the fat green 1940 edition of *The Lives and Times of Archy and Mehitabel*, other favorites, oversize bound copies of *The New Yorker*, various edi-

tions of his own books. The shelves fluttered with notes that
Andy taped up as reminders to himself.

He situated his pine desk perpendicular to the window, with
the light coming in behind him to the right and his typewriter
table forming the left leg of a U in which he worked, seated in
an old oak swivel chair. Thus while typing he faced the doorway. He could look up and see Katharine at her desk, wearing
a pale sweater over tweeds and girlishly sitting on one leg. Smoke
from her cigarette spiraled up around tortoiseshell glasses, which
sat halfway down her nose, as her pencil moved along an oversize page of *New Yorker* galleys. Occasionally one or the other
read aloud from a letter received or an article undergoing revi-
sion, but seldom from what they were actually writing. Andy
wrote Comment and his essays in staccato bursts of typing separated by long, thoughtful silences. At a young age, her son Roger
noted how much effort and time Andy invested in these seemingly casual paragraphs.

An aromatic woodshed linked house and barn, a common
adaptation in the north that facilitated animal care and milk-
gathering during subzero winters, and there were also a henhouse and a cowshed, an icehouse and a garage. Andy wrote
that the connection between house and barn meant that "without stepping out of door you can reach any animal on the place,
including the pig. This makes for greater intimacy." From the
first, he found the huge, lovely barn evocative. Its high loft,
piled with aromatic clover and timothy hay, sparked memories
of the stable behind the house in Mount Vernon, where he had
spent so many golden hours as a child. As soon as he closed the
lift-latch on the kitchen door and stepped down into the barn,

he smelled the tang of straw, cow breath, tack, rubber boots, and manure. Stalls and alcoves testified to the many skills that farming required. They held milk pails and looped rope, rusty rat traps and empty grain sacks, a harness rack here, an old wooden vise there, on one wall a penciled worming calendar and on another an agricultural-service spraying chart for pesticides. Overhead, canoes slept upside down across rafters. Everywhere tools hung on pegs or nails: axes, wooden hay rakes and metal leaf rakes, both round-headed and square-headed hoes, a primordial scythe, a curving, three-tined pitchfork. Angled light from the south windows glittered on the mean gapped teeth of two-handed saws and the metal pneumatic tubes of Crystal Duster pesticide sprayers still mounted to their Mason-jar reservoirs.

When they moved in, Andy began immediately to envision more occupants to fill his barn and his days. From childhood he had always experienced an urge to care for animals; he had seldom been without a dog, usually supplemented with a canary, a goldfish, or some other pet. He envisioned a farm full of animals before they even found the house. The morning sun shone through these windows and side-lit the nineteenth-century cattle stalls. Their thick handmade stanchions that could still lock with hewn pegs and tumblers, and their hoof scars in the plank floor, conjured like a genie the barn's own memories of and need for cows. A museum-worthy milking stool all but demanded that Andy sit on it and acquire a cow to complete the picture. Many animals came through this barn and the other buildings—not only cattle but chickens, pigs, ducks, cats, dogs, sheep, the occasional goat. Andy was as self-conscious about farming as he was about everything else. Suspecting that neighboring farmers were skeptically watching this citified newcomer, he was embarrassed to find himself doing such things as walking across the barnyard carrying a paper napkin.

Andy noted early on that in one year his 148 laying hens produced 5,784 eggs. He still loved eggs, the first glimpse of their not quite roundness and their potent weight in his hand— "a morning jewel, a perfect little thing," he wrote about finding one in the dawn. He recalled the collection of wild-bird eggs that had graced the attic on Summit Avenue, that hot, close space where he could be alone with Meccano and William J. Long's animal stories. Now, decades later, the reality of hen and goose fertility never undermined eggs' symbolic value for him. One goose laid her eggs in a nest she made beside the feed rack in the sheep shed so that when she was off the nest, the lambs would climb in for the cozy straw and incidentally warm her eggs. This was an unusual burst of imagination. Usually the members of these two groups—sheep in their solemn cliques and yammering klatches of geese—moved together in such a way that they seemed to have little individual identity. Other aspects of his birds' behavior fascinated him, such as how during the war anxious chickens mistook the silhouettes of patrol planes for hawks.

A couple of years after Andy bought this place, his mother wrote to him about his new life in the country. She recalled the toy barnyard of her own childhood, with its miniature sheep and pigs and cows and a barn with a painted sky behind it. Quite secular, lacking an infant Jesus and Wise Men, this farm by the Christmas tree nonetheless acquired in young Elwyn's mind an aura of sacred nativity. His formal, elegant mother had fondly called this toy world her "dream farm." Here in Maine, one day when Andy was using desk scissors to trim lambs' wool before entering them at the fair, he realized that he was gently biting his tongue the way he had as a child when performing such a task with one of his pets. When he finished trimming the lambs, he saw that they looked half like the sheep-bulletin photos he had used as a model and half like the little wooden lambs in his mother's toy farm. To instinctively further the emotional connections between childhood and newfound playground, Andy anchored a metal loop in the beam over the north door of the barn and ran a thick, coarse rope through it. He and Joel would climb up into the loft, grasp the rope with both hands, wrap their legs around it, settle upon the heavy knot at the base, and swing down toward the earth and back up toward the sky. It was a dizzy, joyful sensation he hadn't experienced since the Strattons' barn in Mount Vernon.

Andy was not a gentleman farmer. He didn't sit on the veranda and direct a subordinate who in turn bossed those who worked the land and tended the animals. He worked the land and tended the animals himself. True, when writing about his tasks on the farm Andy neglected to mention Katharine, Joe, their cook, their housemaid, and the full-time hired man who often employed assistants. (Eventually a Brooklin neighbor, Henry Allen, replaced Howard Pervear.) But even surrounded by help, Andy was always in the midst of the work. When he decided to dynamite boulders in his field, to create a pasture for the ideal cow he envisioned, he hand-drilled holes for dynamite, helped maneuver the blasted rock fragments onto drags with chains, drove a tractor with its Paleolithic burden scraping broad flat furrows in the field, and unloaded each stone for deposit in the edge of the woods. "People have quit calling me an escapist," he once remarked, "since learning what long hours I put in." He thought it funny that after moving to Maine and reducing his workload at *The New Yorker*, he found himself addicted to a venerable weekly farm paper called *The Rural New Yorker*.

From the barn the east windows framed the cove where they had first anchored. This stretch of Maine coast resembled Andy's beloved Belgrade Lakes region farther inland except that here the sea gave the land a hardscrabble air. But bleakness appealed to Andy's Romantic sensibilities. Sunlit days alternated with sudden fog that could trap a sailor but made the world look mysterious and poetic to a writer safely moored on shore. Fog was always a threat in the back of Andy's mind when he was out in a boat. On land it could be so thick it smothered a cigarette after a few puffs and would leave forgotten tennis shoes sopping merely from having wicked moisture out of the air. In this damp climate some homes and businesses smelled of mildew.

Andy considered that the farm extended far beyond its official property lines, into the bay and what he described as "the restless fields of protein." Always Andy needed to feel self-sufficient. He liked knowing that he could walk past his barn and henhouse, past the garden with its potatoes and asparagus and beets and cucumbers, down the lane of pigweed and thistles, through the pasture where the heifers and calves dodged granite rocks in the soil to nibble wild strawberries, stroll in between the low blueberry bushes and past the ground-hugging cranberry vines heavy with crimson fruit, settle into a boat, and find himself still harvesting from the water itself. In fact, he could start harvesting marine animals even before he got into the boat, in the clam beds that he cautiously prowled barefoot. The tide could vary as much as sixteen feet in a day, and in flood tide the dock's pilings attracted flounder, with their surreal condition of two eyes clustered together on the flattened body, and hand-size cunner, a notorious bait-stealer so small that most fishermen threw them back into the water. Just beyond the point, lobsters lurked. Every summer, only two miles out into the bay, schools of mackerel lured a regatta of family boats to a local Sunday social event simply called mackereling. "When you have your own boat," Andy observed, "you have your own world, and the sea is anybody's front yard."

When Katharine and Andy moved in, the farm had no running water. There was, however, a fresh spring in an always damp glade not far away. There, in the shade of tamarack and alder, amid the ethereal calls of woodcock and the splashes of a frog fleeing his approach along the path sprinkled with tiny tamarack cones, Andy often glimpsed an eel that had somehow navigated up the pasture's brook with blind commitment. Trekking all the way here and back to the house seemed a burden at the time. Later, however, after he had the spring encased in stone and concrete and fitted with an electric pump that drew the water out of a copper pipe, he missed the days of carrying heavy, splashing pails through the woods.

In the country Andy reveled in the parade of nonhuman neighbors. Flotillas of fat black coots drifted by with their white bills visible from surprisingly far away, and beyond them toured loons, whose elegant motif and pared silhouette made the coots look frumpy. Gulls screamed and seals barked. In the course of a day Andy met deer and porcupines, skunks, squirrels both red and gray. He might spy the tracks of weasel and mink. Chittering squadrons of barn swallows flew in and out through the open barn door, their rich blue wings flashing. Where could he find a greater range of birds than between the red-throated hummingbird hovering at Katharine's tiger lilies and the great horned owl that dropped silently out of an alder down by the swamp? Whip-poor-wills called and tree toads chirred. The soil itself was populous—chipmunks, snails, moles, snakes, frogs, woodchucks. The margins of Andy's day were busy with their scurry, their naive surprise at his approach and their predictable rush down a burrow.

Later, he enjoyed the company of the raccoon that nested in the big, hollow balm of Gilead tree in front of the house. This particular neighbor gave birth to her young thirty-five feet in the air, just outside and slightly above Andy and Katharine's own bed. Since childhood, especially since the stories of William J. Long about Mooweesuk the raccoon—"a pocket edition" of Mooween the bear—Andy had found raccoons charming. He grew so accustomed to this female's predictable nocturnal habits that he would get out of bed at three in the morning to watch her shimmy back up the tree trunk to her sleeping kits. He liked to glimpse her silhouette against the sky and he admired the watchful way she sniffed around the door of her home to learn if enemies had trespassed in her absence. During Joe's early childhood, Andy guarded his own house and family in a similar way, making the rounds every night before bed, locking all the doors, checking the lamps and stoves, and taking a last quiet peek into Joe's room for a glimpse of his innocent sleep.

IN 1934, DURING Katharine and Andy's first summer on the farm, his now white-haired parents—Samuel was eighty and Jessie seventy-six—came to visit. They enjoyed the bracing country air and the rugged coast so close to where the family had summered every year in Andy's childhood. Married and with a son, happy on a farm, their youngest child seemed to be finally settling into life. The next August, Samuel died at Mount Vernon, and Jessie moved to Washington, D.C., to live with Clara, Andy's middle sister.

In April 1936, Christopher Morley, a founder of and now a contributing editor at *The Saturday Review of Literature*, wrote to invite Andy to become the magazine's new editor. A decade older than Andy, Morley bridged the generations between one of Andy's heroes—Don Marquis—and Andy himself. A close friend of Marquis's, Morley had become, since the publication of his quirky novels *Parnassus on Wheels* and *The Haunted Bookshop*, around the end of the World War, one of the more versatile men of letters in the United States. Poet, journalist, essayist, novelist, and editor, Morley had been one of the first judges of the now decade-old Book of the Month Club and had just been asked to edit the eleventh edition of Bartlett's *Familiar Quotations*. Two years earlier, he had cofounded the Baker Street Irregulars, a loose affiliation of Sherlock Holmes fans who met at the Algonquin Hotel, where Morley had also helped launch the informal and unofficial but already legendary Three Hours for Lunch Club. Andy was touched by Morley's invitation but made clear that he could not seriously consider such an offer. With numerous asides about his congestion and fever—including a reference to "when the Last Great Bronchitis comes"—he protested that he read "so slowly & so infrequently" that he would make a terrible editor, adding, "What a fine, mad bunch of people you must be, anyway, to have cooked up such a notion!"

As Andy's fame grew, his past receded. Four days later, before he was even over the bronchitis, an exhausted Andy had to take a train to Washington, where his mother was having gallbladder surgery. The family had been optimistic about the surgery's ability to cure Jessie's pain and extend her life. But the surgeon found not only that her gallbladder was clotted with a half dozen acorn-size stones, but also that it, her liver, and parts of her colon were eaten up with cancer so badly that he felt nothing could be done. Surgery itself would kill her. He stitched the incision back together and quietly informed the family that their mother *might* be able to hang on for a few more months. They didn't tell Jessie about the cancer, only about the stones. "She is very vague about diseases, anyway," Andy wrote home to Kay, "and she has never been the sort of person to face facts realistically."

Clara had been tending their mother since Samuel's death. Because of her husband's mental breakdown, she needed work and was about to launch a country inn that would serve three dozen guests per day, a venture requiring a huge investment of her energy and money. It was time for someone else to care for Jessie, so Lillian and Andy discussed alternatives. They looked at a nursing home in Chevy Chase, Maryland; Lillian suggested that she could rent a beachside cottage near Washington and move their mother in with her; and Andy considered moving her and a nurse to Maine to be near him and Kay.

But Jessie's energy and will to live raced downhill over the next couple of weeks. On Wednesday, May 13, Andy was back in Washington, arriving at the Catholic hospital during a hot and noisy thunderstorm—ominous dark clouds, lightning flashing, the heat and air pressure wreaking havoc with Andy's always delicate respiratory system. Jessie lay in her hospital room, small and frail amid the antiseptic white sheets and metal bed frame, frightened by the loud, bright lightning and suffering almost unbearable pain. Her tormented children stood around in a helpless tableau, looking at the tortured limbs of silent Christ on a crucifix at the foot of her bed.

The storm cleared the air. During the night the humidity and temperature both fell, and Thursday morning was clear, the blue sky fresh and clean. Back at the hospital, Andy found his mother also looking cleansed and calm. She seemed to be past the pain, at least for now. Light flooded in the window and showed Jessie small and weak in the bed, yet almost alarmingly bright-eyed.

The contrast between last night and this morning prompted Andy to indicate the benign weather and say, "Isn't it beautiful, Mother?"

But Jessie was thinking about death, not weather. With surprising fervor she exclaimed, "Oh my, oh my—it's perfectly beautiful."

Her mood seemed exalted, transcendent. Knowing she had little time, apparently worried she might even run out of energy to speak, she assured them that the approach of death was actually a beautiful experience. They could hear children singing in the parochial school across the street, and Jessie said she loved the sound of their voices. Andy didn't know how much she was influenced by painkillers—she could barely focus her gaze on them—and how much her own internal system was deluding itself.

Clara took Jessie's hand and asked, "Mother, you're perfectly comfortable, aren't you?"

"Perfectly comfortable."

"And you're perfectly happy?"

"Perfectly happy," Jessie sighed. She seemed to need desperately to reassure her children, as if to soften their loss of her. Whenever a spasm of pain went through her, making her whisper "Oh" again and again, she would soon manage to conjure a weak smile and murmur, "That means absolutely nothing at all."

She died that night, with Clara beside her in the darkness.

That summer the long, slow rhythms of life were more visible than usual. As he grieved over the deaths of his parents only nine months apart, Andy's mind kept journeying down old back roads to revisit the best days of his childhood. He was only thirty-seven, but he kept looking back. He decided to risk returning to Belgrade Lakes, to try to recapture his magical experiences there. He took the train again, the Bar Harbor Express, and watched mist rise from the pastures as the tracks skirted around Lake Messalonskee. He revisited old sensations and renewed their potency: the chime of a distant cowbell, the scent of woodsmoke and lumber and coffee, the taste of birch beer at Bean's old lakeside store, the sparkle of whitecaps in the wind, his bare feet on the warm wooden boards of a dock. It all seemed reassuringly familiar, as if he had returned to the one place in the world where time didn't move, where nothing changed, where childhood and parents lived forever. Toward the end of his visit there, overwhelmed with observations and memories, Andy sat down to write a long letter to Stan, detailing a few changes but mostly reminiscing and emphasizing the similarities between then and now. "Yes, sir, I returned to Belgrade, and things don't change much," he wrote. "I thought somebody ought to know."

★   ★   ★

ANDY'S CAREER HAD proven as unpredictable as his personal life. In a surprising 1934 critique of *The New Yorker* in *Fortune*, Andy and Katharine's former colleague Ralph Ingersoll had taken the magazine in general and Andy in particular to task. He referred to Andy's "gossamer" writing, describing him as "frightened of life," complaining that his recurring themes were terriers, guppies, and a crusade "against the complexity of life." The latter criticism was true and not necessarily wounding. The charge of ephemeral irrelevance, however, stabbed Andy in his most sensitive doubts about himself. Ingersoll was right about another point: Andy had indeed been a part of the magazine's decision to resist for too long commenting upon the poverty and strife of Depression-era America. This kind of attitude had kept Hollywood producing comedies—*Swing Time*, *Bringing Up Baby*, *Show Boat*—at which hard-earned quarters could be traded for escape from breadlines and rumors of war.

Ingersoll's mockery helped fuel Andy's restlessness with *The New Yorker* and with New York itself. Despite glowing reviews of his 1935 collection of Comment pieces, *Every Day Is Saturday*, he was unable to persuade Ross to let him write a longer signed column and thus escape from the anonymity and lightweight reputation of the Comment pieces. *The Atlantic* and *Scribner's* rejected his essays, leaving him yearning for the opportunity to prove himself, or perhaps find himself, in a more demanding form. But his growing fame led to a timely invitation from *Harper's* to write a monthly essay-length column, roughly twenty-five hundred words, for three hundred dollars apiece. "I was a man in search of the first person singular," he wrote. He continued to write Comment for *The New Yorker*, but in his *Harper's* column, "One Man's Meat," he explored new ground. He published a lighthearted tribute to, yes, his long-deceased Boston terrier, a survey of a new kind of field guide invented by a man named Roger Tory Peterson, nostalgic snapshots of the journals young Elwyn had kept in high school during World War I, passionate meditations on freedom and democracy in the new world situation, lyrical glimmers of mortality, and an ode to his favorite writer, Henry David Thoreau. Andy seldom wrote about books or other writers, but he returned often to Thoreau. He once described *Walden* as the only book he "owned," that others merely lived with him. "The note he sounded," he wrote of his hero, "was like the white-throat's—pure, wavering, full of the ecstasy of loneliness."

Often Andy thought of Thoreau and Walden Pond. The neon distractions of Times Square could not compare in Andy's mind with the seals that swam beside his boat in the cove, raising their slicked wet heads out of the water like mermaids and barking through the fog. In 1938 the White family moved to the farm full-time—despite the looming obstacles of long-distance editing and writing, despite having to pull Joe out of a private New York school and move him to a one-room schoolhouse in a village—and despite Katharine's decision, in wanting Andy to be happy, to leave what their colleague Wolcott Gibbs called "the greatest job in the world," a prime editorial position at one of the most influential literary magazines in America.

Having moved as the war was building up in Europe, Andy often felt that his new preoccupations were trivial and even futile. Why was he so fortunate as to be able to milk his cows and write his sly *New Yorker* paragraphs rather than die on a battlefield? One cold early-spring evening he was tending the fickle brooder stove in his henhouse, trying to maintain a maternal fire for the 254 innocent chicks gathered around it—depending upon its warmth for survival—when Joe came out to tell him that dinner was ready and the war news on the radio was bad. A few months earlier, Germany, Italy, and Japan had signed the Tripartite Pact to form the Axis. Clearly they were planning to invade Russia. When Andy wrote up this particular evening for his *Harper's* column, he thought of recent Third Reich propaganda claiming that Aryan domination was the spring (*Frühling*) that would not end, so he said, "I soon knew that the remaining warmth in this stubborn stove was all I had to pit against the Nazi idea of *Frühling*." He redistributed a hundred or so chicks to areas where they were likelier to stay warm and went indoors to be with his family. The kitchen was cozy and the lights bright. In his essay he crafted a home-front manifesto featuring his favorite symbol of life: "Countries are ransacked, valleys drenched with blood. Though it seems untimely I still publish my belief in the egg, the contents of the egg, the warm coal, and the necessity for pursuing whatever fire delights and sustains you."

In the summer of 1941 he further sustained himself by turning again to Belgrade Lakes, this time with Joe. He worried that time would have tarnished what he thought of as a holy spot, but the major change was in Andy himself. Emotionally disoriented, he kept seeing his own childhood in Joe's every move with a fishing pole or canoe. And if Joe was the young Andy, then Andy had to face that he, now orphaned, had become his father.

Chapter 11

THE MOUSE OF THOUGHT

Creation is in part merely the business of forgoing the great and small distractions.

ONE OF ANDY'S early essays for *Harper's* concerned the shipments of children's books that Katharine received every autumn for her annual review roundup in *The New Yorker*. Publishers' nominees, forwarded to Maine from the magazine's offices, flooded into the house, sometimes ten or twenty in a single package. Because the Whites' shelves were already full, the new books teetered in stacks, stealing floor space and climbing onto the furniture like unruly pets, until eventually most wound up donated to the Brooklin area's public schools.

Katharine briefly reviewed as many books as possible and listed others, thereby covering an average of fifty volumes per review, sometimes as many as eighty. She chose books she found well written or amusing or that particularly appealed to Joe, her in-house junior critic. She quoted him, for example, on the author of *The Little Prince*: "He seems to be writing about grownup things in a childish way." Her own comments were similarly brisk but often salty. Of *The Travels of Babar*, the second install-ment in Jean de Brunhoff's series about an orphaned elephant, Katharine wrote, "This year Babar is officially blessed by A. A. Milne in a prefatory paragraph, an unnecessary and misleading condescension, since de Brunhoff is witty without being Poohish, and Babar is an elephant who can stand on his own feet."

Every year Andy began the season by resenting the influx of books, then soon found himself sprawled on the hearth and im-mersed in a tome about how to build a tree house. He read many of the books, from William Karl Harriman's *The Story of Tea* to Lynnwood M. Chace and Evelyn M. Chadwick's *Little Orphan Willie-Mouse*, which featured photographs of an actual wood mouse. Impressively detailed historical accounts stretched from Los Angeles to Tibet, from Williamsburg to Bali. Frances Cava-nah's *Boyhood Adventures of Our Presidents* featured on the front, stamped in red on the beige cloth, a Tom Sawyerish lad appar-ently running away from home; chapters were along the lines of "Tom Jefferson Climbs a Mountain." The hero of the lushly col-ored *Soomoon, Boy of Bali*, who seemed to have the same idea as the boyhood presidents, was carrying his belongings on a pole, along with a white rooster in a cage. *Bumblebuzz*, by Rosalie K. Fry, drew Andy in with a painting on the cover of a bumblebee strolling along with a two-spotted ladybug.

Many of the more practical volumes struck him as unwit-tingly humorous—especially tirades about safety. "It is an odd place, this front yard of World Crisis," he wrote, "where adults with blueprints of bombproof shelters sticking from their pants pockets solemnly caution their little ones against running down-stairs with lollypops in their mouths." A disappointing number of the books, he thought, lacked imagination and a sense of language. One that had plenty of both was an odd prose narrative entitled *The 500 Hats of Bartholomew Cubbins*, by someone calling himself Dr. Seuss (which Andy misspelled in his essay).

"Close contact with the field of juvenile literature," he wrote, "leads me to the conclusion that it must be a lot of fun to write for children—reasonably easy work, perhaps even important work. One side of it that must be exciting is finding a place, a period, or a thing that hasn't already been written about." He pointed out that "with science dominating life nowadays," perhaps it wasn't surprising that the authors of many children's books at least nodded dutifully toward an animal's actual behavior. "Even the cute animals of the nonsense school move against impeccable backgrounds of natural history," he noted; "even a female ant who is sufficiently irregular to be able to talk English lays her eggs at the proper time and in the accepted manner."

WHEN HE CAME to write a children's book himself, only a few years after this essay, Andy casually mixed human and animal characters. Although Katharine and Andy purchased the Maine farm more than a decade before *Stuart Little* was published in 1945, the characters in it weren't based upon the animals in their daily lives. Long before, Stuart had arrived in Andy's mind in a direct shipment from his subconscious. In the spring of 1926 he had visited the lush Shenandoah Valley in Virginia. During his return train ride to New York, while he slept in an upper berth to the rhythm that he had loved since his first rail trip to Maine, he dreamed of a tiny, mouselike child—adventurous, polite but straightforward, dapper, and even supplied with hat and cane. The next morning, when Andy awoke, he remembered this odd character and scribbled a few notes about him.

Soon he made use of them. By then, between his various siblings, he had eighteen nieces and nephews, but no children of his own, so he often found himself called upon at family gatherings to amuse the youngsters with a story. Fond of children and popular with them, he was nonetheless embarrassed in the spotlight. He stammered and struggled, worrying that his poor performance was disappointing as he tried to invent a story on the spot. So he turned to the mouse-child in his mind and wrote up a few adventures for him, providing himself with narrative ammunition that he could pull from a desk drawer whenever a child begged for a story.

These typed manuscripts appealed to others besides children—including Katharine, not surprisingly. In 1935 she showed Clarence Day the Stuart adventures that had thus far accumulated. A regular *New Yorker* contributor best known for his humorous autobiographical stories culminating in *Life with Father*, Day was also a respected family friend. When he said, "Don't let Andy neglect *Stuart Little*—it sounds like one of those *real* books that last," the remark counted. But Andy still didn't pursue the stories. Then in late 1938 he published his essay about rambling through Katharine's flood of children's books. At the New York Public Library, the prominent and influential children's librarian Anne Carroll Moore read Andy's essay and wrote to him, encouraging him to tackle the need for great children's literature himself, to create something that would "make the library lions roar." He replied, "My fears about writing for children are great—one can so easily slip into a cheap sort of whimsy or cuteness."

Meanwhile Katharine had spread the gospel of Stuart elsewhere, to Eugene Saxton, Andy's editor at Harper (until his death in 1942), who asked to see whatever adventures already existed. Andy sent the pages, adding up to more than ten thousand words, in March 1939, with the note, "It would seem to be for children, but I'm not fussy who reads it." He pointed out that, while Stuart was an imaginary mouse, he did not in any way resemble Mickey of dubious fame. He explained that because Stuart had appeared to him in a dream, as a gift rather than an invention, he didn't feel free to metamorphose him from a mouse into a wallaby or a grasshopper.

Harper responded enthusiastically and Saxton encouraged Andy to complete the book as soon as possible. Naturally the aim of simply moving forward on a project made Andy nervous. (He had informed Anne Carroll Moore that he resisted goading like a mule.) He replied, "I can't make any promises," and explained that he was currently tending two hundred and fifty chicks. He hoped he might have the book finished by autumn.

It took him six years.

IN EARLY SPRING of 1943, Andy was as busy as ever on the farm. He sold cows and chopped lambs' tails, built sheds and started a new set of chicks. With the war on and many shortages back home, he had to persuade the gas ration board to allow him to drive once a week to Blue Hill's post office to mail in his *New Yorker* "News and Comment" pieces. Now and then he took time out to fish for smelt brought in by the tide. He could also be found gazing upward in the sunset to watch the woodcocks' mating dance in the sky. Thirteen-year-old Joe had noticed that the lovesick male always flew back down to the place from which he took off, so the boy was able to walk a few steps closer during each flight, then stand perfectly still as the male came back to land. Eventually he crept to within ten feet of the plump, long-billed bird.

What Andy was not doing was writing. Despite ongoing depression, he was in a better mood—after a long, lingering winter and the dreary rains of spring—in part because he had yet again renounced a writing commitment. He had written to Frederick Lewis Allen, his editor at *Harper's*, to confess that, although he had no complaints about how the magazine had treated him, he had always had great difficulty in writing his monthly "One Man's Meat" column. He explained that a regular commitment didn't come naturally to him, and he knew that sometimes he sent in subpar work because of a looming deadline. He used the kind of sentence he had employed in many situations when things seemed to everyone else to be going well: "So the only thing for me to do is quit."

When Allen tried to talk him out of it, Andy replied that, yes, having such a commitment was good discipline, but discipline was not what he needed at the moment. "I want," he said flatly, "to write when and if I feel like it."

What he did not know was when the urge might strike him or what he might then want to write. During 1943 he wrote Comment as usual, but mostly he avoided his typewriter. It was a scary time. During this period he experienced what he described as a "nervous crack-up." For many months he had had trouble sleeping. He had been experiencing dizziness, possibly

The home of Samuel and Jessie White in Mount Vernon, New York, where Elwyn Brooks White was born in 1899 and from which he cautiously ventured to explore the neighborhood.

The stable next to the White home in Mount Vernon, where Elwyn tended horses, dogs, rabbits, chickens, and other creatures, and where he first developed his lifelong fondness for barns and domestic animals. Elwyn is in the foreground, in his Buster Brown suit, circa 1905.

The White family on the porch of a summer cabin at Great Pond, Maine, circa 1908. Elwyn is at center on the steps, to the left of his sister Lillian, who was closest to him in age. On the porch, beyond their mother Jessie, are Clara, Stanley, and Albert.

Belgrade Lake

Maine is one of the most beautiful states in the Union, and Belgrade is one of the most beautiful of the lakes of Maine.

This wonderful lake is five miles wide, and about ten miles long, with many coves, points and islands. It is one

②

he first page of Elwyn's handwritten pamphlet about the summer camps in Maine where is family spent every August. He wrote this in his mid-teens for his friend and neighbor 'reddie Schuler.

The recently married Andy and Katharine in a group photo taken in 1930 at a party celebrating the fiftieth anniversary of Andy's parents, Samuel and Jessie White.

Andy and Katharine in the 1940s, with their dachshund Minnie.

Katharine and E. B. White feeding their sheep on the farm in Maine in the 1940s, a few years before he began writing *Charlotte's Web*.

Katharine holding some of the spring pigs whose lives inspired the story of Wilbur.

Andy's drawing of the farm in Maine from across the road. Allen Cove is visible beyond the barn and house, with foreshortening from this angle making the distance across the cove to the mountains look shorter than it really is. Note how the barn is attached to the house in Maine fashion. To the left, beyond the fence, was the road that led down through the woods to the boathouse.

The farm that Andy and Katharine bought in 1933, on Allen Cove in Maine.

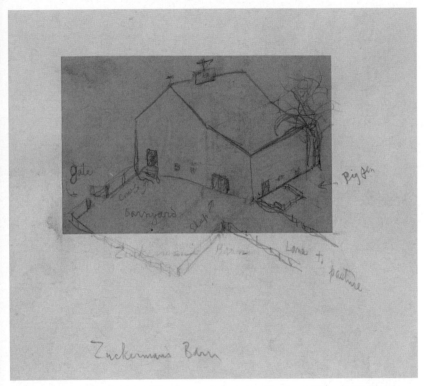

Andy's sketch of the layout of Zuckerman's barn in *Charlotte's Web*, originally begun on a small three-by-five-inch card and then pasted inside a manila envelope and extended beyond the card's edges.

Chapter I. The Barn

A barn can have a horse in it, and a barn can have a cow in it, and a barn can have hens scratching in the chaff and swallows flying in and out through the door — but if a barn hasn't got a pig in it, it is hardly worth talking about. I am very glad to say that Mr. Zuckerman's barn had a pig in it, and therefore I feel free to talk about it as much as I want to. The pig's

name was Wilbur. He was small and white, except when he was dirty — then he was small and brown. Wilbur did not get dirty on purpose, but he lived in the lower part of the barn where

CHARLOTTE

The first page of an early pencil draft of *Charlotte's Web*, with the author's sketch of Charlotte in the upper left corner. White started the story over numerous times and revised each draft extensively as he wrote.

related to his ongoing sinus troubles, for which he finally underwent an operation that seemed to have little effect. He consulted a psychiatrist, took tests, was told that perhaps even his
dizziness and hyperventilation were psychosomatic. What helped
him more than doctors, he thought, was tinkering at his workbench, taking lots of showers, drinking small amounts of dry
sherry, and playing favorite old recordings over and over.

Many changes were taking place. Joe was now attending
Exeter. In 1943 Andy and Katherine gave in to Harold Ross's
wartime pleas for help—and offers of higher salaries—and had
decided to return to full-time *New Yorker* work, which meant
wintering in the city rather than at the farm. The magazine
provided a furnished apartment on East Thirty-fifth Street and
life fell back into a semblance of its old routine—except that
more than ever Andy was experiencing a sense of failure, of
having never accomplished the significant writing of which he
dreamed he might be capable. He complained that his head felt
like an overcharged car battery. He told his brother Stan that he
was going to consult a psychiatrist because his brain also felt
like a tree with a kite tangled in its branches.

The next year, when he published a few clues to his mental
state, a particular image recurred. In February *The New Yorker*
published his poem "Home Song," including the line "Ever at
home are the mice in hiding." In October the magazine published his brief poem "Vermin," in which he confessed, "The
mouse of Thought infests my head . . . He is too quick for me, /
I see only his tail." The next year, 1945, he told Stan that he suffered from "mice in the subconscious." Mice had always been
a recurring theme in his writing. He had identified with them
even more than most children do, especially after the visits to

his Summit Avenue bedroom by his secret mouse friend. His first published writing was about this creature, the childhood poem that won him an award from *Woman's Home Companion* when he was nine, titled "To a Mouse." And once, back in the fraternity house at Cornell, he found a mouse hiding in one of the cubbyholes of his rolltop desk, and both sat unmoving, staring at each other until one of Andy's fraternity brothers walked in and broke up the tableau. In 1926 Andy's first unsigned Comment paragraph for *The New Yorker* had been not about a mouse but about buying a mousetrap.

During the winter of 1944–45, convinced that he was going to die or at least go crazy, Andy sat looking across his desk at West Eleventh Street below, and he was able to complete *Stuart Little* within two months. Originally Stuart's surname was Ade. While Andy was writing the book, however, he and Katharine were also editing an anthology, *A Subtreasury of American Humor*, in which they decided to include a story by George Ade. Maintaining his policy of steering away from resemblance to real people, Andy switched Stuart's name to the more apt Little. Perhaps the oddest aspect of the novel, considering the animal that kept infesting Andy's brain, was that he explicitly stated that Stuart was *not* a mouse, merely a boy who looks like a mouse, weighing so little at birth that "he could have been sent first class mail for three cents." Like his creator, Stuart turned out to be handy, versatile, and plucky, and the opening chapters of the book found him in lighthearted adventures down a bathtub drain and inside a piano. Later, after Stuart's Andy-like decision "to run away from home without telling anybody," Andy's text became more emotional and resonant. The carefree early adventures Andy had written while in his late twenties. The later material emerged from this difficult year in his forties.

Stuart even found himself paddling one of the souvenir birch-bark canoes that Andy had seen at Bean's store on the Maine lake in his childhood. Although he portrayed Stuart's infatuation with the young teacher, Miss Harriet Ames, as a poignant romantic comedy in which Harriet is far wiser, it expressed much of the author's own experience with romance—including a failed date after much anticipation. Following this interlude with another human, Andy kept Stuart's vision of ideal love untainted by the complexities of human interaction, by having it take place not only between a bird and a human mouse, for whom sexuality could never complicate matters, but also mostly keeping his bird friend Margalo offstage and, presumably, unattainable. The book ends not with the culmination of the quest but with his committing to it.

FOR *STUART LITTLE*, Andy was working with a new division at Harper & Brothers—with Ursula Nordstrom, head of the Department of Books for Boys and Girls. In the late-nineteenth century, there had been a movement in the United States to create children's reading rooms in public libraries; by the first decades of the twentieth century, these were commonplace nationwide. Gradually many publishers added departments devoted to children's literature, focusing especially on meeting the needs of the growing library market. Although they had already been producing notable books for generations of children—the company was established in 1817—Harper & Brothers didn't create an official children's department until

1926. Originally it comprised only an editor, an assistant editor, and a secretary. The first directing editor was Virginia Kirkus, who in 1933 founded *Kirkus Reviews*, which quickly became an influential review publication, giving bookstores and publishers a heads-up about the thousands of upcoming titles each year.

A timid New Yorker named Ursula Nordstrom, barely out of her teens, joined Harper's staff in 1931. When she walked in the door, her literary talents were not immediately apparent. She began not as an editor in Books for Boys and Girls but as a clerk in College Textbooks. Despite her intelligence and her interest in the arts, Nordstrom's parents—both actors, her father the famous silent film star Henry E. Dixie—had declined to send her to college and had instead lobbied for secretarial school. Quickly learning the business and outgrowing her shyness, Nordstrom became known as a bright and ambitious young woman with a good sense of humor. After five years of relative boredom in a corner of the company that didn't excite her imagination, Nordstrom was eager to take what she had learned about publishing and apply it in a more congenial environment. When Virginia Kirkus retired in 1936, her former assistant, Ida Louise Raymond, replaced her and took Nordstrom along as assistant editor. Soon, amid messy offices, she was dealing with such writers as Laura Ingalls Wilder.

In 1940 Nordstrom was promoted to director. During the four years since then she had critiqued, encouraged, and cajoled such writers as Margret and H. A. Rey, the married cocreators of a farcical romp entitled *Curious George*, and Margaret Wise Brown, author of a lyrical picture book called *The Runaway Bunny*. Nordstrom was no proponent of artificially sweetened pablum for tots. A witty and talkative workaholic, she believed passionately in the importance of good literature for children, but she did not idealize either children or the world of adulthood to which they were headed. She liked *Stuart Little*'s ambiguities and the unresolved quest at the end.

As Andy well knew from previous experience, the public reaction to a book was unpredictable. One of the stranger responses to *Stuart Little* came from Anne Carroll Moore, the New York librarian who had encouraged him to write the book in the first place. Before it was even published, she wrote again, saying that she had seen the proofs—Harper had sent a set, expecting applause—and she felt that the novel was inconclusive and not affirmative. She actually argued that it was unfit for children. In her surprising battle with Stuart, Moore launched two more salvos: she wrote a letter to Ursula Nordstrom, insisting that the book should not be published, and followed up with a fourteen-page missive to Katharine, advising that Andy cancel the planned publication, insisting that Stuart was unruly and that his story failed in every way to correspond to time-honored patterns for fantasy. Andy ignored her. Katharine replied with restrained politeness.

Nordstrom approached several artists to illustrate the book. Nominees included Aldren Watson, a muralist and illustrator, and Don Freeman, most of whose artwork concerned the world of theater in New York City. Nordstrom and Andy were both also interested in the possibility of getting Robert Lawson, who had gained recognition as illustrator of Munro Leaf's 1936 book, *The Story of Ferdinand*—a tale of a timid bull that, in the prewar years, was denounced as pacifist propaganda. Both author and editor admired Lawson's elegant draftsmanship and commitment to research, but he had long-running commitments to Harper's rival publishers Viking and Little, Brown. (In 1945, the year that *Stuart* was published, Lawson won the Newbery Medal for *Rabbit Hill,* a dream of peaceful coexistence that he wrote and illustrated.)

Then Andy thought of drawings he had seen in *The New Yorker* off and on through the later war years by an ambitious young man named Garth Williams, who had not yet illustrated any books. Under a tight deadline from Harper, Williams submitted preliminary sketches, which included thoughtful attention to detail and respect for the story. Andy chose Williams. He mentioned to Nordstrom how Ernest Shepard had enlarged the proportions of Mole and Toad in *The Wind in the Willows.* Williams tried this approach but found that he couldn't make it work because in the text Andy often referred to Stuart's diminutive size.

When the novel was published in October, reviews were mostly very positive, including praise from critics who treated it as serious literature. Children and adults both read the book and sales were impressive. As far as Andy could tell, Stuart's unnatural mousiness turned out to be a preoccupation only around the *New Yorker* offices. When he ran into critic Edmund Wilson in the hallway, Wilson said in his high-pitched voice, "I read that book of yours. I found the first part quite amusing—about the mouse, you know. But," he confessed, "I was disappointed that you didn't develop the theme more in the manner of Kafka."

Earlier Harold Ross had dropped in to Andy's office. Andy looked up to find him standing in the doorway. He looked jaunty with his briefcase hooked on a walking stick over his shoulder, but his expression was solemn.

"Saw your book, White."

Andy looked at him.

Ross growled, "You made one serious mistake."

"What was that?"

"Why, the mouse! You said he was *born*." Always volatile and always sensitive to implications about sexuality or other behind-the-scenes intimacies, Ross was suddenly shouting. The logistical implications of a mouselike child born to a normal human mother were too much for him. "God damn it, White, you should have had him adopted!"

Meanwhile Stuart had come alive for other readers as he had for his creator. Before publication, Andy had written a letter to Nordstrom, offering his vast barn as a cemetery for unsold copies of *Stuart Little*. (His hero, Thoreau, had once bought up all the unsold copies of *A Week on the Concord and Merrimack Rivers*, remarking in his journal, "I have now a library of nearly nine hundred volumes, over seven hundred of which I wrote myself.") But Nordstrom replied that she wasn't worried because Harper was about to increase the first printing to more than fifty thousand.

Like every other book, Andy's first children's fantasy was out in the world without him, having its own adventures. In the autumn of 1945, for example, a man in New York named Stuart Little wrote to Nordstrom. Despite the name on his letterhead, she thought this claim was a joke and called his number and asked cautiously for Mr. Little. He was real. He wanted only a signed copy of the book. And while riding Manhattan buses in the first few months after publication, Garth Williams kept seeing commuters reading *Stuart Little*, sometimes three at once around him. He found these repeated glimpses of his carefully composed cover—Stuart paddling in his souvenir canoe down a rushing brook—so heartening he decided that, rather than pursue other kinds of artwork, he would concentrate on illustrating children's books. Perhaps he could make a living at it.

Chapter 12

FOREKNOWLEDGE

Confronted by new challenges, surrounded by new acquaintances—including the characters in the barnyard, who were later to reappear in Charlotte's Web—*I was suddenly seeing, feeling, and listening as a child sees, feels, and listens.*

AFTER THE UNITED States dropped atomic bombs on Hiroshima and Nagasaki, eventually killing hundreds of thousands of innocent people, Andy spent the last half of the 1940s expecting Armageddon. The war's ravages, its global reminders of the innate human lust for blood and destruction, left scars on millions who never saw the front, and Andy kept thinking about it. Were human beings really about to annihilate themselves?

In late March of 1948 Andy was in New York, unable to celebrate the vernal equinox in the countryside. Shortly before his favorite seasonal milestone, he went out to a moody lunch alone at the Roosevelt Grill, in the Roosevelt Hotel on East Forty-fifth Street, only three blocks from the *New Yorker* offices. The

Roosevelt's two-story lobby was like a stage set and its grand ballroom complete with Cinderella mural to guarantee a fairy-tale feel to Guy Lombardo's performances. Lombardo's renowned New Year's Eve concerts at the Roosevelt had established "Auld Lang Syne" as a holiday standard. The hotel's other famous in-novation—street-level shops to help replace the income it would lose from Prohibition—had been featured since it opened in 1924, the year after Andy moved to Manhattan and began his job at the Seaman advertising agency, back when he was con-tributing unsigned squibs to F.P.A.'s "Conning Tower" column in the *World*. Andy sat in the dark-paneled restaurant, with Vander-bilt Avenue distantly visible in golden light beyond the blinds, and picked at the sweet white flesh of the weakfish he had or-dered. It was so dark in the grill that he could barely read the gloomy editorials in the *News*. Then the waiter silently appeared beside him, stared out through the blinds, and sighed eloquently. The day outside was beautiful, he said, but the forecast was "To-morrow snow, turning to rain."

Soon Andy wrote up the incident for "Notes and Com-ment," adding a larger perspective on the waiter's and his own melancholy: "He was a man carrying foreknowledge in his breast, and the pain was almost unbearable."

The vague sense of yearning and loss that had haunted Andy's teen years had only grown over the decades. He was the writer who had confessed some years earlier, "A man sometimes gets homesick for the loneliness that he has at one time or another experienced in his life." Even tending animals could leave him half ecstatic and half melancholy. But in 1948 in particular, he couldn't help casting a retrospective eye across his life and work. Over the previous few months he had been awarded three hon-

orary degrees for his contributions to literature, from Yale, the
University of Maine, and Dartmouth. It was difficult for Andy
to maintain his outsider/country-boy pose now that Irving
Penn had photographed him for *Vogue*, sprawling across a burlap-
covered prop, dressed in a flannel suit and with his hands in his
pockets.

As he approached fifty, his married life was mostly serene
and comfortable and so was his professional life, except perhaps
for his ongoing preoccupation with his health. It had always
shown up even in his letters and poems to Katharine, in frequent updates about sniffles, fevers, dizziness, intestinal troubles.
Once, when he omitted such intimate bodily details in a letter,
Katharine replied, "You say nothing about nasal discharge or
stomach upheavals. How are you—*really*?" On a 1934 trip to
Florida with friends, he wrote home to Katharine that he had
experienced a brush with death. The night before, he discovered that his face was swelling. Convinced that he had a brain
tumor, he wrote a loving farewell note to Katharine, unlocked
the hotel room door so that people could find his corpse without trouble, and collapsed on the bed in a panic attack. The
next morning, surprised to find himself still alive, he consulted
a doctor, who informed him that he had a sunburn. Andy considered this diagnosis ridiculous. He argued instead that perhaps he had been bitten by a spider. Even in describing his
deathbed scene to Katharine, he included the detail that he
went to bed "full of flatulence, dizziness & fear." Earlier, while
still in his twenties, he had published in *The New Yorker* a light-
verse ode to how a hot-water bottle could warm and comfort a
sick and lonely man who kept imagining that he was dying.
"Small is the solace in being dead," he observed, "With never a

love at my side." To the water bottle itself he murmured the creepy image "Pretend I'm a woman that's birthed a child / And you are that warm little armful."

ONE ISSUE THAT haunted Andy was the morality of raising farm animals. As he walked along through the early-morning mist, around the corner of the barn and down to the barn cellar, carrying a sloshing pail of slops for a pig, he faced again and again what he thought of as his own duplicity. His pig relied upon him to deliver the food and guard the door, and Andy performed these tasks conscientiously. But in a few months he was scheduled to betray the creature's confidence and slaughter it. Andy had the same troubled relationship with those sheep that were to be eaten rather than merely sheared. He would sit up late in April, tenderly nursing a lamb back to health, only to slaughter it come August. So much gentleness to end in so much blood, in a hammer blow to the head, a knife slash to the throat—only hours after Andy had dutifully served what the lamb did not know was its last meal. There was no bucolic innocence in farming. It seemed a quiet and benign life only from the distant city, much as the lights of Broadway glowed naively festive when recalled from a twilit country porch.

Yet paradoxically he found it even more confusing when nature did the killing and interrupted his own plan. He had been left especially melancholy after the death in September 1947 of a pig whose life he had worked hard to save. With seventeen-year-old Joel assisting, Andy had followed a neighbor's advice, pulled the pig off-balance and turned him upside down, to pour castor oil down his throat—which orifice Andy learned, glimpsing it for the first time at this angle, was a striking corrugated pink.

Fred, the Whites' beloved, arthritic old dachshund, also attended the sickbed. With his two-legged and four-legged assistants, Andy visited the pig at all hours during foggy nights and unseasonably hot days, delivered medicinal slop to an apathetic patient, imitated the pig's own slurping noises to inspire memories of the joy of gluttony, even performed an enema on the poor animal—all to no avail. The veterinarian was unable to help. Andy empathized strongly with the pig. On good days he had often felt a kind of kinship in its noisy appetite, seeing it as a healthy lust for life, so he found it dispiriting to watch the pig lose interest in food and finally even in water. At last the exhausted animal was unable to even push his snout through straw to fluff his bedding. Soon afterward he died. Andy found him outside the barn, stretched on the grass, his face neither anguished nor peaceful.

Andy had also delivered piglets, taking each in hand as it slithered out into the glow of a lantern in the shadowy barn. He had seen both ends of life. He knew the cycle as well as he knew his own breathing. Still, this loss preyed disproportionately upon his mind, and finally he mused over it in a *Harper's* essay, exploring his new job as failed savior and also his usual role as tender executioner. "The loss we felt was not the loss of ham but the loss of pig," he wrote. "He had evidently become precious to me, not that he represented a distant nourishment in a hungry time, but that he had suffered in a suffering world."

A SENSE OF loss, the pig's eventual fate had it survived illness, a farmer's dual role in this ancient drama—these worries had been circling around in Andy's mind for months when, in early 1949, an editor at Doubleday and Company invited him to take a trip down memory lane. Doubleday had been the original publisher of Don Marquis's three volumes about Andy's favorite fictional characters—*Archy and Mehitabel* in 1927, *Archy's Life of Mehitabel* in 1933, and *Archy Does His Part* in 1935. In 1940, three years after Marquis's death, Doubleday had combined all three in a handsome fat omnibus volume, retaining the rakish illustrations by George Herriman, creator of Krazy Kat. Now they wanted a new edition and they offered Andy five hundred dollars to write an introduction for it. This pleasurable assignment took him several weeks. In late August, he wrote to a friend that the Archy introduction was all he had written during the summer.

Although Andy had referred to Marquis numerous times, quoted him, honored him, he had never devoted a full-length essay to him. In 1939 he had been writing a Comment paragraph when he decided to divide its sections with asterisks. He typed

★   ★   ★

across the page and then asked, "Asterisks? So soon?" and typed three more.

★   ★   ★

The look of the page then reminded him of Don Marquis's punctuational and other acrobatics in his newspaper columns. "The heavy pauses between his paragraphs," Andy wrote, "could they find a translator, would make a book for the ages." Andy had typed more asterisks of his own and then remarked out of nowhere, "Don knew how lonely everybody is." Andy suggested to the reader that loneliness might drive reading itself: "You're not out to learn anything, certainly. You just want the healing action of some chance corroboration." A few weeks after Marquis's

death Andy had written to James Thurber, "What a kick in the
pants life gave that guy!" and described Marquis as "one of the
saddest people of our generation."

When thinking about politics, Andy often returned to Marquis. He referred to his own vision of ideal government as "the
perfect state," after Marquis's satirical essay "The Almost Perfect State." In a passionate but playful 1940 *Harper's* essay called
"Compost," Andy wrote the line "A seer a day keeps Armageddon away," only to interrupt himself with a question: "You're
trying to sound like Don Marquis, aren't you?" He admitted to
himself and to the reader that he was indeed.

In the spring of 1946 Andy had invoked Archy and Marquis
again. While contemplating the news about Bikini Atoll in the
South Pacific, where the native islanders were being forcibly
relocated so that the U.S. military could test nuclear weapons as
part of Operation Crossroads, Andy read naturalist Edwin Way
Teale's recent book *Near Horizons*. "If you sat up nights trying
to invent an indestructible bug, especially fitted to survive,"
wrote Teale, "you would have a hard time outdoing the roach."
Andy realized that cockroaches, which were already considered
one of the most ancient forms of life, might be the creatures
likeliest to survive a nuclear holocaust. "Well," he sighed, "Archy's boss is dead, God rest his untransmigrated soul, but Archy
himself is probably good for another hundred million years."
Clearly the same couldn't be said for human beings.

Thus Andy responded congenially, even gratefully, to the
need to re-immerse himself in Marquis's skeptical but compassionate view of life. While writing his introduction for
Doubleday, Andy lingered nostalgically over the virtues of the
era's newspapers, especially the *Evening Sun* itself, and Marquis's

decades of contributions. In doing so Andy was forcefully reminded of how Marquis had freed his own antic imagination, had created what were unquestionably his greatest writings, his funniest and most perceptive and most original, by creating animal characters, especially the humble vermin who served as his avatar. "Archy and Mehitabel, between the two of them," he wrote, "performed the inestimable service of enabling their boss to be profound without sounding self-important, or even self-conscious." Of Archy he said, "The details of his creative life make him blood brother to writing men. He cast himself with all his force upon a key, head downward. So do we all." But Andy couldn't explain the depth and resonance of Marquis's humor. Instead he came back around to his own ongoing preoccupation with a particular kind of animal by stating flatly, "To interpret humor is as futile as explaining a spider's web in terms of geometry."

The doomed pig, and the relationship between humans and animals on a farm, kept running through his mind. Finally, thanks to these natural and literary nudges, Andy began to consider exploring these events in another children's book. Already he envisioned the farm animals' lives as much like his own, half comical and half melancholy. But how might a pig's life be saved from the dastardly farmer's plan?

THE SPIDER LIVED on the underside of the barn's roof. Sheltered from the elements by an overhang, her web was an elegant orb whose loops and strands glittered on dewy mornings like an antique necklace. Every night she made the rounds of her miniature cosmos, tightly wrapping prey, cutting loose and jettisoning debris, reweaving broken strands.

By the time Andy came outdoors in the dawn, she had retired to a corner of the web and only her handiwork was visible. Each morning he was impressed all over again with the spider's industry. That busy autumn of 1948, as Andy went in and out of the shed during the endless daily routine of farm chores, he kept an admiring eye on the work of the tiny creature who lived her equally conscientious life above his head. He had been observing her for several days, watching the dew glitter in the mornings and the web almost disappear as the moisture evaporated by midday, glimpsing the spider herself as she emerged in the twilight to begin the night shift. In the evening he stood below her web and peered up at it, watching his gumdrop-size neighbor scurry toward prey or hang upside down in the center of the web, patiently waiting.

Then one cold October evening he saw that she was clinging to a little roundish object, which upon closer examination turned out to be neither an insect nor another spider. Finally Andy realized that his spider must be spinning an egg sac. This new development required a closer look. He went to get a stepladder and an extension light—a shielded bulb with a hook for hanging, an essential item in every barn—and carried them out to the barn doorway. He climbed up the few steps and hung the lamp nearby and peered closely at the spider's now spotlit trophy. Never having found spiders frightening or repellent, Andy decided that this one was rather beautiful. Her body was an elegant gray and brown, her legs dramatically striped. Now and then as she moved, he could glimpse a curious pattern on her underside reminiscent of the hourglass on a black widow's belly. Andy watched her for a long time. Finally she merely perched atop the object with her eight legs spread over it, and he assumed that she must be laying eggs inside it. She attached the sac to the wood of the projecting roof, not to the web itself. Rounded and soft-looking, the egg sac seemed to have been spun out of peach-colored cotton candy. Finally Andy climbed down from the ladder, put away the light, and left the spider alone in the darkness that was home to her. The next morning her egg sac hung secure under the shed roof, but the spider herself was not in sight. He didn't see her again.

Only a few days after this provocative reminder of the overlooked life-and-death dramas surrounding him every day, Andy had to return to New York for work. Unwilling to leave his new discovery behind, he got out the ladder again, this time bringing along a razor blade. He carefully cut the binding strands of web that held the egg sac to the wood of the barn door and carried it indoors. The sac's material felt like a cross between silk and paper and seemed to weigh nothing at all, but it looked sturdy. He found an empty candy box, punched a few holes in the lid, tucked the egg case inside, and took it with him to the apartment on East Forty-eighth Street. There he put the box on his bureau and forgot about it.

But as he went about his urban business, riding in elevators and dodging cabs and typing at his desk at *The New Yorker*, alchemical mysteries were taking care of themselves inside the candy box. One day several weeks later, he noticed on the bureau a movement so slight it might have been imaginary. He bent down and peered more closely at the box. Tiny spiderlings, so small they were barely visible, were climbing up through the air holes he had punched in the lid. Delighted with this renewal of life so many weeks after the mother's apparent death, Andy stood at the bureau and watched the latest generation of spiders. Even newly hatched, they seemed as busy as a Lilliputian construction crew. Bustling across his daily artifacts, they strung almost invisible web lines from nail scissors to hairbrush, from mirror to comb. Deciding that barn spiders were unlikely to be dangerous to people, Andy let the hundreds of spiderlings cavort across the bureau for the next week or two. Some had departed by the time that he reluctantly evicted the rest because the maid who came in to clean refused to work around a spider refugee camp.

After the spiders left the bureau, they continued to scurry around in Andy's imagination. From childhood he had admired spiders and their webs—the flytraps in the corners of the stable in Mount Vernon, the gleaming tents he found spread in the fields around the Belgrade summer cabins, and nowadays the elaborate webs in his farm buildings on Allen Cove. As early as the *St. Nicholas* days on Summit Avenue, he had seen science-minded but admiring photographs of spiders. In his writing over the decades since, he had often invoked the elegance of their creations. "Nobody styled the orb web of a spider," he acknowledged, but he insisted that it is beautiful because it is "designed to perform a special task under special conditions," like a canoe or (he added in what had become his trademark sudden left turn in sentences) a guillotine. Even in his now extensive political writings, he turned to spiders for his metaphors. In one longer-than-usual Comment piece on academic freedom, he made the analogy that "the elasticity of democracy is its strength—like the web of a spider, which bends but holds."

In his idiosyncratic poem to Katharine, "Natural History,"

he had seen affection and commitment in the spider's tightrope daring. But it was more than a romantic fancy. In the poem he admitted that he saw himself as the spider, groping his way on a tenuous thread of his own creation, hoping eventually that—by trusting the very act of making the web—he would find his way home to where he started.

Chapter 13

ZUCKERMAN'S BARN

I discovered, quite by accident, that reality and fantasy make good bedfellows.

By the end of 1949, Andy was moving forward on research for the book he was calling *Charlotte's Web* in his notes. His longtime editor at Harper & Brothers, the legendary Cass Canfield, who had been president or board chairman since 1931, had encouraged Andy to pull together another collection of *New Yorker* pieces. It had been eight years since the publication of *One Man's Meat*, and Canfield argued that in the interim Andy had written many essays worthy of preservation between the pages of a book.

Early in the writing of *Charlotte's Web*, however, Andy was preoccupied with this exciting new story about a spider and a pig. With unusual optimism, he wrote to Canfield that he couldn't find time to think about work that he had published years ago, but that by fall he might be sending Harper an entirely different kind of book than they had planned, although he remained coy about the subject matter. "I guess it depends on how many rainy mornings we get between now and fall," he added, "rain being about the only thing that brings me and a typewriter together." Rather than a gentleman farmer, Andy liked to pretend that he was a full-time farmer and a gentleman writer.

It turned out to be a hectic year, genuinely busier with farming than with writing. That summer he wrote nothing for "Notes and Comment" and made no progress toward his hypothetical essay collection. Harold Ross was suddenly ill with lung cancer, often unable to be at the office, but keeping up his correspondence as much as possible. He and Andy exchanged letters on various topics, including Andy's new windmill at which to tilt— a campaign for larger taxicabs in New York City. Andy had actually gone so far as to measure the height of the door in cabs. He complained that thirty-eight inches was half the height of a man and a doorway of that size respectable only on an igloo.

That busy summer he didn't completely ignore the world of publishing. He sent a poem to Gus Lobrano at *The New Yorker*, but it was light verse inspired by his experience of sowing rye grass seed that cost an astronomical forty cents per pound. He judiciously critiqued a new manuscript that Jim Thurber had written during his recent stint in the Bahamas, while he was supposed to be writing something else. It was a lyrical fairy tale called *The Thirteen Clocks*. Andy told Thurber that he thought at times the plot might be too fantastic and action-packed for its own good and that the characters' names were confusingly similar; and he complained again about Thurber's muddy habit of not starting a new paragraph for each new speaker in a dialogue. Always Andy advised clarity and straightforwardness.

He aimed for the same goal in his new book. He had faith in clarity of expression even on those days when he lacked any other faith in life. Directness and honesty would carry the day, he believed, bringing alive the story whose mythological simplicity became more compelling for him every day. Two years before, he had found himself empathizing at an almost frightening level with the pig whose demise he chronicled in his *Atlantic Monthly* essay. That story had been true. In *Charlotte's Web* he was free to make everything up as he went along, which meant that he could change the outcome. This time the pig wouldn't die.

> *It is a straight report from the barn cellar, which I dearly love, having spent so many fine hours there, winter and summer, spring and fall, good times and bad times.*

FOR HIS OWN reference, Andy decided, he needed a layout of the stage for his animal drama. He folded a piece of typing paper in half, then in half again to pocket-size, and took it out to the barn. There he diagrammed the barnyard. He drew a horizontal rectangle filling most of this now small page. In its lower right eighth he drew a smaller vertical rectangle and labeled it *Pig*. Outside it to the left he wrote *Sheep+geese*. He drew two small lines indicating the door and faintly sketched a square outside it, which he labeled *Pig pen*. A tiny flat rectangle at the bottom he labeled *trough*. Underneath it all he scribbled *Barnyard*.

For the story he drew a three-dimensional view rather than a diagram. On a small piece of pink scratch paper, about three inches by five, he sketched the barn's southward-facing façade, the left door with a slanting plank ramp, the right with its double doors. He added a hint of a wind vane, a punctuational flourish, atop the steeply slanting roof, and in the upper right corner of the drawing he even sketched in the sycamore tree at the northeast corner of the barn. In cursive he labeled everything— the open *gate*, its door angling outward; the *Barnyard* itself. He drew an arrow pointing toward the ramp and wrote *Cows* and one toward the double door that he labeled *Sheep*.

Realizing that the sketch was growing and would require more space than the small piece of paper could accommodate, he pasted the sheet inside the front cover of the old manila envelope on the front of which he had penciled *Charlotte's Web*. Then he extended the drawing outward from the edges of the pink paper. He added more labels: *Pig pen*, with an arrow pointing toward it on the upper right, and *Lane to pasture* moving toward the lower right. Underneath all of it he wrote *Zuckerman's Barn*.

The setting was now vivid in his mind. His characters were coming insistently to life. He was able to conjure the behavior of the creatures he dealt with every day. Helpless pigs, silly geese, clever spiders, greedy rats—Andy knew all of these characters. He had participated in countless life-and-death dramas and last-minute rescues. He could sit on a three-legged milking stool in the barn, admiring the slapstick of lambs and the gluttony of pigs, while warm sunlight slanted through the doorway and across his back and chattering swallows flitted in and out of the big open doorway. He could recite the ingredients in a pig's daily slop. He could close his eyes and still see every lurking step of a rat—the dastardly thieves on whom he had focused his despair and his .22 rifle during the war, imagining them as Nazis. As long ago as the stable on Summit Avenue, rats had crept into the subterranean pathways of his subconscious as the embodiment of gluttonous dishonesty.

But, try as he might, Andy couldn't envision the intimate details of a spider's life. He could stand in the barn and peer respectfully at one. But she wouldn't sit still for microscopic examination—and even if she did, he wouldn't know what to look for. He didn't have on file in his mind the kind of details about spiders that he possessed about the other characters. He was an observant farmer, not a scientist. What was the spider doing out there in the barn all night by herself? How did she actually go about spinning the web that would be so important in this story? He needed more information. This book would require actual research.

For this reason, he spent many months researching spiders. More than once on his trips to Manhattan during late 1949 and early 1950, Andy returned carrying trophies from a research safari. When he walked down the marble steps of the New York Public Library, past the regal lions with their forepaws like clenched fists, he was carrying scientific tomes full of illustrations of monstrous spider faces and enough Gothic webs to satisfy Dracula. At the apartment in New York or back home in Maine, he eagerly delved into these sources for background information about Charlotte. He was ready to merge his tentative early scenes, his eavesdropped snippets of dialogue and stage notes of action, with the factual support that he craved this time. He hadn't felt this compulsion for natural-history research when writing *Stuart Little*, but then Stuart wasn't really a mouse; he only looked like one.

From the first, Andy's scientific research and his whimsical imagination encouraged each other. He envisioned Charlotte performing certain actions in her web, such as writing letters that showed up well enough for people to see, and immediately turned to the scientists to learn by what chemistry and acrobatics she might accomplish what he had in mind. He pounced upon an unexpected tidbit of information in a source book, such as the detail that some stream-side spiders have been known to catch small leaping fish in their webs, and soon Charlotte was retailing these facts as anecdotes about her extraordinary family.

Chapter 14

SPINNINGWORK

In writing of a spider, I did not make the spider adapt
her ways to my scheme. I spent a year studying spi-
ders before I ever started writing the book. In this, I
think I found the key to the story.

THE OLDEST BOOK of the three research sources that
Andy brought home was *American Spiders and Their Spin-*
ningwork, by Henry C. McCook, who had died when Andy was
twelve. McCook did the work that made him a popular naturalist and author—he even published a series of children's nature
books—on summer holidays and in stolen moments, because
he also served as a Presbyterian minister and a leader in the
Sunday-school movement. He self-published the three volumes
of *American Spiders* over a four-year period beginning in 1889.

McCook's title page showed the interesting detail "Published
by the Author, Academy of Natural Sciences of Philadelphia."
The old-fashioned subtitle read *A Natural History of the Orbweaving*
Spiders of the United States with Special Regard to Their Industry and
Habits. McCook's preface had intriguing subheads running

down the left margin—*A Field Naturalist's Difficulties*, *The Spider's Solitary Nature*, *Study of Spinning Organs*, even *Why the Author Is Publisher*. The contents page revealed an antique anthropomorphism in McCook's thinking, no matter how rigorous his observations. Like Andy, he couldn't resist assigning human personality to animals. Volume II's contents page included phrases such as *Wooing and Mating*, *Maternal Industry*, *Cocoon Life*, and *Babyhood*, even the outrageously unscientific word *Toilet* to describe how the spiders disposed of their waste.

In the preface, McCook bragged about his accomplishment by emphasizing its difficulties: "Summer vacations, and such leisure hours as a most busy life would allow, have been given to the pleasant task of following my little friends of the aranead world into their retreats, and watching at the doors of their fragile domiciles for such secrets of their career as they might happen to uncover." Farther down the page, McCook commented upon one of the spider's traits that had always appealed to Andy, and one he would emphasize in Charlotte's character—their writerlike reclusive industry: "The natural disposition of the spider is a great hindrance to the prosecution of field studies. It is a solitary and secretive animal."

Almost every page also featured an illustration, some in color, from diagrams of web patterns among different species to a double web created by two spiders engaged upon what Mc-Cook called "cooperative housekeeping." In a similar Victorian vein, one subhead read, "A Love Bower." Following a long tradition of projecting onto spiders human and even divine traits, McCook opened his main text with an explanation of why joint-legged invertebrate animals are called arachnids, although Andy surely remembered from his studies at Cornell: "Accord-

ing to the Greek myth, Arachne was transformed into a spider
by Pallas Minerva because she had boasted her superiority over
that goddess in the use of the distaff." Then McCook added the
surprising detail that the word *spider* even derives from *spinder*,
"the spinning one," root of both *spindle* and *spinster*—"by which,"
remarked McCook, "the virgin mistress of the distaff was commonly known in the days of our grandsires." In this context, a
spider as heroine of a novel seems less eccentric and more classical.

Like Andy himself, McCook brought scenes to life with both
a sense of language and a sense of humor:

> I once found a nearly mature Argiope cophinaria hanging in
> the centre of her orb engaged in sucking the juices from a fly,
> which she kept underneath her jaws and appeared to be han-
> dling entirely by the use of her palps. In the mean while she
> held attached to her forefeet on either side two swathed flies,
> one suspended by a single thread, and another by a double
> one. Evidently she was troubled with what the French call
> an embarrassment of riches.

Andy covered many sheets of yellow draft paper with notes
of everything that seemed even possibly relevant to his story—
that young spiders hatch in the fall but remain inside their cocoon until the following spring, that spiders don't kill their prey
with a sting but merely stun it. *Easier to suck blood, probably,* he
added casually, *when prey is still alive.* Sometimes new facts fit into
the story the moment he encountered them: *going to be inconve-
nient for Charlotte to go to the fair, because she is a sedentary spider.
Also, comes about time of egg laying.* Finally he began to think in
prose more than in facts, although his sentences were still in the

tentative present tense in which he wrote notes, not the sculpted past tense of an actual manuscript page: *A spider needs eight legs. She uses 2 sets of forelegs for antennae when she is at work laying out lines.* He noted that an orb weaver has eight eyes in two rows of four each, and at the bottom of the page he wrote an important short sentence: *Charlotte is near-sighted.* Later he underlined it with an editorial blue pencil. This detail explained why Charlotte could see to capture and wrap a fly, but she couldn't see Wilbur himself clearly, down in the straw and manure far below. In the story, he would ask why and she would explain.

Andy particularly wanted to get right the engineering behind Charlotte's fly-trapping and pig-saving webs. He printed the heading ORB WEAVERS and wrote under it:

> *The first thing a spider does is stretch a thread from some high point. Then from the center of this, it stretches other threads like spokes of a wheel. Uses 2 kinds of thread: dry and tough (for the guy ropes) sticky (for spiral).*

Such fascinating details inspired new story developments. *Web never vertical,* Andy noted. *She is under.* On the back of another sheet he asked questions: *Does spinneret have to touch object in order to make an attachment, or can hind leg attach the strand to the object? Does this kind of spider use balloon technique when young?* Eventually, having researched the latter point, he returned to the question and answered it with a firm blunt pencil, *yes.*

He discovered confirmation of what he had witnessed in his own barn and wrote, *The making + repairing of webs almost always takes place just before dark.* He jotted down terms without definitions (spinnerets, attachment disk) and self-explanatory terms (sedentary spiders, wandering spiders). He scribbled the detail that an orb weaver's foundation lines usually form a trapezoid. The Reverend Mr. McCook had a vivid narrative style that fit well with Andy's close-up view of his diminutive spider character: "The first radii that are inserted bend and sway under the weight of the spider, which, as she clambers over them, suggests the idea of a carpenter engaged upon a scaffolding in its first crude state." A few pages later Andy found the helpful detail that sometimes a spider, while spinning a web, will pause at the center, to which she has drawn new lines, and anchor them by wrapping reinforcing silk around where they meet the center.

His notes accumulated on the growing pile of yellow paper.

First they anchor a dry line.
The foundation is an irregular polygon.
The swinging basket
The trial cables.
Mature males spin rudimentary webs on outer margin of females webs. Young males spin regular webs—
Male sends telegrams to female over wires.
Charlotte's husband was quarrelsome little chap.
They pair in spring or summer when weather is serene.

In various ways, McCook emphasized how valuable spiders are even in the human scheme of things. After describing their fragile domiciles among the porches and boat landings of Atlantic City and Cape May, New Jersey, he added, "The proprietors would do well to encourage their presence and propagation as at least some check upon the flies and mosquitoes." This was Andy's own attitude toward his neighborhood spiders. What could attract more flies than dung? Therefore every spider in a barn helped reduce the annoying and unhygienic population of flies.

McCook's next-to-last chapter was called "Death and Its Disguises." It fit well with Andy's thinking about the ending of his own book. Spiders live short and busy lives. If his story were to continue to the next spring, to cover a full rhythmic year in the life of the pig, then his savior, the spider, might well have to die. After noting that a spider's eight widespread legs help it feel any vibration on the strands of the web, that Charlotte's family weave their egg sac under cover of darkness, and that the sac is waterproof and the eggs themselves orange, Andy summed up the arc of his spider heroine's life with a penciled note about her natural history:

> She ~~dies~~ languishes a few days after egg-laying, does not return to the web, and then dies.

THE FIRST PAGE of the first volume of McCook showed an orb weaver of the *Epeira* genus; elsewhere Andy found a dorsal view of another *Epeira*, and a close-up of an *Epeira*'s face and one of its leg joints. Page 34 provided a detail that Andy copied precisely: *Menge observed the pairing of Epeira marmorea on a warm August evening.* Other details made him decide that this was the genus to which he would assign Charlotte. On page 115 Andy found a tidbit he copied onto a sheet of pale yellow paper so thin it was almost onionskin. It was the full scientific identity of his heroine: *Epeira sclopetaria (Ep. vulgaris Hentz), the gray Cross spider, I have not found abundant in wooded spots, but more frequently near bodies of water.*

Charlotte's last name, Andy wrote on another sheet of paper, *is Epeira.*

Then, in John Henry Comstock's volume *The Spider Book*, another of his research sources, he found a more melodious, and arguably more apt, surname for Charlotte. Comstock's book had first been published in 1912, when Andy was thirteen. But he found a new edition that had just been published, revised by an entomologist named Willis J. Gertsch, who had written an admiring introduction. Comstock had been an entomology and zoology professor at Cornell, having already put in more than three decades by the time Andy arrived in the fall of 1917. He had married Anna Botsford, a former Cornell student who became a talented illustrator of her husband's books, as well as a conservationist and activist and a leader of the nature-education movement whose influence included Andy's own early love of natural history. Most of the time Comstock's book was more strictly factual and to the point than McCook's, with only occasional flights of poetic appreciation on the wonders of his subject.

About the clan that Andy was considering for Charlotte, Comstock wrote, "This genus has been commonly known under the name *Epeira;* this, however, is a much later name than *Aranea,* which was proposed by Linnæus in his *Systema Naturæ.*" Three pages later, Andy found a detailed description of his heroine, who turned out to be a barn spider, not a gray cross spider, as he had thought.

Aranea cavatica (A. ca-vat'i-ca).—This spider is dirty white in colour with grayish markings. The abdomen is clothed with numerous whitish or gray hairs, which give it in life a grayish appearance; this is not so marked in alcoholic specimens . . .

On the ventral side of the abdomen there is a broad black band extending from the epigastric furrow to the spinnerets; the basal half of this band is bordered by two curved yellow lines; and near the middle of its length there is a pair of yellow spots.

Andy copied most of this information. A note at the end referred him to Fig. 488, and he found it a couple of pages later: a murky photo in the center of a page, showing a handsomely patterned abdomen but with most other detail lost in the poor quality of reproduction. Rather than changing Charlotte's surname to Aranea, Andy literally made her scientific identification more specific by changing her name to the mellifluous Charlotte A. Cavatica—her genus name shrunk to a middle initial and her species designation promoted to a jaunty Italian-sounding surname.

Some of Comstock's research would prove helpful in Andy's story: "This species, as its specific name indicates, prefers shady situations. Emerton states that it lives in great numbers about houses and barns in northern New England. I have found it in a tunnel at Ithaca, and on the sides of cliffs in a ravine. Its webs are sometimes very large."

On a small white sheet of paper, Andy penciled key aspects of Charlotte's natural history:

Name of spider – Aranea cavatica
Life span – 1 year
Eggs laid 14 October. When would mating have occurred?
How many eggs? 500

Then he listed key research questions: *When will they hatch? When will the young emerge? What does male look like?* Later he returned to this list and answered each point in firm dark pencil: *Fall. Fall or spring. Like female.* One question he didn't answer: *When will the female die after the egg laying?* At the bottom of the page was another question that might prove important: *If the life span is more than a year, do they produce eggs more than once?* He looked up the answer, wrote *yes*, then reconsidered and marked out the whole line. This detail didn't have to be relevant. He wanted his story supported by his character's actual natural history, not enslaved by it.

GERTSCH, THE EDITOR of the Comstock edition, was also the author of the most up-to-date of Andy's sources, *American Spiders*, which had just been published in "The New Illustrated Naturalist" series by Van Nostrand. On the title page, Gertsch was identified as associate curator of the Department of Insects and Spiders at the American Museum of Natural History. Andy checked on him and learned that Gertsch was considered one of the foremost authorities on arachnids in the world. Eventually he visited Gertsch at the museum, to confirm his understanding of spiders and to ask further questions.

In each book Andy found wonderful details that helped inspire the ending of Charlotte and Wilbur's story. Both Comstock and Gertsch wrote lyrically about what Gertsch called "the urge toward ballooning." "Although spiders like man possess only legs as organs of locomotion," wrote Comstock, "like man they are able to travel through the air by artificial means. Long before the invention of balloons or of aeroplanes, spiders had solved the problem of aerial navigation." Gertsch was also poetically inspired by this vision:

> Much of the adventure in the life of the spider is crowded into the first few days of freedom when the young spider-lings, having just broken through the egg sac, strike out for themselves in a world completely new to them. . . . Once the spiderling has reached the summit of the nearest prom-ontory, a weed, a spike of grass, or a fence rail, it turns its face in the direction of the wind, extends its legs to their full-est, and tilts its abdomen upward. The threads from the spin-nerets are seized and drawn out by the air currents.

The balloon builder, Andy scribbled. *Stands on forelegs on a fence post with web streaming out behind in the wind. When ready, he bal-loons.* By now Andy was thinking in scenes and dialogue even as he researched. He imagined Charlotte explaining to the young pig that many spiders are aeronauts. He wrote:

> *"What is an aeronaut?" asked Wilbur.*
> *"A balloonist," said Charlotte. "My cousin used to stand on her head and let out enough thread to form a balloon. Then she'd let go and be lifted into the air and carried upward on the wind."*

Earthbound Wilbur would express skepticism, but Andy foresaw the spider's reply: *"I have some very remarkable cousins."*

In all three books Andy found precise information about how orb weavers spin their intricate webs. He distilled some of it into a diagrammatic sketch. He drew a faint line across the middle of a page, labeled the left end of it *A,* and drew another line coming down from the middle, roughly quartering the lower half of the page. He angled a line from his point *A*, curving it toward the center of the bottom of the page. Then he wrote over this pale diagram, *From the foundation line, the spider makes an attachment and drops down, paying out cable as she goes. She makes this fast to the ground or Something, then climbs back to here*—he drew an arrow pointing at the juncture of the straight and curved web lines—*and runs a diagonal across by ascending the dropline and carrying another line along to point A.*

On the back of another sheet he diagrammed a different web, with its center labeled *hub* and a snaking line labeled *signal line.* He drew two rough diagrams that showed the web in perspective as a flattened oval, with a barely legged circle of a spider body in each, one of them seen from the side. This web engineering was reminiscent of the poem that he had written for Katharine back in 1929, with a spider as unlikely romantic symbol.

Andy noted that Comstock would be his source for "description of Cavatica" and that Gertsch had a good description on page 23 of how spiders eat their prey. *Takes little over an hour to spin orb web,* he wrote, and under it, *Spider that carries air bubble down + lives under water.* Even the facts themselves seemed poetic. On page 2, Gertsch held forth on the glories of spiderwebs:

The orb web has long been a symbol of the spider in the mind of man, who sees in its shimmering lightness and intricate, symmetrical design a thing of wonder and beauty. Such esteem is well merited, for the orb web is the most highly evolved of all the space webs developed by the sedentary spiders. It represents a triumph in engineering worthy of great mechanical ingenuity and learning; yet it was arrived at by lowly spiders, which even by their most ardent supporters are credited with hardly a gleam of what is called intelligence.

Taking advantage of improvements in both photography and printing, Gertsch had much better images than his predecessors. One photo, showing the troubled courtship and mating of black widows, had a caption reminiscent of a Thurber cartoon: "The cautious approach of the small male." There were also excellent diagrams that Andy noted. Early on in Gertsch's book he found Figure I, labeled *External Anatomy of a Spider*. It comprised three illustrations. The first on the left, *A*, was labeled *Dorsal view*, showing the left side of the body as seen from above, with the pear-shaped front part labeled *cephalothorax*, and behind it the more oval, mango-shaped section labeled *abdomen*. In the text Gertsch explained that, unlike insects, which usually have three distinct body parts—head, thorax, and abdomen—spiders have only two visible, because the head and thorax are largely merged into the cephalothorax.

In the center of the page, figure *B* portrayed a *Frontal view of face and chelicerae*. Not for another ten pages did the text inform Andy that chelicerae are the "jaws, which are the offensive weapons of the spider." Scientists thought, explained Gertsch, that these mouthparts evolved from the same appendages that became the second antennae in crustaceans. At the top of figure *B*, like a diagram of a cell, was a semicircle with eight ovals inside it labeled *eyes*—four in a flat row below, four in an arch above. To round out this faceless face, the chelicerae looked vaguely like the fangs of a walrus. This diagram did not resemble anything that Andy thought of as a face.

On the right of the page was the most complex drawing, *C*, labeled *Ventral view, most legs omitted*. It showed the busy-looking underside of the spider's body, like the view of a car overhead on a rack in a garage. It included one of the short, hairy appendages labeled *palpus*, which the text explained was more of a jointed feeler and tongue than an antenna. Where the eight legs joined the cephalothorax, only one was shown in full—the parts labeled, the trail of words moving outward from the body, following the knee crook of the leg downward and then up again to the finely haired last joint.

Andy noted the evocative labels, then penciled, *Legs have 7 joints*, and listed them in a numbered column:

1. *coxa*

2. *trochanter*

3. *femur*

4. *patella*

5. *tibia*

6. *metatarsus*

7. *tarsus*

They discuss legs, + the spinneret, he wrote.

Charlotte ~~enume~~ *names them for Wilbur, who likes to hear her run over the names.)*

   Last of the joints are lined with spines, bristles, and hair.

   "*You have awfully hairy legs, Charlotte.*"

The spines on the hind legs are like the "flyers" of a spinning wheel. They are used for the flocculation of the threads as they pass from the spinning tubes.

On yet another yellow sheet Andy scrawled other identifying terms:

caput	*forehead*	*fang*
thorax	*sternum (plate)*	*hair*
mandible	*falx*	*labium*
palpa or palpi		
palpal claw		

Farther down on Gertsch's page, below the cluttered cephalothorax, was the underside of the abdomen, marked with mysterious, vaguely facelike squiggles labeled *epigynum* and *genital furrow*. On each side of this area was a slit with the intriguing label *opening of book lungs*. Gertsch explained, "The book lungs of the arachnids are closely packed sheets of body surface bound together like the leaves of a book, to give the maximum surface for aeration."

Gertsch's diagram of the spider's body told a story in itself. At the bottom of the oval abdomen, looking in this chassis view like twin exhaust pipes, were the crucial parts of the spider in Andy's growing story, the reason why a spider was the best possible heroine: the spinnerets, the silk-spinning organs with which Charlotte, like the Greek fates, would reweave destiny. The runt pig's life was going to seem insignificant until two unlikely benefactors, a young girl and a spider, cared for him—and changed his fate.

Chapter 15

PAEAN

a paean to life, a hymn to the barn,
an acceptance of dung.

IN 1950 *THE* New Yorker reached the quarter-century mark. "Twenty-five years of working on a weekly magazine," Katharine sighed, "certainly makes one realize the passage of time!" She and Andy had been married for two decades. Joe was halfway through college and, following in his father's footsteps, was working summers as a camp counselor. Katharine's son Roger Angell was thirty already and had a young daughter. His big sister, Nancy, had three children, six and four and eighteen months. Neither Roger nor Nancy lived nearby, so when they brought their spouses and children to visit—often renting a cottage nearby—it was a special occasion.

Katharine was busily working for the magazine still, editing authors such as Jean Stafford, Mary McCarthy, her husband, Edmund Wilson, John O'Hara, and Vladimir Nabokov. Several years before, Katharine had persuaded Harold Ross to lend Nabokov a desperately needed advance against future submissions, resulting in a first-reading agreement. Nabokov had since contributed both stories and a beautiful series of autobiographical essays. Katharine was one of the few editors with whose suggestions Nabokov might comply; he even called her "a subtle and loving reader."

While Katharine maintained her busy schedule of editing stories and writing hordes of letters for the magazine, Andy turned his spare minutes from farming toward *Charlotte's Web*. Often he sat in the boathouse down by the dock, on the simple banquette he had built—with the knothole in the seat that he had to slide across—and faced the stack of yellow copy paper on the plank desk in front of him. A lot of what he wrote went into the nail-keg wastebasket to the left of the table. He had set up a cord and pulley that raised the big, single glass pane to his right to let in the salt air from the bay, with Cadillac Mountain visible over on Mount Desert Island. On cool mornings he lit a fire in the belly of the ancient black iron cookstove, with its two heavy, round burners glowing red at the top.

At first Andy wasn't sure what he wanted to write about the spider and the pig. But he decided that it didn't matter, because he found himself caring deeply about these characters. He knew he had to trust his instincts. What he did not want to do was retell animal life in human terms, or at least he wanted to do so no more than was necessary to tell his story. He enjoyed playful representations of nature such as Archy. He considered Donald Duck an amusing character too, but felt that Walt Disney forced animals to dance the way he wanted them to, with no regard for how the character's natural inspiration in the world might actually behave.

Andy's actors in *Charlotte's Web*, he decided, had to be true
to their nature—as far as possible within the story he was beginning to imagine. For one thing, he considered animals amoral,
so he didn't want to twist their personalities into moral versus
immoral decisions. Charlotte was basically a trapper. She was a
predator waiting patiently at the center of an architecturally
dazzling fly-doom, and he didn't want to overemphasize her
decision to try to help the frightened piglet.

The same rule applied to the rat in his story. Templeton would
not undergo a Scroogean change of heart; he would remain mo-
tivated by rodent selfishness, his help available only for a price.
Andy wanted his own respect and affection for most animals in
their natural state to be implicit in the story. Templeton could get
from Andy only a nod of grudging admiration for his adaptabil-
ity. He had hated rats for too long.

In these first glimmerings, the major characters—except for
the barn itself—were all animals. He sketched out tentative
scenes.

> *The barn—*
> *Wilbur's friends—*
> *Charlotte ~~+ her web~~ Repairing the web—*
> *Wilbur's future*
> *Fog — + an idea*
> *Zuckerman's surprise*
> *Charlotte's busy time—The buttermilk bath*
> *The Fair*
> *Death of Charlotte*
> *~~Return of Wilb~~*

Wilbur's homecoming
or
Wilbur's Return.

He started the story on paper where it had started in his mind—with the spider on her web. For the chapter heading he penciled a firm Roman numeral *I*, stabbed a determined period after it, and began.

Charlotte was a big grey spider who lived in the doorway of a barn.

Immediately he realized that the spider was no more important as a character than the barn itself, so his second sentence became *But there is no use talking about Charlotte until we have looked into the matter of the barn.* He paused to write a sentence at the top of the page and then mark out part of it: *She was about the size of a gumdrop, and she had eight legs, ~~which is enough for anyone~~.* He circled the sentence and drew a line down to where it needed to be inserted, after the first sentence. *This barn was large. It was old. It was white.* He inserted *painted* before *white*, then wrote off to the side, *It smelled of hay and it smelled of manure.* Then he returned to his main block of text, although he kept stumbling, failing to pick up speed.

It was pleasantly warm in winter, pleasantly cool in summer; it had stalls for horses, tie-ups for the cows, an ~~enormous scaffold~~ loft up above for the hay ~~where children would jump and roll~~ and a place down ~~below~~ underneath for sheep, a ~~place~~ pen ~~down below~~ for a pig, a grain bin, a rat trap, a lot of sunlight coming in through the big door.

This false start also petered out, but it established that the barn itself would be an important factor. Eventually Andy moved these details later in the manuscript, to open the third chapter, when Wilbur leaves Fern's home and moves to the Zuckerman farm. Despite his considerable attention to the barn itself and the society within it, he decided not to include the nearby ocean in his story. Thus the Zuckerman and the Arable farms, as well as the portrait of Andy's beloved Blue Hill Fair, wound up feeling like settings in an unnamed American heartland.

Andy tried a number of other ways to get the characters moving around. One day he began a draft on the back of the sheet of paper on which he had written Charlotte's scientific name. He had long since named the spider and had already dubbed the pig Wilbur, but he had yet to name the farmer—the character who, at first, was actually closest to Andy himself in this life-and-death drama.

Wilbur + Charlotte, he wrote at the top of the page, and underlined it. Then he launched into a description of the pig and his habitat together.

Some people might think that Wilbur's place was rather messy. Wilbur liked it, though. He lived ~~underne~~ in the bottom part of the barn~~, under~~ Over him, on the main floor of the barn, the cows were tied up. Every morning and evening the farmer would scrape the cow manure down through the trap door. Wilbur always greeted each new deposit enthusiastically. When the door opened, Wilbur would grunt, and look up. Then the dressing would come slipping and sliding down. Wilbur always investigated it right away

This attempt didn't work out, either. So he tried several other ways to launch the book. In his endless revising as he went along, he wrote new sections below and to the side, circled them, drew arrows to their new location, then crossed out those as well. He drew vertical lines down the left margin of the text and wrote, *Fix. Make better.* Sometimes he scrawled a quick squiggly line, sometimes a hard firm slash. He drew large *X*'s across entire pages.

He wrote a variation on this pig-and-farmer opening with the farmer now named. He tried a slightly different approach to opening with a description of the barn, revising each thought as he went along.

Chapter I. The Barn.

The ~~best~~ + warmest + pleasantest part of Zuckerman's barn was the ~~part under the shed roof on the south side cellar.~~ *part underneath the cows*

He paused to insert *where the cows were.*

on the south side. ~~Mr. Zuckerman had a trap door in the main floor, and twice a day he would take his shovel and open the trapdoor~~ *It was warm because the* ~~cow~~ *manure* ~~kept~~ *pile.*

He paused to insert *of* after *because,* then added at the end, *I can't explain why manure piles are warm, but they are.*

Dung would be a recurring motif in the story. In one scene Andy wrote about Wilbur's environment, *A manure pile is not the cleanest place in the world, but it is warm—and young pigs need warmth.* The topic didn't make him uncomfortable even in writ-

ing a children's book. He referred to it often in his essays. In one
he remarked, "There is no doubt about it, the basic satisfaction
in farming is manure, which always suggests that life can be cy-
clic and chemically perfect and aromatic and continuous." Manure had impressed him ever since his early childhood, when
the warmth of its decomposition had somehow hatched the eggs
that the coachman had already declared infertile.

On one occasion Andy rolled a piece of paper into the typewriter—he composed most of his *New Yorker* paragraphs and
letters on the machine instead of in pencil—and centered the
heading *Chapter I* and the title *ESCAPE*, skipped a few lines, and
began typing, *At midnight, John Arable pulled his boots on.* Arable
goes out into the barn and admires the newborn piglets, only to
find that there is one more than the mother can feed. But Andy
decided that this gambit didn't work, either.

The draft that held together began with the pig:

> *I shall speak first of Wilbur.*
> *Wilbur was a small, nicely-behaved pig living in a manure pile in*
> *the cellar of a barn. He was what farmers call a spring pig . . .*

Other alternatives occurred to him—above *nicely-behaved* he
wrote *beautifully* and below it he wrote *symmetrical*—but this
time he kept going. Over the next several months of 1950,
when he wasn't farming, he was working on the story of Charlotte and Wilbur. He wrote 134 scribbled-over pages in long-
hand. In the middle of October 1949 he had written to Cass
Canfield at Harper's adult division to say with unusual optimism that his next book was in sight. "I keep it in a carton," he
added, "as you would a kitten." Like all his other books, though,

Charlotte's Web took longer than he had imagined. He finished the draft on the nineteenth of January 1951. On the first day of March he wrote a letter to Ursula Nordstrom at Harper's children's division:

> I've recently finished another children's book, but have put it away for a while to ripen (let the body heat out of it). It doesn't satisfy me the way it is and I think eventually I shall rewrite it pretty much, in order to shift the emphasis and make other reforms.

Back in 1939, when he was being encouraged to finish *Stuart Little*, Andy had said firmly, "I would rather wait a year than publish a bad children's book, as I have too much respect for children." He had the same attitude about *Charlotte's Web*. He set it aside for almost a year. While he incubated eggs and sheared sheep and mended fencing, while he corresponded with Jim Thurber and naturalist Edwin Way Teale and his old college buddy Howard Cushman, the manuscript sat in its box, growing as quickly as a kitten. Its images, its scenes and poetry, ripened in Andy's mind and matured into a better form. Gradually he realized that he wanted a more human perspective on the barnyard community. When he went back to the manuscript, he added five chapters, introducing a little girl named Fern, who would be the first person to save Wilbur's life, on the day of his birth.

> *"Alone? My best friends are in the barn cellar. It is a very sociable place. Not at all lonely."*
>
> —FERN

THE CHARACTERS' NAMES Andy chose—or they arrived—from various sources. The spider's name had been in his mind from the first, when he thought she was going to be Charlotte Epeira, before her real species name inspired the designation Charlotte A. Cavatica. He had once owned a pig named Wilbur, besides having known a couple of people with the name, including an office boy at *The New Yorker*. At first the farmhand who works for the Zuckermans was named Larry, but Andy changed it to Lurvy. The name Templeton might have popped into his mind for the rat because it was the name of a New York City telephone exchange that he had called, like Astoria and Murray Hill. It had a nice incongruously fancy air for a rat.

For the little girl who had become a big part of the story—as well as the reader's way into the world of animals—Andy joined in the tradition of Dickens and Shakespeare in assigning a symbolic name: Fern Arable. He couldn't have squeezed any more potent nature symbolism into her given name than by christening her after one of the most ancient forms of life. Andy passed ferns every day as he walked down to write. They flourished throughout the woods and elsewhere on the property, especially along the path to the boathouse, where whole colonies of waist-high ferns grew around the lichen-covered granite boulders strewn underneath the trees. Back in 1944, he had used Fern's surname in "Home Song," the poem in which he referred to mice in hiding; the next winter, he adapted the poem for the family Christmas card. The line was "Home is the part of our life that's arable." In early versions Andy imagined Fern's brother as a twin, Vern, but soon he renamed him Avery. Fern has empathy for other creatures that her brother can't equal. The animals clearly understand human speech, but only attentive young humans such as Fern may respond in kind. Her innocent willingness to sit still and listen affords her a glimpse of other lives, to the point that she says to her mother about Templeton, "None of us like him very much." In Andy's honest approach, this young attitude also had to change. Late in the book he had Fern wander off with a boy named Henry Fussy and leave the animals behind.

Fern's father sounded a bit like Samuel White, Andy's father. When Fern first glimpses Wilbur in the morning light that makes his ears glow, Mr. Arable's remark ("Saved from an untimely death") has a rhetorical swing to it reminiscent of the music-loving businessman who had held forth at the head of the White family's dining table, back in the infancy of a century that was now middle-aged.

Having shown her mother's skepticism about Fern's report of barnyard gossip, Andy invented a doctor for Mrs. Arable to consult about Fern's mental well-being. His name, like most other characters' names, evolved. He began as Dr. Lacey and turned into Dr. Barton and then Dr. Goudy. But eventually Andy decided to sneak in another symbolic name. After painting his bountiful arcadian landscape and naming the farm owner for a Greek epic poet, he continued his classical theme by rechristening the medical man Dorian, after the ancient Greeks who inhabited the bucolic, half-legendary Arcadia. Andy's education at Cornell during World War I had been steeped in classical literature, and one of his early books bore the title *Quo Vadimus?* (Where Are We Going?). In such venerable allusions Andy was again following in Don Marquis's footsteps. The Archy chronicles were rife with classical references of all sorts, from casual puns on the name of the emperor Valerian to the ongoing theme of Mehitabel's former life as Cleopatra.

Other words were going to be as important as the characters' names. Ever since the fateful day when he walked down through the woods to the pig pen, Andy had known that he wanted Charlotte to write something in her web. He debated, however, about how the other animals might deliver words for her to copy. At one point he considered reusing the unnamed dog who snaps at Wilbur's leg during his raucous escape attempt. *They get the cocker spaniel,* he scribbled to himself, *to bring Charlotte a spelling book from the boy's room.* But he decided that the rat could find the words, if bribed.

Then there was the question of what Charlotte might spell out in her web to convince the community of Wilbur's innate wonderfulness. Andy looked around at words the animals could borrow from labels on farm and household products. *Crunchy. Prepotent. Terrific.* From a shirt label they could find *pre-shrunk,* which would be funny. He examined packages of Ivory soap flakes and Hygrade machine oil. A few terms might be amusing for the animals to consider but they would quickly reject them, such as *delicious* and *nutritious.* He wrote down *Pig Supreme* and then added, *(Sounds like a dessert).* He wrote, *"With new Radiant Action,"* then under it, *they settle for just the word RADIANT.* One day when he wasn't at his desk he had another idea and wrote it out on a card to insert into the growing manuscript—at the fair, Templeton returning to Wilbur's stall with a piece of cardboard reading, *Low cost, all-purpose power unit—here is the answer to your problem. Take a good look at this handy power-package. Plenty of clearance, turns on a dime.* He wrote down a couple of amusing ways that Wilbur might respond, then abandoned the idea.

Andy didn't worry about consistency. Charlotte would toss off words such as *untenable* and *sedentary* and recite scientific names for the parts of her leg (once Andy learned these terms, he couldn't resist placing them in her mouth), but be unable to write *humble* in her web without Templeton's fetching a model. In having Charlotte define *sedentary*, Andy wrote that it means she doesn't "go wandering." Then he wrote three fancier words to the side and circled them: *promenading, prancing, gallivanting.* Wilbur is equally inconsistent. After needing *sedentary* defined he immediately uses the word *delectable*. He is also born with the porcine dream of searching for truffles. Andy sketched out a scene in which Wilbur explains his philosophy and defines himself as a sensualist ("I like to be warm and I like to be full"), but he abandoned it. It would have been too self-aware for his innocent protagonist. Although up until then all the characters had been animals or people, in a moment of Disneyesque whimsy Andy wrote that a maple tree down in the swamp suddenly turned red because it became so anxious about the crickets' warning of impending autumn.

After wrestling to get sections of the book right, he often later cut them out of the story or changed them entirely. He wrote a scene in which Avery spies Charlotte and decides to knock her down with a stick, but as he climbs over the pig pen Wilbur rushes up and grabs the stick in his mouth and wrestles it away from Avery. It would have been satisfying in some ways to have Wilbur rescue Charlotte in turn, but Andy decided instead to keep Wilbur passive and not heroic. He changed the scene and made it more ironic: it is Templeton, the villain, whose greed saves the day. Avery falls and breaks open the rotten egg that the rat hoarded. Its stench clears everyone out of the barn. Andy also considered having Charlotte hint that she had eaten

her husband, who was an entertaining rascal and great dancer—
but she said she tired of him: *"What ever happened to him?" "Ask
me no questions, I'll tell you no lies."* He rejected this idea.

He introduced endless small changes along the way. Charlotte brings up the Queensboro Bridge, points out that it took
humans two years to build it, and that in contrast she can build
a web in a single evening. For the final manuscript, he looked
up the number of years and changed *two* to *eight*. He altered ways
in which the heroine might be defensive or unrepentant about
her bloodsucking habits, surrounded as she was by domesticated
herbivores.

> *A man who is dealing in fantasy doesn't worry about*
> *contradictions or inconsistencies.*

ANDY DIDN'T ENVISION for his book the kind of bustling, con-
tentious society that Don Marquis had created for Archy, with
his hero only one of numerous cockroaches and Mehitabel a cat
among peers and rivals. Charlotte, in contrast, would live her
solo invertebrate life among mammals and birds. Andy represented most species by a single individual, as if it were the type
specimen of its race—Templeton the sole rat on the farm, Charlotte the only spider in the barn. This decision was firmly in the
tradition of talking-animal stories dating back to Aesop, and it
had also been the custom in more recent tales. In 1908, when
Andy was nine, Kenneth Grahame's *Wind in the Willows* was
published, with Mole and Rat representing their kind by the
mythic River. About the time Andy graduated from college,
A. A. Milne populated the Hundred Acre Wood with one boy,

one bear, one owl, one donkey—and one exotic invasive, a kangaroo. But Grahame had his animals live in mansions and drive automobiles and brew a cozy pot of tea by the fire, while Milne based his characters upon his son's toys, not real animals. Andy had different inspirations and different goals.

In keeping with his particular anthropomorphic view of his farm community, to each group of animals who demonstrated a distinct herd mentality—the sheep, the geese—Andy assigned a collective identity with no named individuals. A geese's repetitive cackle he interpreted as a stammer. One of the parts of the book he particularly liked was the goose's remark beginning, "At-at-at, at the risk of repeating myself." He also decided to ignore the sad fate of Wilbur's siblings, and to have no other pig show up until the fair, when Wilbur competes with the rude and obese Uncle.

Andy was too much an experienced farmer to allow his pastoral ode to get by on merely golden nostalgia. He had to inject some potent real-world issues—greed and apathy in the form of a rat, the paradoxical fate of most farm pigs, the threat of execution hanging over Wilbur, and the inevitability of Charlotte's own natural death. Mortality stalked the scene from the first line: "Where is Papa going with that ax?" The farm animals spoke with casual familiarity of trouble and death. Andy had learned that spiders don't usually eat dead prey, so Charlotte says that she gives her fly victims an anesthetic as a little free service she throws in. In one draft, Andy had the sheep describe in considerable detail how Wilbur is likely to die—that he would be shot behind the ear, then knifed. Such specificity was too ghoulish even for Andy, so he changed it to having the sheep begin, "Arable arrives with his .22, shoots the—" only to be interrupted by Wilbur's anguished scream that he doesn't want to die. Besides mortality itself, throughout many idyllic scenes Andy dabbed colorful spots of melancholy. He translated the song sparrow's aria as "sweet, sweet, sweet interlude" and informed the reader that it referred to life's brevity. Crickets harped on the same theme. But overall Andy's theme was the joy of being alive, of reveling in the moment with visceral attention. What seemed like two themes were really one.

On these scribbled-over, endlessly revised pages, he spent a lot of his own time on his portrayal of the natural progression of the seasons. He needed time itself to move through the story, with seasonal rhythms determining the arc of the narrative— Wilbur's birth in spring, Charlotte's instinctive urge to lay eggs in fall, her own children's hatching in a new spring. Therefore he had the opportunity to include the kinds of fleeting phenomena he loved about each season, from the secret milk in dandelion stems to the tiny orange eggs of potato bugs. He included the rope swing that he had made for Joe (and himself) that still dangled from the beam over the barn doorway. Early on Andy had listed for himself the ingredients in a pig's food and also the animal's daily schedule. Readers learned that it takes a goose egg a month to hatch, that buttermilk is great for washing pigs. Andy wrote an ode to rain, which he had always enjoyed—he had often wondered in print why meteorologists act as if rain is unnatural—but then trimmed it down considerably from its survey of the fields and house and kept it focused on the barn.

Every few pages, he burst into one of his Whitmanesque

inventories—the contents of Wilbur's food trough, the "rat's paradise" of a carnival midway after fairgoers have gone home, Templeton's thesaurus of ways he doesn't want to be jostled by Wilbur inside the crate. Andy remembered from the day he cut down the spider's egg sac from the shed wall that its material was peach-colored and looked like cotton candy, a nice image for something to be woven and hidden away at a county fair. He had Templeton cut the strands of web that held the egg sac to the ceiling of Wilbur's stall at the fair, just as Andy himself had taken a razor blade and cut down the egg sac under the shed roof—except that Templeton would use his ugly rat teeth.

He hadn't planned the book as a summary of what if felt like to be E. B. White, but by the last page it had preserved in amber his response to the world. He worked in his love of dewy summer mornings and of a lit-up Ferris wheel in an autumn twilight. There were few experiences he enjoyed more than spending an afternoon at a fair, strolling the littered midway, watching a cattle auction, listening to the loudspeaker. Back in the late thirties, he had written a "One Man's Meat" essay for *Harper's* about the worries regarding national security as the United States moved toward what turned out to be World War II. In it he automatically used a Ferris wheel as an everyday symbol of the urge toward transcendence battling with the impulse toward safety. While standing in line with young Joe to board the Ferris wheel at the Blue Hill Fair, Andy had watched people's expressions—the uncertainty, the flickers of worry or excitement. And he also worked into *Charlotte's Web* his first sight of Joe riding a Ferris wheel with a girl. Joe was twenty-two by the time Andy finished the book, but this midway moment from his childhood was one more snapshot of life preserved between its pages like a summer leaf.

Throughout the many days spent writing the book, Andy kept revising, crossing out, starting over. Even the saddest sentence in the book required lots of tinkering: *Nobody, of all the ~~thous~~ hundreds of people ~~in the~~ that had seen the Fair, knew that a grey spider ~~who~~ had played ~~such an~~ the most important part in the ~~Nob~~ No one knew ~~that~~ it ~~she clung~~ when she died.* Andy wrote in caps in the left margin *FIX* and drew an arrow pointing to the sentence. Then he went on to the next chapter.

With this book as with its predecessors, as with every essay and poem, there finally came the question of how to close the story. After the chapter entitled "Charlotte's Death," he needed to end on what he saw as the most positive aspect of life—that although death may be inevitable, so is the next round of living creatures, that because of the inevitability of death we must revel in the moment. In the last three paragraphs, Andy quickly pulled themes together—the slow rhythms of the year, the seasons of a life, the endless recycling of living matter through new generations of spiders and lambs and, again and again, through manure, waste matter itself drawn back into the earth to become another generation of living creatures.

He provided a quick glance at the major characters, inviting his actors to parade across the stage before the curtain fell. This decision required that he again adopt the omniscience glimpsed now and then earlier in the text, this time peering into the future. He backed upward and outward from the close-up view of Wilbur talking with Charlotte's three daughters who decide to remain in the barn with him—Joy, Aranea, and Nellie. He let readers know that Fern soon grows up too much to spend her time in barns listening to animals chat, that throughout Wilbur's presumably long and happy life Mr. Zuckerman never again considers turning him into bacon, that each year a few of Charlotte's descendants remain in the barn, maintaining the cycle of life.

A final ode to the most important character—the barn itself— created the penultimate note that he would sustain through the final paragraph:

> It was the best place to be, thought Wilbur, this warm delicious cellar, with the garrulous geese, the changing seasons, the heat of the sun, the passage of swallows, the nearness of rats, the sameness of sheep, the love of spiders, the smell of manure, and the glory of everything.

Then Andy had to find the closing words. He tried various alternatives for the ending, as he had wrestled with practically every page of the book. In 1943, a writer in the *New York Times* had complained about Andy's writing. He had thrown at Andy's style what Katharine called "fighting words" such as *hogwash*, *soft soap*, and *racket*. Andy had replied and others had joined the fray. Incensed, Katharine fired off a reply. It ended with memorable phrasing:

> A's letter to the Times needs no defense against such words, nor does anything he has ever written. They are not words that should be applied to anyone who is an honest man and an honest writer. Andy is both.

Andy identified closely with Charlotte. Besides her wit and commitment to Wilbur, the spider reminded him of his favorite fictional cockroach. She had been inspired in part by Archy, with whom Andy had felt a kinship since his teen years. She embodied the spirit of the barn, which he had once described as almost a sacred place, a stage for birth and death and the rhythms of life. Over the last couple of years he had gone to as great lengths to learn spiderweb building as he had once done to learn sailing or farming or writing. He had never spent more time on any literary task than in accurately describing the hidden mysteries of spider life. In his poem to Katharine after their wedding, Andy had presented himself as a spider—blindly spinning a web between himself and his newlywed bride. Clearly he hoped that doing so might be a meaningful act in itself, but also that his connection with her would become a greater connection with himself and his origins. Now, in the last moment of *Charlotte's Web*, Katharine, whose love and devotion had anchored Andy emotionally and helped him achieve greater satisfaction and deeper work than before, was present again. He closed with a description of Charlotte that he adapted from Katharine's description of Andy himself:

It is not often that someone comes along who is a true friend and a good writer. Charlotte was both.

Andy skipped a few lines and wrote firmly in the center of the page, THE END.

Chapter 16

SOME BOOK

The web glistened in the light and made a pattern of
loveliness and mystery, like a delicate veil.
—FROM *CHARLOTTE'S WEB*

"THAT'S THE BEST news I've had in a long time," Ursula
Nordstrom replied to Andy in March 1951, when he told
her that he had completed a draft of a new children's book but
had set it aside to ripen. She went on to say that she didn't mean
to sound pushy but that Harper & Brothers would welcome the
manuscript whenever it was finished. In the six years since its
publication, *Stuart Little* had been one of Harper's bestsellers.
"We assume that you will want Garth Williams to illustrate it,"
she said, and added that she hoped Williams would be free when
the book was ready. Whenever Williams worked for Harper,
he always knew that any assignment they had given him could
be put on hold if another E. B. White book came in. Other publishers, of course, didn't have the same rule for him. Since *Stuart
Little*—and with that book as his debut—Williams had become
a respected, in-demand illustrator. Simon & Schuster's popular

Golden Books imprint lured him, as well as other illustrators, with lucrative contracts.

A year later, in March 1952, Nordstrom was, as usual, in her office at Harper & Brothers on Thirty-third Street. She was working back in the labyrinth of old offices that smelled of paper, printer's ink, and rubber cement, when the receptionist left her desk out front and came back to report that E. B. White had just arrived and was asking to see her. She went out to the large front room, which bookcases and glass walls divided into offices, and found Andy waiting near the elevator, small and neat as always, with a package in his hand. He held it out and said, "I've brought you a new manuscript."

Nordstrom was surprised and delighted. She hadn't heard any news about Charlotte in many months and hadn't realized that Andy was even close to finishing the book. Her first thought was that probably it was already too late in the year to have the manuscript edited, illustrated, printed, and bound in time for publication in Harper's fall list. But possibly she could make it. Realizing that she would have to get Garth Williams to work immediately, she asked, "Have you given me a carbon copy, too, so I can rush it off to Garth?"

"No," he said casually, "this is the only copy. I didn't make a carbon copy." He got back on the elevator to go to his *New Yorker* office, leaving Nordstrom with the realization that she was holding the only copy in existence of a new book by one of Harper's favorite authors.

Usually, like most editors, Nordstrom was too busy with correspondence, meetings, and other editorial and production matters to actually find time to read manuscripts at the office. Yet, afraid that she might somehow lose this one on the train if she took the pages home, Nordstrom sat down in her office and began to read:

> *"Where's Papa going with that ax?" said Fern to her mother as they were setting the table for breakfast . . . .*

The first person to read *Charlotte's Web* particularly admired the turn of events foreshadowed when a voice in the dark barn asks the pig, "Do you want a friend, Wilbur? I'll be a friend to you." She liked Wilbur's tone when, the next morning, he spoke to the air around him and asked his mysterious nighttime friend to please make her presence known. As she read through the typed pages, Nordstrom found the story remarkably engaging. Soon she decided that she knew a great book when she met one, and before she even finished the manuscript she called Andy at *The New Yorker* to share her excitement.

She wasted no time. Four days after Andy turned in the manuscript, she told him that the Advertising Department would soon be sending catalog copy for his approval. The description of the book for its jacket copy could wait, but catalog materials had to be prepared months in advance.

URSULA NORDSTROM TURNED forty-two the month before Andy delivered the manuscript of *Charlotte's Web* to her office. She had been director of the Department of Books for Boys and Girls for twelve years, following nine spent working her way up the ladder. Writers knew that they could speak their mind to Nordstrom and she would reply in kind. Famous for defending her authors' books and careers, risks and gambles—and for flattering, cajoling, and coercing them into producing ever better work—in

1946 she had instituted the Nordstrom Award for the Most Amiable Author of the Year, which a Harper staffer designed and hand-set annually. Often her letters included profane complaints about an uncooperative typewriter or sly parodies of the pablum that many writers manufactured for the children's market.

After more than two decades in the business, she had long outgrown her insecurities about not having a college education, as well as most other worries about her inadequacies. In 1952 she was confident enough about her status and worth to admit to horrified Harper colleagues that she had bought a television set, which was considered the mark of a philistine because of the poor quality of programs available. Commercial network programming, which was now four years old, was slowly growing more diversified. For the rare evenings when she wasn't editing manuscripts at home, Nordstrom could choose between programs such as *The Texaco Star Theater, The George Burns and Gracie Allen Show, Howdy Doody,* or a recently launched morning news-and-talk program called *Today.*

Nordstrom was well-known in her field and highly respected, having worked with many of the established and promising names in children's literature, from Crockett Johnson, who wrote *Harold and the Purple Crayon,* to Margaret Wise Brown of *Goodnight Moon* fame. Recently Johnson's wife, Ruth Krauss, had published her first book with Nordstrom, *A Hole Is to Dig,* illustrated by a promising young man named Maurice Sendak. But no children's book that Harper had published was more popular than *Stuart Little.* From her first quick reading, Nordstrom knew that *Charlotte's Web* was possibly even better. She asked Andy his opinion about the contract and advance and he suggested she follow whatever Harper had done for *Stuart Little*, which was basically the same contract he had had for *One Man's Meat*. It called for an advance of five hundred dollars against future royalties. When she sent him two copies of the contract later in March, she told him that she had had two more copies typed up as well, one for Garth Williams, who would soon be in touch. She then added, *It is a wonderful book.*

Andy ran the contract by Milton Greenstein, a lawyer who in his few years at *The New Yorker* had become invaluable. Andy wanted to take advantage of the Internal Revenue Service's maximum-payment clause, which would permit Harper to hold the majority of profits on the book and to dispense them to Andy in a fixed amount per year to reduce his tax rate. He chose an annual payment of seventy-five hundred dollars. "It sounds like an extravagant dream to me," he wrote to Nordstrom, "as I never believe that any book is going to sell."

Only a few days after seeing Nordstrom in her office, Andy sent her a report from the barnyard—a newborn lamb already exploring the snowy pasture, a goose nesting atop a manure pile. Spring was struggling to break through the Maine winter. "Charlotte's children," Andy added, "are due shortly." He also brought up a topic that had been worrying him. He asked Nordstrom if she had read elsewhere any story that included as plot element a spider writing in its web. He insisted that he wasn't any better read in children's books than in adult books, which left him anxious that he might inadvertently have used an idea already claimed by another author.

"I believe Charlotte is the first spider since Miss Muffet's," Nordstrom replied. She did, however, recount key details from the old story about Robert the Bruce. The hero of Scottish independence was crowned in the spring of 1306 and defeated at the Battle of Methven less than four months later. He fled to an island off the northern coast of Ireland, where, legend claims, he encountered an inspirational spider. He watched it trying to attach the necessary lines to launch a web. Six times it tried and six times it failed. Robert supposedly admired this perseverance and considered the demonstration an omen, because he had tried and failed six times in his attempts to rout the English. Heartened, he went on to win many battles against the English, culminating in the decisive Bannockburn victory in 1314. Nordstrom didn't mention similar stories perhaps more analogous to Charlotte's method of rescuing Wilbur, tales in which a fugitive hides in a hollow tree (or similar shelter) and a spider quickly weaves a web over the entrance to the sanctuary. The pursuers assume that no one could possibly have hidden there without disturbing the web. This kind of unlikely rescue had been told about Muhammad, King David of Israel, and lesser personages, but wasn't too similar to Charlotte's behavior.

Certainly there had been few arthropod protagonists in children's literature. A spider writing in a web, however, had been a minor point in a children's book published only eight years earlier, in 1944—in a series that also featured a group of talking barnyard animals. *Freddy and Mr. Camphor* was the eleventh in Walter R. Brooks's acclaimed series of smart, amusing, and literate novels about a pig named Freddy and his animal friends on the Bean Farm in upstate New York. The pig and the spider and the other farm creatures had been appearing in the series since 1927. In Brooks's story, however, the web's sign, created by a spider named Mr. Webb, plays no role in the plot. It reads, "Patriotic Mass Meeting. Tonight at 8:30. All Bugs, Beetles, and

Caterpillars Invited. Fireworks, Music, Dancing. Mr. Webb will speak." Brooks, who also wrote a series of stories about a talking horse named Mr. Ed—similar to the premise behind the Donald O'Connor movie *Francis*, about a talking mule, which had appeared in 1950—had published stories in *The New Yorker*.

On April 9, a week after Nordstrom's mistaken assurance that a spider hadn't been seen in children's fiction since Mother Goose, both Katharine and Andy dined with her in New York City. They discussed the draft of Harper's catalog copy for *Charlotte's Web* that Nordstrom had sent to Andy, and she made notes of their suggested changes. She also reported that Garth Williams loved the story and, eager to illustrate a second White volume, was already sketching. During dinner Nordstrom, with some hesitation, brought up the title of the last chapter, which in the manuscript Andy had called "Charlotte's Death." Apparently she felt that the title foretold too much information and in too blunt a form. At home, later the same evening, she consulted a favorite book of hers, *Little Women*, to learn how Louisa May Alcott had heralded the demise of an important character. The title of the chapter in which Jo learns of Beth's approaching death is "Beth's Secret." The death itself occurs four chapters later, in "The Valley of the Shadow." The next morning at work, Nordstrom typed up some of these details and sent them to the Whites.

Nordstrom picked the perfect example with which to sway Andy. A few years earlier, during the winter of 1940–41, he and Katharine and Joe had read *Little Women* aloud every evening. Andy called it their after-dinner mint. He found it a wrenching experience to read about Laurie and Amy's troubles during the

Civil War, while a new and larger war was raging across Europe. In the final version of *Charlotte's Web*, on the page proofs, Andy changed the chapter title to "Last Day."

Nordstrom also conveyed to Andy the concern within Harper about his decision to kill off the heroine. On this point Andy refused to budge. Natural history could not be dodged: Charlotte's species of spider dies after spinning its egg sac. He could arrange to have a pig rescued by the spider's concerted efforts, but even her compassion and determination couldn't alter her own fate.

GARTH WILLIAMS HAD been told to work as quickly as possible so that *Charlotte's Web* could be published in the fall despite its spring delivery. The morning after the Whites dined with Ursula Nordstrom, Williams was heading out the door of his apartment with sketchbook in hand, to draw spiders in the arachnid displays at the American Museum of Natural History, when the phone rang. Ursula Nordstrom was calling to discuss further ideas about illustrations. Williams explained that he wanted Fern to appear in a number of the early drawings. It was good that she wouldn't appear in all of them, because her looming presence would keep the animals too small—and Charlotte would be invisible. Those scenes in which Fern was not present could thus be opportunities to zoom in on the animal characters and explore their world more fully. Williams emphasized that he was open to suggestions of any kind. But clearly, as an experienced professional, he had ideas of his own and was already pursuing them.

At forty Williams was in demand. He was so well thought of at Harper's that, while he was undergoing financial troubles the year before, Nordstrom had offered to reinstate a monthly stipend of five hundred dollars, a regular advance against royalties. Since his start illustrating Andy's first children's book in 1945, he had provided drawings and paintings for a dozen other books in the field and outside it. They ranged from a reissue of Henry Gilbert's version of the Robin Hood saga to Damon Runyan's famed story collection *In Our Town*. The year before he tackled Charlotte and Wilbur, Williams illustrated Simon and Schuster's anthology *Elves and Fairies*. His style varied from project to project—delicate and evocative pencil work for one book and for the next ink drawings in great detail. Some of his illustrations were in color, beginning the year after *Stuart Little* with Margaret Wise Brown's *The Little Fur Family*, which was bound in actual rabbit fur whose previous owner hadn't fared as well as Brown's characters. But Andy's new book was to have black-and-white drawings reminiscent of those chronicling the adventures of Stuart.

In his wide-ranging work, Williams drew upon constant travel and knowledge of both urban and rural ways of life. He was born in New York City in 1912 to English parents and had a peripatetic life practically from birth. He spent his infancy in France, preschool years back in New York, the next few years in Canada, and at the age of ten was in England again. Williams particularly enjoyed drawing Andy's New England farm in *Charlotte's Web*, because some of his earliest memories were of what he called his barefoot Huck Finn years in farm-country New Jersey and in Canada. His mother was a French-trained painter and his father a cartoonist for the British humor magazine *Punch*. With everyone in his home drawing or painting in some way, he naturally gravitated toward the same kind of activity. His father claimed that at the age of nine months, while strapped in a high chair, young Garth had reached a finger over to draw a simplified pine tree in the condensation on a window. Unlikely or not, it was a story full of family pride in the arts. Once in his childhood Garth had found a portfolio of his father's drawings that were ready for presentation. He calmly proceeded to add to them, sketching in what he thought of as improvements. His father merely said, "I'm afraid he's going to be an artist," and erased his son's contributions.

Williams grew up wanting to also become an architect, but came of age just after the crash on Wall Street in 1929. His family could afford to send him for only three months to Westminster Art School, but with talent and hard work he promoted this experience into a full scholarship to the Royal College of Art. Winning the British Prix de Rome for sculpture in 1936 gave him the opportunity to study further in various European countries. He was back in England a couple of years later, where his participation in a planned new women's magazine was cut short by the war. Soon he was an ambulance dispatcher with the Civilian Defense arm of the British Red Cross. He continued to work as both painter and sculptor. After being wounded in the spine while driving an ambulance, Williams returned to the United States and began looking for outlets for his urge to draw. Eventually *The New Yorker* gave him a chance, and Andy soon noticed and recommended him to portray Stuart.

Williams felt that an illustrator must strive to see the characters and the setting through the eyes of the author, to try to achieve a kind of graphic equivalent of the resonance that first inspired the writer to record or imagine these people and places. He understood that Andy's goal of natural behavior for his imaginary creatures needed to be reflected in their appearance. When drawing animal characters, he liked to begin by sketching a realistic portrait of the creature as his guide. This initial image he would rework in successive drawings, gradually incorporating human expressions and postures. In drawing the nesting geese watching Templeton roll away their egg that wouldn't hatch, Williams turned their bills downward just enough, and narrowed their eyes just enough, to suggest a human scowl of distaste. He showed Templeton's smug self-satisfaction by drawing the rat leaning on his left elbow with his chin resting in tiny rodent fingers and his right arm akimbo at his waist. To portray rudeness in the lamb who refuses to play with young Wilbur, Williams drew it with head held high as it walked away, turning to speak over its huffy shoulder.

In some ways Williams found *Charlotte's Web* less interesting to illustrate than *Stuart Little*. With Stuart, he had had fun drawing the contrast in size—the telephone repairman towering above Stuart like Gulliver, Stuart himself climbing a fire hydrant as if it were the Washington Monument. There were also lively fantastic elements such as a trash can hit by the invisible car that a dentist gives Stuart. Williams found the human characters in *Charlotte's Web*, in contrast, rather ordinary to draw, except for Fern herself. Williams employed his own daughter Fiona as a model for Fern, which may be why she turned out such a beguiling figure: courageously grabbing the ax that her father holds, smiling maternally while feeding the newborn Wilbur, flying through the air on the rope swing in the barn. Wanting, like Andy, to reflect the passage of time in the book, toward the end Williams drew Fern looking taller and older, even in an unaccustomed frilly dress, as she strolls off toward the midway with a boy named Henry Fussy.

FROM THE FIRST, the question of Charlotte's appearance was the most difficult obstacle that Williams faced. For *Stuart Little* Andy had suggested numerous illustration ideas; he even sent a clipping from a Sears & Roebuck catalog that showed a girl who fit his mental image of diminutive Harriet Ames. This time he had many new ideas and didn't waste time in passing them along. On March 28 he wrote the first letter to Nordstrom in which, after seven years of knowing her, he addressed her as Ursula. "I am too exhausted to call you Miss Nordstrom any longer," he explained. "Too much typing for a man of my years." (He was fifty-two.) He suggested that Williams ought to consult some of the books that Andy himself had read while researching the scientific background of spiders. He mailed Nordstrom his own copy of Willis Gertsch's recent book *American Spiders*, so that she could lend it to Williams. He also sent her the New York Public Library call number for Henry McCook's three-volume compendium *American Spiders and Their Spinningwork*.

Andy particularly advised Williams to examine McCook's plate 23, opposite page 85 in Volume I. It showed a spider standing on six legs and holding up two like a dancer. From the front, it appeared to have only two eyes—in the location where human beings would expect to find eyes—and three smaller ones below seemed to form a frowning mouth. On the top of its head it wore what looked like a sporty little haircut. "The eyes and hair," Andy remarked, "are quite fetching." He also pointed out a plate that showed an orb weaver's web spangled with dew. "Garth might find it helpful to thumb through these majestic tomes," he added. "He'd better watch out, though—once a man gets interested in spiders, there's no time left for art."

Aside from the question of accuracy, Williams faced another challenging issue: how could he make a spider—with numerous eyes and a pincerlike mouth—charming? He did not share Andy's affection for spiders and found the photographs in Gertsch and McCook gruesome. Williams had told Nordstrom that he wanted to tackle the challenge of portraying a spider in close-up, but would he be able to convey human emotion on such an alien face? Determined at first to be as realistic as he had with the sheep and the pig, he drew Charlotte's face as a portrait, with the scattered eight eyes that real spiders possess—two in front where eyes are in human beings, two near what Williams intended to be a nose, two on the top of her head, and two low on the sides. Then he also sketched a portrait of Charlotte with a simple human-looking visage, one he thought of as a Mona Lisa face.

Despite his remark to Nordstrom that he was going to start slowly, Williams delivered sketches to her office on the morning of April 28, barely a month after Andy had arrived with the manuscript. She was thrilled with his portrayal of Wilbur, declaring that he looked "darling." She also liked the way that he had envisioned Mr. Arable and Lurvy.

The sketches of Charlotte were more problematic. Nordstrom pointed out that giving a spider a human face didn't necessarily accomplish the goal of portraying a spider, that perhaps the less Charlotte looked like a person the better. Perhaps, Nordstrom suggested, the many-eyed drawing might be modified to make Charlotte more spiderlike by omitting the line that Williams had intended for a mouth and enlarging some of the eyes.

Williams turned over the sheet with the eight-eyed Charlotte and roughly sketched a simpler face on the back. He agreed that if White didn't like Charlotte with either the human face or the eight eyes, he would draw a new round of samples more along the lines of this sketch.

Later the same day Nordstrom messengered the sketches to the author. She asked Andy to cover portions of various drawings with a small piece of paper to imagine how they might look revised, but assured him that if he liked Charlotte as she was in these drawings, then Harper was satisfied. Andy didn't like them. He rejected the first round of spider sketches and Williams submitted more. Finally Andy wrote to him, "You better just draw a spider and forget about a countenance."

Charlotte and her habitat weren't to appear in the book until the twelfth illustration, a view of the barn door with Wilbur standing on his hind trotters to peer up at his new friend. Readers would already have met Fern and Wilbur, Mr. and Mrs. Arable and Avery, the Zuckermans and Lurvy. Williams drew the first of his more close-up pictures to be next in the book, accompanying Charlotte's explanation to Wilbur of how to catch and kill a fly. He portrayed Charlotte extruding silk from a spinneret on her abdomen and using six of her legs to wrap it around the fly. He carefully drew the two hind legs clinging to radial lines of the web, even showing how her weight and activity stretched the line downward. Nor did Williams ignore the murder victim. Even through the mummy-wrapping of silk, he made visible the fly's compound eyes and folded wings.

For Charlotte thinking about how to save Wilbur's life, Williams drew her hanging head down in the web, its radial strands taut with the weight of her long, spindly legs. With her front leg positioned like an arm resting its elbow below on another strand of web, she leans her head in one hand. Williams drew her roughly diamond-shaped abdomen with something close to the real-life pattern of *cavatica* on it—"sort of like a keystone," as Andy said—but below that he left her round face blank. Andy liked this illustration, which showed the spider with smooth legs and abdomen. "Actually," he wrote later to Nordstrom, "Charlotte's legs are equipped with fine hairs, and these are mentioned in the book, but the overall effect is of smooth, silk-stocking legs."

Finally Andy took it upon himself to revise this latest portrait. To the bottom edge of Charlotte's blank face he added two tiny dots, barely visible, to serve as eyes. Above them, at the top of the oval, he drew a few short vertical lines that gave the faint impression of hair. With these almost subliminal marks he somehow gave Charlotte a thoughtful expression. But Williams privately thought that doing so was a form of cheating.

When he designed the cover, Williams took a different approach from what he had used for Andy's first children's book. On the jacket of *Stuart Little*, the two-inch-tall mouse-boy was alone in his souvenir birchbark canoe, *Summer Memories*, paddling his way down a rushing brook, away from a New England village and toward adventure. The more ambitious and accomplished cover of *Charlotte's Web*, in contrast, draws all the characters' eyes to the pivotal heroine in the plot. Sheep, goose, Wilbur, and Fern all peer hopefully upward at the loyal-hearted spider, as she coolly descends on a silken strand down through space, or at least from the cobwebby initial letter of her own name. These sloppy web strands did not sneak by without notice. When Nordstrom sent Andy a copy of the eleven-by-fourteen cover drawing, Andy grudgingly admitted that the "rather mussy Charles Addams attic web" was acceptable for the cover, but pointed out that it was inaccurate for a book portraying an orb weaver. "I'm sure," he added, "that Garth realizes that."

On June 20, three months after Nordstrom first called him, Williams delivered the finished drawings, except for one he decided at the last minute to revise. As requested, he had made Templeton more scruffy and ratty, further from the possibility that he might be seen as a cute mouse. Nordstrom had questions and he had answers: Was the word TERRIFIC legible enough in the web? He thought so. Why hadn't he portrayed Wilbur at the fair? Because every time he tried, the picture looked just like the barn scenes.

Soon Nordstrom was sending Andy "dummy cuts" of the illustrations and even the jacket design. "I like everything," he replied. Then he complained that the goose on the jacket looked too snakelike and suggested that this herpetological effect might be because her beak was open and her eye too round. He could accept it, but "no goose-lover in this house is satisfied."

IN JUNE, NORDSTROM presented *Charlotte's Web* to the Harper sales force. Usually the salesmen didn't have patience for much synopsis of a book, but Nordstrom found to her surprise, as she distributed copies of some of Garth Williams's illustrations, that the men were examining the pictures closely and asking for more and more details. They seemed to find the premise of the book touching—and they quickly became enthusiastic about its sales potential. Later in the summer, one of the salesmen told Nordstrom that his newfound appreciation for spiders was hampering his home repair. He had been painting his front porch when he discovered a spiderweb on the ceiling. Deciding to not disturb this creative animal at its work, he painted around its web.

Andy had been having his own new experiences with spiderwebs. Every day in the barn he used a shovel to push fresh manure from the cattle tie-ups to the trapdoor, where it fell down to the barn cellar that he had described with such affection in *Charlotte's Web*. Lately a spider—he thought of her as one of Charlotte's daughters—had taken to weaving her web in the tie-up itself, between posts just behind a bull calf. Each morning Andy would be busily working and forget that the web was there, which meant that yet again he would accidentally tear it down. Consequently, the spider had to spend her time repairing instead of enjoying her painstaking work and waiting for flies to wander into her parlor. Each night she rebuilt the web. Each morning Andy tore it down again. Then one evening she must have had an arachnid brainstorm. The next day, while doing his cleanup chores, Andy realized that he hadn't encountered a spiderweb yet. He examined the stall. This time the spider had spun her foundation lines to attach to different parts of the stall, outside Andy's path. He was impressed with what appeared to be her ability to learn from experience.

When he described this encounter to Nordstrom, Andy added that he was teaching the spider to write in her web. Then, he claimed, he planned to lend her to Brentano's Bookstore in New York for their display window, where she could weave a web and spell out the words SOME BOOK.

Chapter 17

COMPLETION

the terrible excitement of so great a concentration of
books in one place under one roof, each book wanting
the completion of being read.

—E. B. WHITE DESCRIBING A BOOKSTORE

AS PUBLICATION TIME neared, Andy was busy as usual
with a number of other projects. Richard de Rochemont
had approached him about making a film based upon Andy's
long essay "Here Is New York," which had also been published
as a small volume. Rochemont was a documentary filmmaker
who had worked on the newsreel *The March of Time*, which had
been appearing in theaters since 1935 and had ended in 1951. In
1949 he produced the first documentary series on TV, *Crusade
in Europe*, based upon General Dwight D. Eisenhower's account
of his career in World War II. Rochemont sent Andy a treatment. Andy explained in his usual careful way precisely what
he thought was wrong with it, arguing that because the script-
writer, Lois Jacoby, had been torn between story and spectacle,
she had produced something that was "neither fish nor fowl." The

project, like several others based on Andy's work that occurred to various stage and film people, never reached fruition.

Family and friends and colleagues occupied much of his time with more serious issues than a documentary film that might not come to pass. Life was swirling around them, as always. Andy's oldest sister, Marion, who had married when he was not quite three, reached her golden wedding anniversary in April 1952. That spring Andy and Katharine had five grandchildren hunting for Easter eggs in the living room. In the summer, as Andy and Ursula Nordstrom worked out publishing details on *Charlotte's Web*, Katharine was diagnosed with hepatitis, a little-known disease that Andy misspelled when notifying Nordstrom, and after a hospital stay she required a slow convalescence. Andy secretly advised to Gus Lobrano, who had replaced her in much of the fiction department dealings, to accede only slowly if she requested that work be sent to the hospital.

Harold Ross had died in December 1951, during surgery to remove a tumor from his lung. Andy was saddened and Katharine was devastated. For a quarter of a century, Ross had been like a force of nature in their lives. At the helm of the magazine that had brought Andy and Katharine together and given both the opportunity to develop their talents, Ross had been a friend, a daily presence, the focus of a high percentage of their daily correspondence and phone calls, the inspiration for many of their favorite anecdotes. Now they seemed adrift. Andy told a friend they felt "disemboweled." The funeral was a dismal affair—so many usually lively, even disorderly, people, sitting quietly in their shared misery. "In retrospect," Andy wrote of Ross, "I am beginning to think of him as an Atlas who lacked muscle tone but who God damn well decided he was going to hold the world up *anyway*." Andy kept thinking aloud about Ross's impact on his life and career. "The things that matter a great deal to me, most of them, were of not much interest or importance to Ross, and vice versa, and we really only met at a rather special level and at one place—like a couple of trolley cars hitched together by a small coupling. The thing I thank God for is that that connection proved flawless and was never even strained." With William Shawn, Andy wrote an appreciative eulogy for the magazine, which elicited many encouraging remarks from *New Yorker* writers. J. D. Salinger, who had been publishing stories in the magazine since "A Perfect Day for Bananafish" in 1948, and who had published a novel, *The Catcher in the Rye*, only the year before, wrote to thank Andy for his comments about Ross.

In early April 1952 Andy and Katharine hosted a party whose 131 guests showed up to celebrate the appointment of Ross's heir apparent, William Shawn, as the next editor of *The New Yorker*. Shawn himself was one of many who took a turn at the piano, and the last to do so was popular cartoonist Peter Arno. Dancing went on erratically during the party, which lasted until almost dawn. At one point a drunken partygoer accidentally opened the wrong door while looking for his coat and found the Whites' cook in bed. She politely suggested he close the door and go away.

However much Andy's opinion of his own work varied from day to day, professional validation kept arriving. Some came from surprising directions, including two in quick succession from England. He graciously turned down an invitation from the British humor magazine *Punch* to contribute regularly. And after George VI, the British king, died in February 1952, an editor at Hamish Hamilton, Andy's English publisher, wrote to Cass Canfield at Harper to tell him and Andy that *Stuart Little* had been one of the king's favorite books, a copy of which he often carried with him on trips, and that as recently as Christmas the queen had also given him *The New Yorker Album*. From less exalted directions, strangers occasionally sought Andy's advice about writing, now that he had acquired a respectable and apparently lasting reputation. A college student wrote to him, expressing dissatisfaction with her education and the frivolity of college life, which seemed unlikely to stimulate her yearning to write. He urged her not to give up on frivolity, to get a dictionary that would enable her to never again misspell the word *apparel*, and to "remember that writing is translation, and the opus to be translated is yourself."

> *I write largely for myself and am content to believe
> that what is good enough for me is good enough for a
> youngster.*

CHARLOTTE'S WEB WAS published on October 15, 1952. One of the most important and perceptive reviews came early. It was written by a Mississippi writer named Eudora Welty, who had published several story collections and a couple of novels, most recently *Delta Wedding*. In the *New York Times Book Review*, in a review entitled "Along Came a Spider," she raved about *Charlotte's Web*. She found herself unable to distill its meaning, so instead she summarized its themes: "What the book is about is friendship on earth, affection and protection, adventure and miracle, life and death, trust and treachery, pleasure and pain, and the passing of time. As a piece of work it is just about perfect, and just about magical in the way it is done."

Like a comet on an elliptical orbit, Anne Carroll Moore, the New York Public Library librarian who had attacked *Stuart Little* in 1945, had left Andy alone for years but reappeared in 1952 to complain about *Charlotte's Web*. By late October Nordstrom had received advance notice that Moore was expressing her dissatisfaction. "As her reservations about *Stuart Little* preceded a wonderful success for that book," Nordstrom joked to Andy, "I am taking all this as good news for *Charlotte's Web*." She pointed out that, because Eudora Welty had declared *Charlotte* perfect for readers over the age of eight or under the age of eighty, Moore was disqualified because she was eighty-two.

In December Moore's review appeared in the column "The Three Owls Notebook," in *Horn Book Magazine*, which had become an influential periodical in the field of children's literature since its founding in 1924. She praised a number of new books, from Esther Averill's *Jenny's Adopted Brothers* to H. A. Rey's *Curious George Rides a Bike*. She saved most of her complaints for *Charlotte's Web*. She said again that *Stuart Little* had disappointed her but conceded that "thousands of people liked it." She explained that she herself grew up on a farm in Maine and that E. B. White portrayed farm animals with "great beauty and rare understanding." Then she added the almost incoherent qualifying clause "as a children's book it never came clear from the preoccupation of an adult who had not spent a childhood on a farm." She liked the opening. She liked Fern but thought her mother an idiot. Then she informed Andy what his story ought to have been:

Fern, the real center of the book, is never developed. The animals never talk. They speculate. As to Charlotte, her magic and mystery require a different technique to create that lasting interest in spiders which controls childish impulse to do away with them.

Back when Katharine was first reviewing children's books for *The New Yorker*, she had told Andy about the candlelit meetings with librarians that she had attended at the New York Public Library. When he read Moore's review of *Charlotte*, he wrote to Nordstrom, "Would it be all right if I sent the librarians some candles for Christmas, for use in their candlelight meeting? I mean the kind that explode."

In mid-December *Newsweek* ran a cryptic little note about the book: "Charmingly sentimental tale for children and adults about a spider and a pig, written with many a fearful glance backward for fear of horse laughs from the left." Unaware of having glanced back for any reason, and unaware of why he might fear the left, and for that matter of what comprised "the left" in this reviewer's estimation, Andy wrote to Cass Canfield, who later blasted the reviewer for making no sense. Canfield sent Andy the reply letter from Robert Cantwell, *Newsweek*'s book editor. "I didn't know while writing *Charlotte's Web*," Andy replied, "I was sitting behind a psychological barrier created by child psychologists, but one lives and learns."

Most reviews, however, were quite positive. Bennett Cerf proclaimed that he was glad to know that Wilbur would not suffer the ignominious fate of starring in a Christmas dinner with a candied apple in his mouth. "Though I am not usually attracted by stories that personify animals," M. F. Kieran wrote in *The Atlantic Monthly*, "this one is absolutely delicious." *The New Yorker*, not surprisingly, raved. "This is really more than a work of sheer fantasy," wrote Katherine Kinkead, "for it creates not an impossible world of witches and giants and the like but a world that, as Mr. White proceeds to rub his jinni's lamp, the adult reader begins to feel uneasily might actually exist and that children, of course, know exists."

Andy was pleased to note that one perceptive review came from P. L. Travers, author of *Mary Poppins* and its sequels—including *Mary Poppins in the Park*, which had just appeared. She wrote in the *New York Herald Tribune* that "such tangible magic is the proper element of childhood," and that she felt the book had "an absorbed and dreamlike air such as one sometimes surprises in a child playing alone." Andy also liked a remark that Travers had made elsewhere, that a writer who writes successfully for children is probably actually writing for one child—the writer.

Like most of Andy's other projects, *Charlotte's Web* attracted some unexpected interest. Louis de Rochemont, brother of the documentary film producer who wanted to adapt "Here Is New York," and himself a producer of noir films such as *The House on 92nd Street* and the recent Dana Andrews semidocumentary *Boomerang!*, was after Andy to sell him movie rights to the story of Charlotte and Wilbur. He threw Andy an expensive luncheon party at the Cloud Club, atop the Chrysler Building. When Andy stepped out of the elevator in such elegantly appointed surroundings, he suddenly remembered an adventure from his early days at *The New Yorker*. Ralph Ingersoll, the managing editor in 1928, exploited Andy's comfortable feeling about heights that would dizzy anyone else by suggesting that he go over to the skyward-climbing Chrysler Building, then half built, and see if he could get to the top. Andy had spent many hours climbing up twenty-three floors on the two-inch-pipe scaffolding, surrounded by workmen splattered in white plaster from above, with the East River blinding in the sunlight far below. Now, twenty-four years later, he hadn't even wrinkled his best suit in the ascent to the top. "Jesus," he said to himself as he walked in, "I'm getting ahead."

IN LATE OCTOBER, Andy wrote to Nordstrom that so far it seemed his book was mostly being read by adults. "I have had only a sprinkling of childhood reaction to the book—those vital and difficult precincts—and will not know for a little while how it sits with the young." There were glimpses, of course. *The New Yorker*'s reviewer, Kinkead, described a ten-year-old boy she knew who took time away from football to read *Charlotte's Web*: "After a period of unusual silence in his room, broken by occasional loud laughs, he emerged with his face drawn but under rigid control. 'It's terrible to have to say goodbye to Charlotte,' he said."

Some of the surprising childhood reaction had been within the author's own family. Roger Angell read *Charlotte's Web* aloud to his quiet four-and-a-half-year-old daughter, Caroline, who listened thoughtfully. When the story was over, she said to her father, "I think there was an easier way to save Wilbur, without all that trouble. Charlotte should have told him not to eat, then he wouldn't have been killed because he would have been too thin."

When Andy recounted this story to Nordstrom, he added, "Trust an author to go to a lot of unnecessary trouble."

By December, however, Andy was already receiving responses from children far beyond his own family. When the students of Mrs. Bard's fifth-grade class at a Larchmont school sent a collection of letters asking about the author behind *Charlotte's Web*, and asking if E. B. White really lived on a farm, he replied in detail. As he had always loved to do, he listed again the many animal neighbors who populated his forty acres. First he took a census of the barn: the eighteen hens and ten sheep, a pair of geese, the bull calf on whose stall Charlotte's daughter had built her web, and a chipmunk. Although Andy unrealistically listed only a single rat, he admitted that the real barn held "many spiders." Then he listed the wild animals, from skunk to frog. The letters came just as Ursula Nordstrom informed Andy that Harper & Brothers' first printing of fifty thousand copies had not been too optimistic, and that she had just ordered a second printing.

Soon the influx of cards and letters from readers became more than Andy could even consider answering personally. Finally Nordstrom asked him to write a public letter that they could print many copies of and keep on hand to mail to readers. He wrote a chatty two-page account of how he came to think of the story of *Charlotte's Web*. In this note as in the novel, he didn't speak down to children. He told how he began to feel guilty about his relationship with pigs, that it made him feel treacherous, the daily feedings and ever greater familiarity ending up with a sudden murder. "I do not like to betray a person or a creature," he wrote, "and I tend to agree with Mr. E. M. Forster that in these times it is the duty of a man, above all else, to be reliable." About Charlotte he said, "Once you begin watching spiders, you haven't time for much else—the world is really loaded with them. I do not find them repulsive or revolting, and I think it is too bad that children are often corrupted by their elders in this hate campaign."

Closer to home, Roger's ten-year-old daughter, Alice, found a way to convey to the author the power of his compassionate story in *Charlotte's Web*. The next summer, after she had read the book several times, she was spending the summer in Brooklin—staying with her father and mother at a nearby cottage—when she learned that her grandfather was planning to slaughter a pig. It was a spring pig and apparently it was doomed to die in the fall, just like Wilbur—in September, sometime after Alice left Maine. Horrified, she connived a clever plan to remind her grandfather of his own book. She got out her crayons and drew a large copy of the SOME PIG illustration, the first hint that Wilbur was either extraordinary himself or had extraordinary friends. Then she persuaded her father to drive her to her grand-parents' farm in the night. Quietly Alice and Roger went down the dark lane to the pigpen, with Allen Cove visible beyond it. There Alice thumbtacked her poster to the boards of the pen.

The next morning, when Andy carried a pail of slops down to feed the pig, he was surprised and amused to find the drawing. But the pig's destiny lay in the future. For now there were other animals to feed and other chores to do, and he was eager to tell Katharine about this sign that had appeared during the night. The pig was eating happily when Andy walked back up to the barn.

Coda

AFTER *CHARLOTTE*

E. B. WHITE'S colleagues in the creation of *Charlotte's Web* continued to rise in their fields after its publication in 1952.

The next year, after the book had proved to be one of Harper & Brothers' great successes, a company executive treated Ursula Nordstrom to a grand lunch and made a show of offering her a position in the adult division. Offended at the implication that the department to which she had devoted so much passion was merely a stepping-stone to adult publishing, she resisted the urge to push the restaurant table "into the lap of the pompous gentleman opposite," as she said later. Instead she calmly explained that her job was publishing children's books. She insisted that she could not imagine being interested in publishing books for "dead dull finished adults."

Nordstrom wound up legendary in her field. She edited everyone from Laura Ingalls Wilder to Shel Silverstein, and her own children's book, *The Secret Language,* appeared in 1960. Nordstrom fearlessly championed many controversial innovations in books that she edited: the first mention of menstruation in a book for girls in Louise Fitzhugh's *Long Secret* in 1965; John

Donovan's references to homosexual experiences in his 1969 novel, *I'll Get There. It Better Be Worth the Trip*; Maurice Sendak's naked boy floating through *In the Night Kitchen* in 1970; and M. E. Kerr's drug background in the 1972 novel *Dinky Hocker Shoots Smack!* Loyal authors whose work had been supported by Nordstrom responded with affectionate nicknames. Margaret Wise Brown called her Ursula Maelstrom; to Russell Hoban, author of *Bedtime for Frances* and its sequels, she was Ursa Major. Eventually Harper & Row, the company's later incarnation, offered their in-house legend her own imprint, Ursula Nordstrom Books. She retired in 1973 and died in 1988 at the age of seventy-eight, leaving behind her longtime companion, Mary Griffith.

Garth Williams became one of the most renowned illustrators in twentieth-century children's literature. In 1947, after his success with *Stuart Little* and a couple of other books, Nordstrom had approached him about creating new illustrations for a uniform edition of Laura Ingalls Wilder's *Little House* books. He confessed that he felt more comfortable drawing animals than people, but he dived into research, including a visit to the eighty-year-old Wilder herself on Rocky Ridge Farm in Missouri. The new edition was published the year after *Charlotte's Web*. Williams also wrote several books and illustrated them. The most controversial was *The Rabbits' Wedding*, a 1958 picture book. To Williams's astonishment, his lyrical color illustrations of the romance between a black rabbit and a white rabbit were denounced as "integrationist propaganda" in Alabama, where the state library system withdrew the book from circulation.

Williams went on to illustrate Margery Sharp's charming 1959 novel *The Rescuers* and its sequels about Miss Bianca and the

Mouse Prisoners' Aid Society. His masterpiece may have been his beautiful illustrations for George Selden's Newbery Honor Award–winning *Cricket in Times Square* and its sequels. When E. B. White completed his third children's book, *The Trumpet of the Swan*, in 1969, both he and Nordstrom were disappointed to find that the by then hugely popular Williams was unavailable to illustrate it. (The job went to Edward Frascino, who would later illustrate a collection of previously unpublished Archy and Mehitabel adventures, *Archyology*.) Garth Williams died in 1996 at the age of eighty-four. In 2010, his original drawing for the cover of *Charlotte's Web* was sold at auction for $155,000, more than five times the auction house's advance estimate. Forty-one other pieces of his original artwork, including other images from White's novel, were sold at the same time, for a total of $780,000.

IN 1957 ANDY and Katharine finally moved permanently to the farm in Maine. Katharine's favorite pastime there was gardening. Andy noticed that when she was in the mood to garden, she simply went out to the flower beds, sometimes even in a tweed suit and Ferragamo pumps. The next March, Katharine launched an occasional *New Yorker* column, "Onward and Upward in the Garden," employing a style of title used in other contexts in the magazine. On the last day of 1960, after thirty-five and a half years at *The New Yorker*, she officially retired. Other than for an occasional consultation, she was out of the office for good. William Shawn had been editor for a decade and the magazine was flourishing, and from every direction came letters and articles praising Katharine's contributions to literature. The young John Updike, whose work she had edited since his first appearance in

The New Yorker, wrote, "I am very sad, for myself and for the magazine, for I think as an editor you are irreplaceable, and probably personally responsible for a giant part of the magazine's excellence in the last thirty years."

Unfortunately retirement was not a time of relaxation for Katharine. "I must say," Andy wrote to a friend on January 2, 1961, "she looks a little as though she were entering Leavenworth." Two days later, she began experiencing dizziness, numbness in her arm, and headaches. Doctors theorized neurological disorders and tumors; finally she underwent an angiogram, which revealed a blocked artery. Later she had to have an emergency appendectomy, wound up with terribly painful dermatitis, and contracted osteoporosis of the spine from medication for her skin disorder. She was in pain for much of the last several years of her life, but nonetheless enjoyed her role as a doting if old-fashioned grandmother. She died in 1977, to glowing obituaries about her crucial position at *The New Yorker*. Two years later, Farrar, Straus & Giroux published an acclaimed collection of her garden essays under the same title as the column, *Onward and Upward in the Garden*.

Andy, now a white-haired eighty, broke his no-interviews rule and talked to the *New York Times* about Katharine's book. With a white West Highland terrier named Suzy on his lap, he discussed his few remaining animals on the farm—two noisy geese and eight laying hens—and how much he missed his wife of forty-eight years. He imitated how she used to wind her long hair around and around and hold it in place with hairpins, and how she would reach for the phone with one hand while already holding a cigarette in the other. "This place," he said of the farm, "doesn't fit me since Katharine died."

Over the years he had published several other books. His essay collection *The Second Tree from the Corner* came out in 1954, two years after *Charlotte's Web*. In 1959, after writing an essay about his old Cornell professor William Strunk Jr., he was invited to write a new introduction to Strunk's book *The Elements of Style*, a commitment that resulted in a complete overhaul and his own essay about writing. His 1962 essay collection, *The Points of My Compass*, showed him in top form, and the next year he was awarded a Presidential Medal of Freedom. *The Trumpet of the Swan* came in 1970—an adventurous tale of a trumpeter swan, named Louis after Louis Armstrong, who is born mute and must therefore learn to play a trumpet (and write on a portable chalkboard) to replace his natural voice. Andy gave Louis's father, the regal old cob, his own father's grandiloquent manner of speech: "Welcome to the pond and the swamp adjacent! Welcome to the world that contains this lonely pond, this splendid marsh, unspoiled and wild!" After her companion, Mary Griffith, commented to Ursula Nordstrom that she always seemed particularly pleased to receive a letter from E. B. White, Nordstrom suggested to him that Harper publish a volume of his collected letters. It appeared in 1976, with a revised edition following in 2006. In 1977, the year of Katharine's death, Andy's collected essays were published, and the following year he received an honorary Pulitzer Prize for his lifetime of writings.

In August 1984, at the age of eighty-five, Andy loaded a canoe onto his car and drove to nearby Walker Pond to paddle around and admire the animals. Later, back at home, he was unloading the canoe from the car's roof rack when it slipped and hit his head. The next day he went to dinner at the cottage where Roger Angell and his wife, Carol, were staying. During the meal he confessed that he was feeling disoriented and confused. That fall, after Roger and Carol left Brooklin, an ever more confused Andy began spending most of his time in bed. Doctors speculated that what might appear to be sudden onset Alzheimer's was probably dementia resulting from a concussion inflicted by the canoe.

Joe, who still lived nearby with his wife Allene—and ran the acclaimed Brooklin Boat Yard that he had founded in 1960—managed medical care for his father during his decline. Joe hired nurses who attended Andy day and night. Often during the next several months he came to read to his father and discovered that Andy seemed to enjoy hearing his own books and essays read to him. But gradually Joe realized that his father couldn't always remember who wrote the words he was hearing. At times he dismissed the writing with a quick wave of his hand, and Joe would go on to read something else. At other times, seeming more peaceful, as if able to concentrate longer, Andy would listen through to the end.

Then he would stir and look at Joe and ask again who wrote what had just been read to him.

"You did, Dad."

Andy would think about this odd fact for a moment and sometimes murmur, "Not bad."

Although he remained able to identify family members, he became increasingly disoriented. He died on the first day of October 1985. After Katharine's death eight years earlier, Andy had not accompanied the rest of the family to her private burial service in the Brooklin Cemetery. Knowing Andy's aversion to public events, no one had been surprised or upset. Now his legendary fear of crowds became part of his own memorial service. "If Andy White could be with us today," Roger Angell said to the assembled family, "he would not be with us today."

ON A WARM early morning in spring, one day in the late 1980s, a yellow school bus pulled into the farm's circle driveway and parked in front of the barn. The children were already excited and laughing when they came down the steps, peering at the barn and the outbuildings and talking about Charlotte and Wilbur. Would they see Templeton? No geese were in sight. Where was Mr. Zuckerman?

When Joe White sold his parents' farm in 1987, two years after Andy's death, he stipulated that the property must never be set up as an E. B. White museum or commercialized in any way. His father had hated publicity, and as his fame grew, he had left town every year on his birthday to avoid reporters. (Townspeople knew where he went but refused to reveal the location, even after his death.) Robert and Mary Gallant, a retired couple from South Carolina, were avid E. B. White fans. They had already bought a farm in the area when they learned that the White farm was for sale, but they hastened to buy it too and then sell the first one. They shared the family's distaste for exploiting the legacy of E. B. White. They had given in, however, to a schoolteacher's request to host a classroom visit to the farm where *Charlotte's Web* had been inspired and written. The school was in an impoverished inland region and the students had helped raise money for the trip.

The Gallants came out of the house to welcome the children

and their teacher. They showed them the barn cellar where pigs were raised, the stalls for sheep, the wide doorway in which Charlotte's web appeared. They pointed out the rope swing that still hung in the doorway. Soon the kids were gathered in the barn, seated on hay bales, with the big doors open to the farmyard and the sparkle of Allen Cove down beyond the pasture. The Gallants usually invited Joe and Allene to join them for such occasions, but they hadn't accepted. Today Joe happened to be at the farm to borrow some equipment. He met the children and spoke a little about his father. Mary Gallant asked if he might like to read aloud from *Charlotte's Web*, but Joe declined. Then they turned on a recording of *Charlotte's Web* being read by the author.

Having bought this farm because it belonged to E. B. White, Mary and Robert Gallant stood listening to the recording—to Andy's strong, calm voice with its Northeastern accent—and felt as if the years had vanished. As he casually read the words that had come to him with such effort decades earlier, his real animals seemed to be back in the barn, the silly geese and sly rat, the sheep and cows and pigs. For a moment the Gallants couldn't tell the difference between fiction and reality, between the spider in the barn that had inspired the story and the fictional spider Andy had created on the page.

Joe watched as the children sat rapt, transported by the story that embodied the life he had known as a child in this barn—helping feed the pigs and milk the cows, swinging on the rope, going to the Blue Hill Fair. He had tended the pig whose death had helped inspire *Charlotte's Web*. Finally in a pause he told the Gallants that he had changed his mind, that he would like to read a little of the book himself. He stood up and flipped through the pages to find the place in the story where Mary Gallant had turned off the recording. Around him the children looked up and waited expectantly. Then he cleared his throat and began to read. It was as if the recording hadn't been turned off, as if Andy were still telling the story himself. It was the same voice.

ACKNOWLEDGMENTS

In late 2010 my wife and I were in New York City for Penguin's Seventy-fifth birthday party. A couple of hours before it began, Laura and I met for a drink at the Algonquin with Heide Lange, my wonderful agent. Heide has been guarding and advising my career for fifteen years. As we sat there talking about *The Story of Charlotte's Web*, which I had not yet completed, I said to her, "You have *always* been behind this idea. You read five drafts of the proposal before we were ready to even show it to anyone!"

And Heide murmured sweetly, "Only five drafts?"

Perhaps it was ten. My heartfelt thanks to Heide and to her excellent assistants, Jennifer Linnan and Rachael Fried.

At some point, anyway, we decided that the proposal was ready to show to editors. George Gibson bought the U.S. rights for Walker & Company, as well as U.K. rights for Bloomsbury, the publisher that is now Walker's parent company. For at least a decade I had been hearing what an extraordinary editor George is, and his reputation is not exaggerated. Besides his sense of language and nuance, he looks at a manuscript with the eye of a structural engineer. His thoughtful suggestions about matters large and small vastly improved this book. Thanks also to the rest of the fine crew at Walker & Company—George's assistant, Margaret Maloney, production editor Nathaniel Knaebel, copy editor Steve Boldt, jacket designer Natalie Slocum, and publicist Carrie Majer.

While writing *The Story of Charlotte's Web*, I have accrued many debts. First, thanks to Robert and Mary Gallant, the current owners of the farm in Brooklin, Maine, where E. B. White and Katharine S. White lived, and to their son Robert Gallant Jr., who helped me get in touch with his parents. The amiable Gallants hosted a two-day ramble around their house and property and answered countless questions in person, on the phone, and via e-mail.

At Cornell University's Carl A. Kroch Library, where I researched in the E. B. White Papers in the Division of Rare and Manuscript Collections, everyone was cordial and helpful, but gratitude goes especially to Ana B. Guimaraes, Eisha Prather, and curator Katherine Reagan. Martha White, granddaughter of E. B. White and curator of his estate, graciously provided information, permissions, and contacts. Access to much of White's printed work is available through *The New Yorker*'s digital edition of its entire run, every page of every issue since 1925, with a subscription to the magazine. I used it constantly.

My longtime friend Amy Garner Jerome has been cheering on this project since its inception, and I want to thank her, Aaron, Dahlia, and Satchel. Jon Erickson was helpful at every turn, as usual. Other particular encouragement came from Josephine Humphreys, Ross King, Denny Adcock, Jody and Barry Kammerud, Ron Watson, Michele Flynn, Collier Goodlett,

Rebecca Flynn-Goodlett, Luiza Flynn-Goodlett, and Ben Flynn-Goodlett. Thanks to Rhonda and Bill Patterson, in whose home and beach house I worked on this book. Several friends read and commented upon snippets of the manuscript, including Pamela Burdett, Laurie Parker, Mark Wait, John Spurlock, and several of the people already mentioned above. Thanks, as always, to Cesare Muccari and his fine staff at the Greensburg Hempfield Area Library, especially Diana Ciabattoni, Cindy Dull, and Linda Matey.

Last and yet first, because the book's dedication is not enough to commemorate her, I welcome this opportunity to express gratitude and admiration to my wonderful wife, Laura Sloan Patterson, who shakes up my thinking and keeps my life surprising and entertaining. She has nurtured this book from inception to completion.

ABBREVIATIONS FOR FREQUENT SOURCES

(See bibliography for full publication information on cited sources.)

Cornell: *E. B. White Papers, Division of Rare and Manuscript Collections, Kroch Library, Cornell University*

Charlotte: Charlotte's Web, *by E. B. White*

Davis: Onward and Upward: A Biography of Katharine S. White, *by Linda H. Davis*

EBW: *E. B. White*

Elledge: E. B. White: A Biography, *by Scott Elledge*

Every Day: Every Day Is Saturday, *brief* New Yorker *pieces by E. B. White*

KSW: *Katharine Sergeant White, although at various times in the book she is known as Katharine Sergeant, Katharine S. Angell, or Katharine White*

Kunkel: Genius in Disguise: Harold Ross of The New Yorker, *by Thomas Kunkel*

Letters: Letters of E. B. White. *Because of various*

editions, including a revised 2006 edition containing letters absent from the 1976 first edition, citations of letters are by date, not page number.

Neumeyer: The Annotated Charlotte's Web, by Peter F. Neumeyer

NY: The New Yorker

Nordstrom: Dear Genius: The Letters of Ursula Nordstrom, edited by Leonard S. Marcus

OMM: One Man's Meat, essay collection by E. B. White

Points: The Points of My Compass, essay collection by E. B. White

Second Tree: The Second Tree from the Corner, essay collection by E. B. White

Stuart: Stuart Little, by E. B. White

Wild Flag: The Wild Flag: Editorials from The New Yorker on Federal World Government and Other Matters, by E. B. White

Writings: Writings from The New Yorker, 1927–1976, brief pieces by E. B. White

NOTES

xi   "But real life" (book epigraph): EBW, Harper & Brothers flyer replying to letters about *Charlotte*, Cornell, Box 242.

Introduction: TRANSLATING YOURSELF

1   "I didn't like": EBW, letter to "Pupils of Grade 5-B, Larchmont, New York," 26 December 1952, in *Letters*.

3   Fadiman . . . "the standing problem": Clifton Fadiman, "Professionals and Confessionals: Dr. Seuss and Kenneth Grahame," in *Enter, Conversing* (Cleveland, OH: World, 1962).

4   "This boy . . . felt": EBW, "A Boy I Knew," *Reader's Digest*, June 1940.

4   "Remember that writing": EBW, letter to Elizabeth S——, 10 December 1951, in *Letters*.

4   "I discovered": EBW, letter to G. Deitch, 12 January [1971], in *Letters*.

6   *"Where's papa going"*: *Charlotte*, ch. 1.

Part I: ELWYN

7   *"Our rich experiences"* (Part I epigraph): EBW, "Notes and Comment," *NY*, 8 February 1936, quoted by Elledge, p. 21.

Chapter 1: ENCHANTED

9   *"He lived a life of enchantment"*: EBW, "A Boy I Knew," *Reader's Digest*, June 1940.

9   The birds were scurrying: EBW, "Was Lifted by Ears as Boy, No Harm Done," *NY*, 9 May 1964.

10   The stable: Ibid.; stereopticon photos, Cornell, Box 221, especially Photo N3891; occasional details in letters and essays.

10   Jimmy Bridges: EBW, Introduction, *Letters*.

10   coachmen in the neighborhood: Elledge, p. 20.

11   loving mice and hating rats: EBW, "Sanitation," *Harper's*, in *OMM*.

11   "My dream farm": EBW, "Fall," *Harper's*, in *OMM*.

11   collie named Mac: Guth, *Letters*, p. 15, n. 1; and countless notes.

11   pee into the coal bin: EBW, Introduction, *Letters*.

12   high-button shoes: See photo insert in *Letters*.

13   *"My first and greatest love affair"*: EBW, "Freedom," *NY*, July 1940, in *OMM*.

13   built eight years before Elwyn's birth: Elledge, p. 3.

14   leafy neighborhood, the scent of honeysuckle, etc.: EBW, Introduction, *Letters*.

14   their windows: Cornell, photo in Folder 220B.03.

14   carriages: See stereopticon photos, Cornell, Box 221, for

surrey parked in drive, as well as horse hitched to it, and other photos showing carriage drive and side of house; scattered references to carriages in EBW letters (especially early) and essays.

15   tall windows on the third floor: See photo insert in *Letters*.

15   In the dawn he woke: EBW, quoted by Elledge, p. 16.

15   (soon nicknamed En): Elledge, p. 21.

15   Elwyn's earliest faint memory: EBW, letter to Marion White Brittingham [April 1952] in *Letters*.

16   Little Lord Fauntleroy suit: EBW, introductory notes to *Letters*, p. 6.

16   suit precisely like Buster's: Cornell, Folder 220A.07.

16   nicknamed Bunny (further shortened to Bun): Innumerable letters between EBW and Stanley, from EBW's early childhood onward.

16   Stan also taught Elwyn: EBW, Introduction, *Letters*, p. 6.

16   To demonstrate centrifugal force: EBW, letter to Janice H. White [February 1979].

17   in early childhood, Elwyn became aware: EBW, "Freedom," *Harper's*, in *OMM*.

Chapter 2: FEAR

19   *"I don't know whether"*: EBW, letter to Stanley Hart White, 11 March 1954, in *Letters*.

19   a handful of songs: Elledge, pp. 5–8.

20   "that there was an inexhaustible fund": Quoted in Elledge, p. 15, who cites in his n. 25 for ch. 1 an undated obituary from the *Register*.

20   uncanny ability to remember: Ibid., p. 14.

20   painting might fetch five thousand dollars: Ibid.

21   beard of a Civil War general: See any photo of William Hart online.

22   For a formal portrait: Cornell, Folder 220A.15.

22   recovering from a harrowing ride: EBW, Introduction, *Letters*.

22   "All hail!": Quoted in Elledge, p. 4.

23   trip to the New York Zoological Park: EBW, letter to John Tee-Van, 29 June 1948, in *Letters*.

23   extravaganza *The Wizard of Oz*: EBW mentions his memory of the play, particularly of actor Fred Stone, in *Here Is New York*; my description of the performance comes from *The Annotated Wizard of Oz*, edited by Michael Patrick Hearn, pp. lviii–lxii.

23   Once at the Hippodrome: EBW, "Hippodrome," *NY*, 9 February 1929, in *Writings*.

24   supplied with musical instruments: EBW, Introduction, *Letters*, p. 3.

24   "I know eight pieces out of it already": EBW, letter to Albert Hunt White, 21 October 1908, in *Letters*.

24   Every Christmas Eve: EBW, *NY*, 22 December 1928.

25   *"I suffered nothing"*: EBW, Interview by Frank H. Crowther, *Paris Review*, Fall 1969.

25   Elwyn loved weather: EBW, "A Boy I Knew," *Reader's Digest*, June 1940.

26   Lincoln School: Elledge, p. 21–22.

26   the Misses Kirby: EBW, "My Day," *Harper's*, in *OMM*.

27   "I pledge allegiance": See Francis Bellamy, *The Youth's Companion*, 1892. During the rise of the Nazis in Germany in the 1930s, the similarity of the Nazi oath to the

U.S. Pledge of Allegiance prompted the deletion of the salute from the American version and it was turned into a gesture of placing the right hand over the heart. In 1954 the U.S. Congress added to the Pledge of Allegiance the words *under God*, turning it into a public prayer as well as a patriotic oath.

27   The school: Cornell, Box 221.

28   intimacy of the bathrooms: EBW, Interview by Frank H. Crowther, *Paris Review*, Fall 1969.

28   A crowd of any kind: EBW, "A Boy I Knew," *Reader's Digest*, June 1940.

29   Meccano: Elledge, p. 15.

29   The eggs were arranged: Ibid.

29   swing wildly down on a rope: Ibid., p. 20.

29   he would call upon Freddy: EBW, "October," NY 12 October 1929 in *Every Day*.

30   turtles lay eggs: In a section of his poem "Zoo Revisited," in *Second Tree*, EBW reimagines himself as a boy named Olie Hackstaff, who learns from his friend Kenny Whipple that turtles lay eggs. Because the final poem closely matches EBW's journal-like notes for it, and because it appears among other autobiographical scenes in an avowedly autobiographical poem, I have included this detail as an actual experience in EBW's own life. Commentators agree that Olie's friend Kenny Whipple in the poem clearly represents Elwyn's friend Kenny Mendel, because of his personality and the menagerie belonging to both. EBW portrays a full scene with details that seem to me a bit too precise to be autobiographical, so I didn't include them, keeping only the mention of the incident.

30   a cute mongrel pup: EBW, "Dog Training," *Harper's*, in
       OMM.

31   something . . . about being female: Ibid.

31   After Christmas 1908: Elledge, p. 22.

31   Sometimes Lillian rode: See photo insert, *Letters*.

32   sunbathed in the nude: EBW, "Cult," *NY*, 20 June 1931,
       in *Every Day*.

32   he swam in the darkness: Ibid.

Chapter 3: TRUSTWORTHY

33   *"This seemed an utterly"*: EBW, "Once More to the Lake,"
       in *OMM*.

33   "Douse his head in cold water": EBW, "The Summer Ca-
       tarrh," *Harper's*, in *OMM*.

34   Inland freshwater lakes: Thorson, *Beyond Walden*, espe-
       cially chapter 7, "Family Lake Culture"; Aron, *Working
       at Play*, especially chapter 6, "'Unfashionable, But for Once
       Happy': Camping Vacations"; Kammen, *A Time to Every
       Purpose*, especially chapter 3, "Nostalgia, Nationalism, and
       the American Seasons, 1854–1914."

34   back-to-nature movement: Schmitt, *Back to Nature*.

35   lakeside camp on Great Pond: Elledge, p. 27; EBW,
       "Once More to the Lake," and many other mentions.

35   "axehead capital of the world": http://en.wikipedia.org/
       wiki/Messalonskee_Lake_and_Stream.

35   The trip began: EBW, Introduction, *Letters*; "Once More
       to the Lake," in *OMM*.

35   Grand Central was undergoing reconstruction: "Grand
       Central Terminal Opens," *Railway Age*, September 2006.

35 Bar Harbor Express: Maiken, *Night Trains.*

35 seasonal night train: http://faracresfarm.com/jbvb/rr/run_
    thru.html.

35 last stops before Bar Harbor: http://en.wikipedia.org/
    wiki/Bar_Harbor_Express.

36 The family boarded the Express: Details about the White
    family's summers in the Belgrade Lakes region come es-
    pecially from EBW, "Once More to the Lake," *Harper's,*
    in *OMM;* EBW, letter to Stanley Hart White, 17 October
    1935, in *Letters;* EBW, Introduction, *Letters;* EBW, scat-
    tered single details and recapitulations in various essays
    and letters. See also captioned stereopticon photographs,
    Cornell (especially Boxes 220A and 221), for details of cab-
    ins, canoes, outdoor lunches, clothing, whole family and
    family subsets in boats, activities, paths through woods,
    and so on.

40 Often Samuel interrupted: EBW, letter to Stanley, 17 Oc-
    tober 1935, in *Letters.*

Chapter 4: A WRITING FOOL

42 *"In those days":* EBW, "Coon Tree," *NY,* 14 June 1956, in
    Points.

42 nature writers were lining up: Aside from more specific
    primary sources cited, see also Schmitt, *Back to Nature,* es-
    pecially chapter 4, "Nature Fakers"; and Ralph H. Lutts,
    The Nature Fakers.

43 He enjoyed books by both Long and Seton: EBW, Inter-
    view by Frank H. Crowther, *Paris Review,* Fall 1969. In
    this interview EBW specifies favorite childhood authors

but not titles; for both Long and Seton I choose what seem to me a representative volume from the era and describe what seem to be representative aspects of it. For influence of Long's *A Little Brother to the Bear*, see EBW, "Coon Tree," *NY*, 14 June 1956, in *Points*.

44   "To Plato, the owl": Long, *Ways of Wood Folk*.

44   "Two things must be done": Long, *A Little Brother to the Bear*.

45   "a pocket edition of Mooween in all his habits": Long, *A Little Brother to the Bear*.

45   "emphasise our kinship": Seton, *Lives of the Hunted*. See also anonymous review in *The Nation*, 13 March 1902.

45   "Lobo stands": Seton, *Wild Animals I Have Known*.

46   "nature fakers": Burroughs, "Real and Sham Natural History."

46   "To absorb a thing is better": Burroughs, "The Gospel of Nature," *Time and Change*.

46   "I have reaped my harvest": Burroughs, Introduction, *Wake-Robin*.

47   "We don't in the least mind impossibilities": Theodore Roosevelt, *Everybody's Magazine*, September 1907.

47   *"I was a writing fool"*: EBW, letter to Judith W. Preusser, 10 November 1963, in *Letters*.

48   "Maine is one of the most beautiful states": EBW, handwritten pamphlet; see photograph inserts in Elledge; see Cornell, papers of EBW.

48   "This is where I belong": EBW, letter to Stanley Hart White [January, 1947], in *Letters*.

48   "I wonder . . . what I'm going to be": EBW, journal entry, quoted in Elledge, p. 32.

49   writing down his day: EBW, Introduction, *Letters*.

49   a poem, "To a Mouse": Elledge, p. 30.

49   *St. Nicholas* magazine: Gannon et al., *St. Nicholas and Mary Mapes Dodge*; Marcus, *Minders of Make-Believe*, pp. 55 ff.

50   "Glad to see us?": See image of article, *St. Nicholas* magazine, November 1873, online at http://flyingdreams.home .mindspring.com/nickopeningpages.jpg.

50   one about Lincoln: See image of article, *St. Nicholas* magazine, 1912 (no issue date shown), online at http://flying dreams.home.mindspring.com/nickbiooflincoln.jpg.

50   ("Next to its usefulness"): See image of article, *St. Nicholas* magazine, 1907 (no issue date shown), online at http:// flyingdreams.home.mindspring.com/nickinventionhis tory.jpg.

51   Faulkner: Blotner, *Faulkner: A Biography*, p. 39.

52   the name of the dog: Long, *A Little Brother to the Bear*, pp. 92–93.

54   "A True Dog Story": Cornell, EBW Papers, Cornell, Box 222.

Chapter 5: LIEBESTRÄUM

55   "*The only sense that is common*": EBW, "The Ring of Time," *Harpers's* in *Points*.

55   awkwardly translated Caesar: EBW, "First World War," *Harper's*, in *OMM*.

55   Naturally girls: EBW, Introduction, *Letters*; EBW, various essays; Elledge, p. 34 ff.

56   Somewhere out there in this busy world: EBW, "Getting Ready for a Cow," *Harper's*, September 1942, in *OMM*.

56   "To get in right with the girls": EBW, letter to Stanley
      Hart White [14 May 1916].

57   Lillian . . . tried to teach him popular dances: EBW, "Af-
      ternoon of an American Boy," *NY*, 29 November 1947.

58   Elwyn went along with her: ibid

59   greeted Eileen's mother: All dialogue from EBW, "After-
      noon of an American Boy," *NY*, November 29, 1947 in
      Second Tree.

60   skating with a pretty blue-eyed girl: Elledge, p. 35; EBW,
      Introduction, *Letters*; EBW, "First World War," EBW, poem
      "Zoo Revisited," in *Poems and Sketches*.

61   in a blissful romantic haze: Ibid.

61   Elwyn was assistant editor: Ibid.

61   he reimagined Henry Wadsworth Longfellow's:
      Elledge, p. 34

62   Most of his literary heroes: EBW, "Don Marquis," *OMM*.
      An earlier version of this essay appeared as the introduc-
      tion to Doubleday's 1950 edition of Don Marquis's *Lives
      and Times of Archy and Mehitabel*. See the index for infor-
      mation on Marquis throughout the text.

62   Don Marquis: Sims, "A View from the Under Side,"
      Introduction to *Annotated Archy and Mehitabel*.

63   "We came into our room": Don Marquis, *Archy and Me-
      hitabel*, or Sims, *Annotated Archy and Mehitabel*.

64   Elwyn admired the literate cockroach: EBW, "Don
      Marquis," *OMM*.

64   graduated from high school: EBW, "First World War."

64   "civilization itself seeming to be in the balance": Wood-
      row Wilson, 2 April 1917, in a joint session of Congress in

Washington, D.C. The full sentence from his speech:
"It is a fearful thing to lead this great peaceful people
into war, into the most terrible and disastrous of all
wars, civilization itself seeming to be in the balance."

65   sale of the big Summit Avenue house. Elledge, p. 9.

65   One friend had already enlisted: Ibid.

65   "I don't know what to do": EBW, "First World War," in
     Harper's, *OMM*.

66   "My birthday!": EBW, Ibid.

66   carefully packed the strip of bicycle tape: Elledge, p. 36.

Part II: ANDY

67   *"All writing is both a mask"*: EBW, letter to Scott Elledge,
     16 February 1964, in *Letters*.

Chapter 6: OLYMPUS

69   white-bearded emeritus figure: Cornell yearbook, 1918,
     in the Cornell archives.

70   described in a fanciful list: EBW, "I'd Send My Son to
     Cornell," *University* 1, n. 5 (1933); quoted in part in Elledge,
     p. 51.

70   he was invited to join: Cornell yearbooks, 1918–21, in the
     Cornell archives.

70   senior year he was elected fraternity president: Elledge,
     p. 54.

70   On October 13, 1917: EBW, "First World War," *Harper's*,
     dated October 1939, in *OMM*.

70   served on several Cornell committees: Cornell yearbooks, 1918–21, in the Cornell archives.

71   sang in the secular choir: Elledge, p. 50.

71   He registered for the draft: EBW, "First World War," *Harper's*, in *OMM*.

71   paragraphs that hid internal rhymes: EBW, letter to Jessie Hart White [December 1918], in *Letters*.

71   "I think I must have consumption": EBW, "First World War."

71   English 8 with William Strunk Jr.: EBW, "Will Strunk," *NY*, 1957, in *Points*.

72   Fall Creek Drive: Guth, note in *Letters*, p. 19.

72   home of Professor Bristow Adams: EBW, letter to Luella Adams, 24 November 1957, in which he quotes from his journal entries of the time; reprinted in *Letters*.

72   its eight pages: Guth, notes on *Letters*, pp. 17ff.

72   national and international news: Elledge, p. 59.

72   unprecedented confidence: EBW, quoted by Guth, notes to *Letters*, p. 17.

72   a catchall column: Ibid., p. 18.

73   sprawled across the flatbed press: Elledge, p. 53.

73   compared her eyes to the deepest: Ibid., pp. 61–62.

73   *"All beginnings are wonderful"*: EBW, "Danbury Fair," *NY*, 18 October 1930, in *Writings*.

73   Lillian was commuting: Elledge, p. 69.

74   to read the news: Examples taken from various mentions in paragraphs for *NY*, in *Every Day*.

74   promoted it on giant billboards: Jane McMaster, "A Glance Back to 1924 in First E&P Directory," *Editor and Publisher*, 29 July 1950. Available at the comic-strip history site http://

strippersguide.blogspot.com/search/label/News%20of
%20Yore.

74 The building had Corinthian columns: From my own
observation; see also photos at http://www.nyc-architec
ture.com/SOH/SOH029.htm.

75 *"My heart has followed"*: Marquis, "The Name," *Dreams &
Dust.* EBW quotes this line from Marquis in both his introduction to *The Lives and Times of Archy and Mehitabel*
and his *Paris Review* interview.

76 "He is one of the men who saw": Anonymous introduction to article by Frank Seaman, "Merchandising and
Advertising Abroad," *The Americas*, December 1916, a
publication of the National City Bank of New York.

77 One day in late February 1925: Elledge, 102; EBW, notes
in *Letters.*

77 to survey a newsstand: These magazines were on newsstands during this week; images of front covers and text
available at various online sources.

78 The first issue arrived on newsstands: Sources disagree
about the first day of distribution.

78 The first issue of *The New Yorker*: See *NY*, online archive;
I consulted it constantly.

79 "Into every one of this season's song sparrows": Elledge,
p. 102.

80 two-bedroom apartment on the third floor: Ibid., p. 147.

80 He described a lunchtime encounter: EBW, "Child's
Play," *NY*, 26 December 1925.

80 Childs restaurant: "Business: Childs' War," *Time*, 11 February 1929; Christopher Gray, "Streetscapes: The Childs
Building," *New York Times*, 6 November 1988; David W.

Dunlap, "Fade from White: Memories of Pancakes at Childs," *New York Times*, 31 July 2007.

82   The woman striding: EBW, quoted by Guth in *Letters*, p. 72, without source attribution; EBW, quoted by Nan Robertson, "Life without Katharine: E. B. White and His Sense of Loss," *New York Times*, 8 April 1980.

82   Angell had majored: Davis, p. 32ff.

83   she also participated in almost every other decision: Ibid., p. 59ff.; Elledge, p. 118; see also Kunkel.

83   At thirty-four, Harold Ross: Details of Ross's description come from Kunkel, Grant, Thurber, Elledge, Davis, and EBW.

83   Angell and Ross invited Andy: Elledge, p. 115.

84   Ross's friends . . . coming aboard: Thurber, *Years with Ross*, pp. 22–24; Kunkel, various citations under names of Round Table members.

84   searching for the right "formula": Kunkel, p. 105, and many other sources.

84   Each owed a debt to nineteenth-century forebears: Yagoda, *About Town*, pp. 84ff; Sims, "A View From the Under Side," introduction to *The Annotated Archy and Mehitabel*.

84   Andy agreed to contribute: Guth, note in *Letters*, p. 72; Elledge, pp. 113–14.

Chapter 7: INTERVIEW WITH A SPARROW

86   *"New York is part"*: EBW, Interview by Frank H. Crowther, *Paris Review*, Fall 1969.

87   identifying the birds: Ibid.

87   peaceful snowfall one February day: EBW, "Cold Thought," *NY*, 4 February 1928, in *Every Day.*

87   "its skinny ailanthus tree": EBW, "Soil," *NY*, 5 May 1928, in *Every Day.*

87   he explored Bronx Park: EBW, "Distant Borough in April," *NY*, 21 April 1928, in *Every Day.*

88   the newly opened Reptile and Amphibian Hall: EBW, "Seeing Things," *NY*, 18 February 1928, in *Writings*; Eugene Bergmann, "Design and Production of a New Herpetology Hall," *Curator: The Museum Journal*, September 1978.

89   he commented on everything from: EBW, *Every Day* throughout; Elledge, pp. 123, 155, among many others.

89   "A lot has been done by novelists": EBW, "Old and Young," *NY*, 18 October 1930, in *Every Day.*

89   General Treaty for the Renunciation of War: See the text of the pact at http://www.yale.edu/lawweb/avalon/imt/kbpact.htm.

89   "While the pacific ink": EBW, "A Treaty," *NY*, 8 September 1928, in *Every Day.*

90   back to writing about nature: EBW, "Mysteries of Life," *NY*, 22 September 1928, in *Writings.*

90   "They glance in the right direction": EBW, "Crossing the Street," *NY*, 16 July 1932, in *Writings.*

90   speculated that Ziegfeld Follies: EBW, "Duck Welcomers," *NY*, 28 January 1928, in *Every Day.*

90   "Down in the Village": EBW, "October," *NY*, 12 October 1929, in *Every Day.*

91   "As we grow older": EBW, "Disillusion," *NY*, 16 February 1929, in *Writings.*

91   Freud had used the term *locomotor phobia*: Siân Morgan, "The History of a Phobia," *Encyclopedia of Psychoanalysis* 6, p. 179.

91   Andy casually revised Freud: EBW, "Locomotophobia," *NY*, 3 October 1931, in *Every Day*.

91   paradoxes of Einstein's theories: EBW, "Mysteries," *NY*, 14 February 1931, in *Every Day*.

94   Andy imagined interviewing the bird: EBW, "Interview with a Sparrow," *NY*, 9 April 1927, in *Writings*.

Chapter 8: CRAZY

96   *"The whole scheme"*: EBW, "Foreword," *Points*.

96   *"I could not then unbend"*: Quoted in Elledge, pp. 147–148.

96   "Too small a heart": EBW, "Belated Christmas Card," *NY*, 7 January 1928.

97   "rub shoulders with the famous": EBW, "Rubbing Elbows," *NY*, 11 June 1927.; Magdol, in later interviews with Elledge, insisted that she said "rub shoulders."

98   *"He goes his way"*: EBW, "Portrait," in *The Lady is Cold*.

98   a conversation between himself and the canary Baby: EBW, "Bye Low Baby," *NY*, 17 March 1928. All quotations here from same source.

99   *"I'm in love, and I'm going crazy."*: EBW, "A Boston Terrier," *Harper's*, in *OMM*.

100   In Paris, Thurber liked to sneak: Holmes, *Clocks of Columbus*, pp. 75–76.

100   a managing editor . . . a "jesus": Ibid., p. 87.

100   doughnuts and cocktail-party anchovies: Holmes, *Clocks of Columbus*, p. 82.

101   "Take this down, Miss Terry": Thurber, *Years with Ross*,
      p. 48.

101   "Which elephant is talking?": Ibid., p. 41.

101   closet-size office: EBW, note in *Letters* (Guth edition), p. 73.

101   Rose's first drawing: See Rose's own account on the Na-
      tional Cartoonists Society Web site, http://www.reuben
      .org/ncs/members/memorium/rose.jpg.

101   "It's broccoli, dear": *NY*, 8 December 1928; reprinted in
      Complete Cartoons of The New Yorker, p. 15. According to
      Thurber in *The Years with Ross*, p. 53, White ran the cap-
      tion by him and he merely replied, "Yeh, it seems okay to
      me," but neither of them "cracked a smile."

102   Ross hesitated . . . Katharine published it: Ross, letter to
      George W. Stark, 5 June 1931, in Ross, *Letters*, p. 61.

102   a drawing of a seal: Thurber, *Years with Ross*, pp. 53–63.

103   "Just the minute another person": Thurber and White, *Is
      Sex Necessary?*, p. 162–63.

104   "There are apartments in New York": Ibid., p. 102.

104   "To kiss in a dream": Ibid., p. 174.

105   "I gather," one of them asked: Thurber, *Years with Ross*,
      p. 50.

105   "I don't know what you think of it": EBW, journal entry,
      3 November 1929, quoted in *Letters* (Guth edition), p. 82.

                    Chapter 9: AS SPIDERS DO

106   "What a life": EBW, letter to Reginald Allen, 2 January
      1971, in *Letters*.

106   "God, how I pity me!": Holmes, *Clocks of Columbus*, p. 87.

107   close friend of and poker player with: Ross, *Letters*, p. 72.

107 an excerpt from a feeble stage routine: Julius H. Marx, "Vaudeville Talk," *NY*, 11 April 1925.

107 Andy found Ross a fascinating hybrid: EBW and William Shawn, eulogy for Harold Ross, *NY*, 15 December 1951; EBW, letter to H.K. Rigg, 11 December 1951, in *Letters*; Davis, p. TK.

108 an overworked portfolio crammed: EBW, quoted in Davis, p. 114.

108 "This is to introduce Mrs. Angell": Kunkel, p. 144.

109 took Katharine home to his native Cleveland: Davis, p. 48.

109 the first-ever insurance system for soldiers: Davis, p. 46.

110 Katharine went along and wrote two powerful articles: Davis, pp. 49–54.

110 French notions of marriage: KSW, letter to Callie Angell, 20 January 1975, quoted in Davis, pp. 231–32; Davis, pp. 71ff; Roger Angell, "Hard Lines," *NY*, 7 June 2004.

111 Ernest suggested that she herself have an affair: Davis, 71.

111 Katharine had also been a prizewinner: Ibid., p. 24.

111 "Now grows my heart unruly": EBW, "Desk Calendar," *NY*, 14 November 1928, p. 23; Elledge, pp. 149ff; Davis, pp. 77ff.

112 "No man is lonely": EBW, letter to Harold Ross, 16 June [1928], in *Letters*.

112 spent well beyond their financial means: Davis, pp. 62–67.

113 Roger innocently called out: Ibid., 71.

113 Ernest slapped Katharine: Ibid., p. 80.

113 To tell eight-year-old Roger: Roger Angell, "Hard Lines," *NY*, 7 June 2004.

114 wondered if he ought to leave: EBW, journal entry, 1 January 1919, quoted in *Letters* (Guth edition), p. 82.

114 "the animal alertness to the other's heart": EBW, quoted by Davis, p. 79.

115 They wrote letters.: Ibid., p. 88

115 she and Andy were married: Elledge, pp. 170ff.

115 "If it lasts only a year": Ibid., p. 173.

115 Andy took Roger for a ramble: Roger Angell, "Andy," *NY*, 14 February 2005.

116 Andy wound up moving: Elledge, p. 174.

116 using an interoffice memo form: Guth, *Letters*, p. 88.

116 "People slowly accustomed themselves": Guth, *Letters* pp. 88–89.

117 his investment in Camp Otter: Elledge, p. 173.

117 *"The spider, dropping down from twig"*: EBW, letter to KSW [30 November 1929]; "Natural History," in *Poems and Sketches*, p. 72.

118 Harris's revival of Chekhov's play: EBW, "Unwritten," *NY*, 26 April 1930, in *Writings*.

118 Elena and . . . Mikhail: Description from photo of Gish and Perkins in costume onstage for this run of this play, from the Billy Rose theater papers at the NYPL.

118 throat began to tighten up: EBW, letter to KSW [spring 1930], in *Letters*.

119 Jim Thurber's Scottish terrier: Holmes, *Clocks of Columbus*, pp. 103–4.

119 "It takes courage": James Thurber, "The Thin Red Leash," *NY*, 13 August 1927, in Thurber, *Dog Department*.

119 "an opinionated little bitch": Guth, introducing EBW's spring 1930 letter to KSW as Daisy, *Letters*, p. 91.

119 "Dear Mrs. White": EBW, letter to KSW [spring 1930] in *Letters*.

120 Their son, Joel, was born: "Certainly not": EBW, letter to Scott Elledge, 16 June 1982, quoted in Elledge, p. 178.

121 "White tells me you are already": EBW, letter to Joel White, 31 December 1930, quoted in Elledge, pp. 178–79.

121 a nursemaid for Joe and a cook: Elledge, p. 179.

122 anchoring for the night: EBW, letter to Stanley Hart White, quoted by Elledge, p. 214, n. 32, not in *Letters*.

122 a decrepit, old dock: EBW, letter to KSW [early September 1937], in *Letters*.

123 Katharine and Andy explored: Elledge, p. 183.

Part III: CHARLOTTE

125 *"I knew of several barns"*: EBW, "Fro-Joy," in *Harper's*, in *OMM*.

Chapter 10: DREAM FARM

127 *"Animals are a weakness with me"*: EBW, "Pigs and Spiders," Harper publicity flyer for *Charlotte*, Cornell.

127 Andy and Katharine were able to buy: Elledge, pp. 183ff.

127 profits passed six hundred thousand dollars: Ibid., p. 183.

128 the house encountered strong winds: Davis, p. 114, in a footnote quoting KSW's father, Charles Sergeant.

128 built around 1800: Ibid., pp. 114–15.

128 ground-floor studies: I borrowed many of these details from Roger Angell's vivid glimpse of his mother's and

stepfather's work habits in his essay "Andy," *NY*, 14 February 2005; others come from Cornell photographs and my own visit to the EBW farmhouse.

129   "without stepping out of the door": EBW, "A Shepherd's Life," *Harper's*, April 1940, in *OMM*.

129   As soon as he closed the lift-latch: I merged passing details from numerous comments by EBW in his essays and letters, as well as his descriptions in draft notes on *Charlotte's Web* (Cornell, Box 2, Folder A), and my own visit to the site and my photos of older tools that had been left in the barn when White died and kept in situ by the current owners. See also Roger Angell, "Andy," *NY*, 14 February 2005.

130   nineteenth-century cattle stalls: EBW, "Getting Ready for a Cow," *Harper's*, September 1942, in *OMM*.

131   carrying a paper napkin: Roger Angell, "Andy," *NY*, 14 February 2005.

131   "a morning jewel, a perfect little thing": EBW, "Morningtime and Eveningtime," *Harper's*, August 1942, in *OMM*.

131   mistook the silhouettes of patrol planes: EBW, "Foreword," *OMM*.

132   using desk scissors to trim lambs' wool: EBW, "Fall," *Harper's*, in *OMM*.

132   Andy anchored a metal loop: From my own visit to the White barn and my interviews with the current owners, who recounted stories told by Henry Allen, the Whites' caretaker, who remained with the Gallants after they bought the house. As I mention in the introduction, the rope swing is still there.

132   When he decided to dynamite boulders: EBW, "Getting Ready for a Cow," *Harper's*, September 1942, in *OMM*.

132 "People have quit calling me an escapist": EBW, "A Shepherd's Life," *Harper's*, April 1940, in *OMM*.

133 *The Rural New Yorker*: EBW, "Farm Paper," *Harper's*, in *OMM*.

133 Fog was always a threat: EBW, letter to Stanley White, 11–21 July [1945], in *Letters*.

133 the farm extended beyond: EBW, "Salt Water Farm," *Harper's*, January 1939, in *OMM*; EBW, early draft of *Charlotte*, Cornell, Box 2, Folder B; EBW, occasional remarks in letters and essays.

133 "the restless fields of protein": EBW, "Salt Water Farm," *Harper's*, January 1939, in *OMM*.

134 "When you have your own boat": EBW, "Second World War," *Harper's*, September 1939, in *OMM*.

134 a fresh spring: EBW, "Progress and Change," *Harper's*, December 1938, in *OMM*.

134 parade of nonhuman neighbors: EBW, "Report," dated December 1939, in *OMM*; *Charlotte*, chapter 9, "Wilbur's Boast"; EBW, many occasional remarks in letters, essays, and *Charlotte* drafts.

135 the raccoon that nested: EBW, "Coon Tree," *NY*, 14 June 1956, in *Points*.

136 Christopher Morley . . . wrote: EBW, letter to Christopher Morley, 27 April 1936, in *Letters*.

137 his mother . . . died: EBW, letter to KSW, 1 May 1936, in *Essays*; White, letter to Stanley Hart White, "Thursday / Bert Mosher's. / Belgrade Lakes, Maine / [1936?]," in *Letters*; Elledge, pp. 203–4.

140 Ralph Ingersoll had taken the magazine: Ralph Ingersoll, "The New Yorker," *Fortune*, August 1934.

140   a timely invitation from *Harper's*: Elledge, p. 211.

140   "I was a man in search of the first person singular": EBW,
      Introduction, *OMM*.

141   "The note he sounded": EBW, "Visitors to the Pond,"
      NY, 23 May 1953, in *Writings*.

141   seals that swam beside his boat: EBW, letter to "Pupils of
      Grade 5-B," Larchmont, NY, 26 December 1952, in *Letters*.

141   In 1938 the White family moved: Elledge, pp. 210–14.

142   "I soon knew": EBW, "Spring," *Harper's*, dated April 1941,
      in *OMM*.

Chapter 11: THE MOUSE OF THOUGHT

143   *"Creation is in part"*: EBW, "Here Is New York," *Holiday*,
      July 1948.

143   most wound up donated: Davis, p. 138.

143   Katharine briefly reviewed as many: Ibid., p. 106.

143   "He seems to be": Ibid., p. 107.

144   He read many of the books: EBW, "Children's Books,"
      Harper's, in *OMM*. All EBW quotations here from this
      essay. Descriptions of covers are from online searches.

145   In the spring of 1926: EBW, "The Librarian Said It Was
      Bad For Children," *New York Times*, 6 March 1966; Elledge,
      pp. 253ff.

146   "Don't let Andy neglect *Stuart Little*": Elledge, quoted
      p. 254.

146   children's librarian Anne Carroll Moore: Ibid., from let-
      ter to EBW from Anne Carroll Moore, 16 January 1939.

146   "My fears about writing": EBW, letter to Anne Carroll
      Moore, 15 February 1939, in *Letters*.

147 "It would seem to be for children": EBW, letter to Eugene Saxton, 1 March [1939], in *Letters*.

147 He informed Anne Carol Moore: EBW, letter to Anne Carol Moore, 25 April 1939, in *Letters*.

147 had to convince the gas ration board: EBW, letter to Harold Ross, [April? 1943], in *Letters*.

148 to watch the woodcocks' mating dance: EBW, letter to Gustave S. Lobrano, [March? 1943], in *Letters*.

148 "So the only thing for me to do is quit": EBW, letter to Frederick Lewis Allen, 13 March [1943], in *Letters*.

148 "I want," he said flatly: EBW, letter to Frederick Lewis Allen, 20 March 1943, in *Letters*.

148 what he described as a "nervous crack-up": EBW, letter to Harry Lyford, 28 October 1943, in *Letters*.

149 a furnished apartment on East Thirty-fifth Street: Elledge, pp. 250–51.

149 "Ever at home are the mice in hiding": EBW, "Home Song," *NY*, 5 February 1944.

149 "The mouse of Thought": EBW, "Vermin," *NY*, 6 October 1944.

149 "mice in the subconscious": EBW, letter to Stanley Hart White [January 1945], in *Letters*.

150 he found a mouse hiding: Elledge, p. 263.

150 about buying a mousetrap: EBW, unsigned, untitled Comment, *NY*, 2 October 1926.

150 to complete *Stuart Little* within two months: EBW, "The Librarian Said It Was Bad for Children," *New York Times*, 6 March 1966; Elledge, pp. 253ff.

150 Andy switched Stuart's name to the more apt Little: Neumeyer, p. 105.

150   "he could have been sent first class mail": *Stuart*, ch. 1.

152   amid messy offices: *Nordstrom*, pp. xxixff.

153   unfit for children: EBW, "The Librarian Said It Was Bad for Children," *New York Times*, 6 March 1966.

153   insisting that Stuart was unruly: KSW, letter to Anne Carroll Moore, quoted (without date) in Guth, *Letters*, p. 267.

153   Nordstrom approached several artists: *Nordstrom*, pp. 8, 9.

153   *Ferdinand* . . . pacifist propaganda: Sue Lile Inman, "Robert Lawson," *Dictionary of Literary Biography*, v. 22, p. 233.

153   author and editor admired Lawson's: Nordstrom, letter to KSW, 30 March 1945, in *Nordstrom*.

154   a preoccupation only around the *New Yorker* offices: Wilson and Ross quotations from EBW, *New York Times*, 6 March 1966. I italicized *born* in Ross's exclamation.

155   "I have now a library": Thoreau, *Journal*, 28 October 1853.

155   increase the first printing to more than fifty thousand: Nordstrom, letter to EBW, 12 September 1945, in *Nordstrom*.

155   a man in New York named Stuart Little: Ibid.

156   Perhaps he could make a living: Marcus, *Minders of Make-Believe*, p. 176.

Chapter 12: FOREKNOWLEDGE

157   *"Confronted by new challenges"*: EBW, Introduction, *OMM*.

157   In late March of 1948: EBW, "Tomorrow Snow," *NY*, 20 March 1948, in *Writings*.

157   Roosevelt Hotel: Much of the Roosevelt Hotel information came from historical photos on their own Web site, http://www.theroosevelthotel.com.

158   "He was a man carrying foreknowledge": EBW, "Tomorrow Snow," *NY*, 20 March 1948, in *Writings*.

158   "A man sometimes gets homesick": EBW, "My Day," *Harper's*, in OMM.

158–   awarded three honorary degrees: EBW, letter to KSW
59   [June 1948], Guth, note to *Letters*, p. 296.

159   Irving Penn had photographed him for *Vogue*: See photo insert in Elledge, after p. 278.

159   "You say nothing about nasal discharge": Quoted in Davis, p. 115; her source note, p. 267, says "KSW to EBW, Tuesday [1935]."

159   Convinced that he had a brain tumor: EBW, letter to KSW [26 March 1934], in *Letters*.

159   how a hot-water bottle: EBW, "To a Hot Water Bottle Named Jonathan," *NY*, 18 February 1928.

160   the morality of raising farm animals: EBW, "Death of a Pig," *Atlantic Monthly*, January 1948.

161   delivered piglets: EBW, quoted by Neumeyer, p. 2.

161   "The loss we felt": EBW, "Death of a Pig," *Atlantic Monthly*, January 1948.

162   This pleasurable assignment: EBW, letter to John McNulty, dated 21 August 1949, in *Letters*.

162   "Don knew how lonely": EBW, "Hot Weather," *Harper's*, in *OMM*.

163   "A seer a day": EBW, "Compost," *Harper's*, in *OMM*.

163   "If you sat up nights": Teale, *Near Horizons*, New York: Dodd Mead, 1942.

163   "Archy's boss is dead": EBW, untitled paragraphs, *NY*, 9 March 1946, in *Wild Flag*.

164   "Archy and Mehitabel, between the two of them": EBW,

"Don Marquis," *OMM.* Actually White doesn't capitalize Archy's name, following common newspaper practice then because Archy himself could not work the shift key of Marquis's typewriter; but in White's introduction to the Marquis omnibus White rejects this idea and follows Marquis's own practice, which was to capitalize the names of his characters.

164 "The details of his creative life": Ibid.

164 "To interpret humor": Ibid.

165 his gumdrop-size neighbor: *Charlotte*, ch. 5.

166 peach-colored cotton candy: Ibid.

166 The sac's material felt: This description comes from my having examined and held such egg cases myself.

167 "Nobody styled the orb web of a spider": EBW, "The Motorcar," *Harper's*, in *OMM.*

167 "the elasticity of democracy": EBW, "Academic Freedom," *NY*, 26 February 1949, in *Every Day.*

Chapter 13: ZUCKERMAN'S BARN

169 *"I discovered, quite by accident"*: EBW, letter to Gene Deitch, 12 January [1971], in *Letters.*

169 "I guess it depends": EBW, letter to Cass Canfield, 19 May 1950, not in *Letters*; quoted by Elledge, p. 293.

170 wrote nothing for "Notes and Comment": Elledge, p. 293.

170 campaign for larger taxicabs: EBW, letter to Harold Ross [January?] 1950," in *Letters.*

170 *The Thirteen Clocks*: EBW, letter to James Thurber, 6 June 1950, in *Letters.*

171   *"It is a straight report"*: EBW, letter to Gene Deitch, 12
      January [1971], in *Letters*.
172   focused his despair and his .22 rifle: EBW, "Fall," *Harper's*,
      in *OMM*.

Chapter 14: SPINNINGWORK

175   *"In writing of a spider"*: EBW, letter to Gene Deitch, 12
      January [1971], in *Letters*.
175   McCook: All quotations from *American Spiders and Their
      Spinningwork*.
177   Andy covered many sheets of yellow draft paper: Cornell.
      All quotations, as well as descriptions of EBW's manu-
      script drafts of *Charlotte*, are from Cornell, especially Box
      2, Folders A, B, and C. In same folders see EBW's dia-
      grams of spiderwebs and barn layout, some within text,
      some separate.
181   Comstock: All quotations from *The Spider Book*.
181   Gertsch: All quotations from *American Spiders*.

Chapter 15: PAEAN

189   *"A paean to life"*: EBW, letter to Gene Deitch, January 12
      [1971], in *Letters*.
189   "Twenty-five years of working": Quoted in Davis, p. 157.
189   Joe was halfway through college: Ibid., p. 156.
189   to lend Nabokov a desperately needed advance: Ibid., p. 144.
190   "a subtle and loving reader": Ibid., p. 151.
190   he found himself caring deeply: EBW, letter to Dorothy
      Joan Harris, 28 June 1974, in *Letters*.

190   Walt Disney forced animals to dance: EBW, letter to
       Gene Deitch, 12 January [1971], in *Letters.*

191   didn't want to twist their personalities: Ibid.

191   *"The barn——"*: All quotations from EBW's drafts of *Charlotte*, Cornell, Box 2.

195   "the basic satisfaction in farming is manure": EBW, "A
       Winter Diary," *Harper's*, January 1941, in *OMM.*

195   "I keep it in a carton": EBW letter to Cass Canfield,
       dated 19 October [1949], in *Letters.*

196   He finished the draft: Elledge, p. 295.

196   "I've recently finished another children's book": EBW letter to Ursula Nordstrom, dated 1 March 1951, in *Letters.*

196   "I would rather wait a year": EBW, letter to Eugene Saxton, 11 April 1939, in *Letters.*

197   owned a pig named Wilbur: EBW, letter to J. Wilbur Wolf,
       25 March 1953, in *Letters.*

197   Andy changed it to Lurvy: Neumeyer, p. 18, n. 11, citing
       Folder B from Cornell archives.

197   "Home is the part of our life": EBW, "Home Song," *NY*,
       5 February 1944.

198   "None of us like him": *Charlotte*, ch. 7.

198   Fern's father sounded a bit like Samuel White: Peter F.
       Neumeyer makes this point in his *Annotated Charlotte's Web*, p. 5.

198   Dorian, after the ancient Greeks: I didn't notice this myself. I ran across it in Neumeyer, p. 105, n. 1. It seems to
       me a convincing argument that White deliberately chose
       this uncommon name. He was fully aware of the ancient
       pastoral themes in his story and even referred to the book
       as a "paean," the ancient Greek word for a hymn of praise.

199   *They get the cocker spaniel*: Neumeyer, p. 20, n. 14, and p. 97, n. 9, citing Cornell, Folder A.

201   she said she tired of him: Cornell, Box 2, Folder B.

201   *"A man who is dealing"*: EBW, letter to Childhood Revisited Class, 9 March 1973, in *Letters*.

202   One of the parts of the book he particularly liked: EBW, from Cornell archives, cited by Neumeyer, p. 17, n. 8, cites Cornell, Box II, Folder II.

205   the saddest sentence in the book: EBW, Cornell, Box 2, Folder B.

206   "A's letter to the Times": KSW to Mrs. George F. Murray, 27 April 1949, quoted by Davis, p. 140.

Chapter 16: SOME BOOK

208   *"The web glistened"*: EBW, *Charlotte*, ch. 11.

208   "That's the best news I've had": Nordstrom, letter to EBW, 19 March 1951, in *Nordstrom*.

209   in March 1952: Neumeyer, p. 207.

209   her office at Harper & Brothers: Harper office description: Jean Craighead George, *Journey Inward*, pp. 213–14, quoted in *Nordstrom*, pp. xxix–xxx.

209   Nordstrom was too busy: Most of the details about White's delivery of the *Charlotte's Web* manuscript come from an article Nordstrom wrote, "Stuart, Wilbur, Charlotte: A Tale of Tales," *New York Times*, 12 May 1974. Neumeyer, p. 207, says White delivered the manuscript on March 29, but he and Nordstrom were exchanging letters about it a few days before this date.

210   Nordstrom sat down in her office: Nordstrom, quoted by

Susan Heller Anderson, "Ursula Nordstrom, 78, a Nurturer of Authors for Children, Is Dead," *New York Times*, 12 October 1988.

210 Nordstrom found the story remarkably engaging: Ursula Nordstrom, "Stuart, Wilbur, Charlotte: A Tale of Tales," *New York Times*, 12 May 1974.

210 She wasted no time: Nordstrom, letter to EBW, 2 April 1952, in *Nordstrom*.

211 had bought a television set: Nordstrom, letter to Ruth Krauss, 29 January 1952, in *Nordstrom*.

212 five hundred dollars against future royalties: Nordstrom, letter to EBW, 21 March 1952, in *Letters*.

212 Milton Greenstein, a lawyer: Guth, *Letters*, p. 311, n. 1.

212 "It sounds like an extravagant dream": EBW, letter to Ursula Nordstrom, 27 March 1952, in *Letters*. See also editor Guth's note to this letter.

212 "Charlotte's children": Ibid.

212 "I believe Charlotte is the first": Ursula Nordstrom, letter to EBW, 2 April 1952 in *Nordstrom*.

213 A spider writing in a web: Walter R. Brooks, *Freddy and Mr. Camphor*. Originally published in 1944; reprinted, New York: Overlook Press, 2000.

214 They discussed the draft: Nordstrom, letter to KSW, 10 April 1952, in *Letters*.

214 Garth Williams . . . was already sketching: Nordstrom, letter to EBW, 2 April 1952, in *Letters*.

215 changed the chapter title: Letter from Nordstrom to KSW, 10 April 1952, in *Letters*.

215 he had ideas of his own: Nordstrom, letter to EBW, 10 April 1952, in *Nordstrom*.

216   a regular advance against royalties: Nordstrom to Garth
       Williams, 29 March 1950, in *Nordstrom*.

216   a dozen other books: Entry on Williams in *Something about
       the Author* 66.

216   peripatetic life: Joan Brest Friedberg, "Garth Williams,"
       Dictionary of Literary Biography.

216   his barefoot Huck Finn years: William Anderson, "Garth
       Williams after Eighty," *The Horn Book Magazine* 69.2 (1993).

217   "I'm afraid he's going to be an artist": Garth Williams,
       quoted in entry in *Something about the Author* 66.

217   Williams felt that an illustrator: Garth Williams, "Illustrat-
       ing the Little House Books," *Horn Book*, December 1953.

218   This initial image he would rework: Quoted by Silvey,
       Children's Books and Their Creators, p. 685.

218   Williams found *Charlotte's Web* less interesting: Garth Wil-
       liams, unpublished letter to Peter F. Neumeyer, 2 October
       1983, quoted in Neumeyer, p. 121.

219   he even sent a clipping: Ursula Nordstrom, "Stuart, Wil-
       bur, Charlotte: A Tale of Tales," *New York Times*, 12 May
       1974.

219   sent her the New York Public Library call number: EBW,
       letter to Nordstrom, 28 March [1952], in *Letters*; Nord-
       strom, letter to EBW, 2 April 1952, in *Nordstrom*.

219   "The eyes and hair": White, letter to Nordstrom, 28 March
       [1952], in *Letters*.

220   photographs in Gertsch and McCook gruesome: Garth
       Williams, unpublished letter to Peter F. Neumeyer, 2 Oc-
       tober 1983, quoted in Neumeyer, p. 121.

220   with the scattered eight eyes that real spiders possess:
       Nordstrom, letter to EBW, 28 April 1952, in *Nordstrom*.

220   a Mona Lisa face: Guth, *Letters*, n. on pp. 353–54; Garth
      Williams, unpublished letter to Peter F. Neumeyer, 2 Oc-
      tober 1983, quoted in Neumeyer, p. 121.

220   Despite his remark to Nordstrom: Nordstrom, letter to
      KSW, 10 April 1952, in *Nordstrom*.

220   the less Charlotte looked like a person: Nordstrom, letter
      to EBW, 28 April 1952, in *Nordstrom*.

221   sketched a simpler face on the back: Ibid.

221   if he liked Charlotte as she was: Ibid.

221   "You better just draw a spider": Guth, *Letters*, n. on pp.
      353–54.

222   "sort of like a keystone": EBW, letter to Nordstrom, 28
      March [1952], in *Letters*.

222   "Charlotte's legs are equipped": EBW, letter to Nord-
      strom, 24 May 1952, in *Letters*.

222   With these almost subliminal marks: Neumeyer, p. 66.

222   But Williams privately thought: Garth Williams, unpub-
      lished letter to Peter F. Neumeyer, 2 October 1983, quoted
      in Neumeyer, pp. 200–201.

223   "rather mussy Charles Addams attic web": EBW, letter to
      Nordstrom, 24 May 1952, in *Letters*.

223   Nordstrom had questions: Nordstrom, letter to EBW, 20
      June 1952, in *Nordstrom*.

223   "no goose-lover in this house": EBW, letter to Nord-
      strom, 24 May 1952, in *Letters*.

224   he painted around its web: Nordstrom, "Stuart, Wilbur,
      Charlotte: A Tale of Tales," *New York Times*, 12 May 1974.

224   thought of her as one of Charlotte's daughters: EBW, let-
      ter to Ursula Nordstrom, 23 July 1952, in *Letters*.

Chapter 17: COMPLETION

226 *The terrible excitement*: EBW, "Poetry," November 1939, in *OMM*.

226 Richard de Rochemont: EBW, letter to Richard de Rochemont, 28 April 1952, in *Letters*.

227 hepatitis: EBW, letter to Ursula Nordstrom, 23 July 1952, in *Letters*.

227 "disemboweled": EBW, letter to H. K. Rigg, 11 December 1951, in *Letters*.

227 The funeral: EBW, letter to Frank Sullivan, [17? December, 1951], in *Letters*.

227 "an Atlas who lacked muscle tone": Ibid.

228 "The things that matter": Ibid.

228 J. D. Salinger: EBW, letter to J. D. Salinger, 17 December 1951, in *Letters*.

228 turned down an invitation: EBW, letter to Kenneth Bird, 28 December 1951, in *Letters*.

229 George VI: See copy of unpublished letter in Cornell, 28 March [1952], originally from Hamish Hamilton office, signed only "Jimmy."

229 "remember that writing": EBW, letter to Elizabeth S——, 10 December 1951, in *Letters*.

229 *"I write largely for myself"*: EBW, letter to Childhood Revisited Class, 9 March 1973, in *Letters*.

229 *Charlotte's Web* was published: Elledge, p. 298.

229 Eudora Welty . . . raved: Eudora Welty, "Along Came a Spider," *New York Times*, 19 October 1952.

230 Moore was expressing her dissatisfaction: Nordstrom, letter to EBW, 23 October 1952, in *Nordstrom*.

230 Moore's review appeared: Anne Carroll Moore, "The Three Owls Notebook," *Horn Book Magazine*, December 1952; reprint available at http://www.hbook.com/maga zine/articles/1950s/dec52_moore.asp.

231 "Would it be all right": EBW, letter to Ursula Nord strom, 5 December 1952, in *Letters*.

231 "Charmingly sentimental tale": Guth, note to EBW, letter to Cass Canfield, 29 December 1952, in *Letters*.

231 Bennett Cerf proclaimed: Bennett Cerf, "Trade Winds," *The Saturday Review*, 15 November 1952.

231 "Though I am not usually attracted": M. F. Kieran, review of *Charlotte, Atlantic Monthly*, December 1952.

232 "This is really more": Katherine Kinkead, review, *NY*, 6 December 1952.

232 "such tangible magic": P. L. Travers, *New York Herald Tribune Book Review*, 16 November 1952.

232 Andy also liked a remark: EBW, letter to Cass Canfield, 29 December 1952, in *Letters*.

232 Louis de Rochemont: EBW, letter to Stanley Hart White, 11 January 1953, in *Letters*.

233 Andy had spent many hours: EBW, "Ascension," *NY*, 17 March 1928, in *Writings*.

233 four-and-a-half-year-old daughter, Caroline: EBW, letter to Ursula Nordstrom, 22 October 1952, in *Nordstrom*, and p. 55, n. 2 to Nordstrom's letter to White, 23 October 1952, in *Nordstrom*.

234 When the students: EBW, letter to "Pupils of Grade 5-B, Larchmont, New York," 26 December 1952, in *Letters*.

234 "I do not like to betray": EBW, letter distributed by Harper & Brothers, in *Cornell*.

235   Roger's ten-year-old daughter: Roger Angell, "Andy,"
       NY, 14 February 2005.

CODA: AFTER *CHARLOTTE*

236   treated Ursula Nordstrom to a grand lunch: and quotations
       in paragraph: Nordstrom, letter to Meindert DeJong, 4
       March 1953, *Nordstrom*, pp. 63–64.

237   affectionate nicknames: *Nordstrom*, p. xix.

237   more comfortable drawing animals than people: William
       Anderson, "Garth Williams after Eighty," *The Horn
       Book*, March/April 1993.

237   denounced as "integrationist propaganda": Unsigned As-
       sociated Press story, *Los Angeles Evening Mirror News*, 22
       May 1959.

238   his original drawing for the cover: Michael Cavna,
       " 'Charlotte's Web' Cover Art Snares $155K at Auction,"
       Washington Post, 16 October 2010.

238   tweed suit and Ferragamo pumps: Nan Robertson, "Life
       without Katharine: E. B. White and His Sense of Loss,"
       New York Times, 4 April 1980.

239   "I am very sad": John Updike, letter to KSW, 27 Decem-
       ber 1959, quoted in Davis, p. 180.

239   "I must say . . . she looks": EBW, letter to Morris Bishop
       [2 January 1961], in *Letters.*

239   emergency appendectomy: Davis, p. 191.

239   talked to the *New York Times*: Nan Robertson, "Life
       without Katharine: E. B. White and His Sense of Loss,"
       New York Times, 4 April 1980.

240   Andy gave Louis's father: EBW, *The Trumpet of the Swan*, ch. 4.

240   Nordstrom suggested . . . collected letters: *Nordstrom*, p. 363, n. 1.

240   Andy loaded a canoe: Roger Angell, "Andy," *NY*, 14 February 2005.

241   managed medical care for his father: Ibid.

241   "You did, Dad" and "Not bad": Ibid.

242   a yellow school bus: All information in this scene comes from Mary and Robert Gallant, in interviews with the author, July 2009 and December 2010.

SELECTED BIBLIOGRAPHY AND FURTHER READING

This bibliography comprises all books cited within the text or the notes to the book, as well as others useful for the student or general reader interested in E. B. White. It omits articles that are cited only once or twice in the notes, unless they have special significance.

BOOKS BY E. B. WHITE

Charlotte's Web. New York: Harper & Brothers, 1952.

The Elements of Style, New York: Macmillan, 1959 (Based upon Strunk's privately printed 1919 edition.) by William Strunk Jr., and E. B. White.

Every Day Is Saturday. New York: Harper & Brothers, 1934.

The Fox of Peapack and Other Poems. New York: Harper & Brothers, 1938.

Here Is New York. New York: Harper & Brothers, 1949.

Introduction, *The Lives and Times of Archy and Mehitabel*, by Don Marquis. Garden City, NY: Doubleday, 1950.

Is Sex Necessary? or, Why You Feel the Way You Do, by James Thurber and E. B. White. New York: Harper, 1929.

The Lady Is Cold. New York: Harper & Brothers, 1929.

Letters of E. B. White, edited by Dorothy Lobrano Guth. New York: Harper & Row, 1976. Revised edition, edited by Martha White. New York: HarperCollins, 2006.

One Man's Meat. New York: Harper & Brothers, 1942.

Poems and Sketches of E. B. White. New York: HarperCollins, 1983.

The Points of My Compass. New York: Harper & Row, 1962.

Quo Vadimus? or, The Case for the Bicycle. New York: Harper & Brothers, 1939.

The Second Tree from the Corner. New York: Harper & Row, 1954.

Stuart Little. New York: Harper & Brothers, 1945.

A Subtreasury of American Humor, coedited with Katharine S. White. New York: Coward-McCann, 1941.

The Trumpet of the Swan. New York: Harper & Row, 1970.

The Wild Flag: Editorials from The New Yorker *on Federal World Government and Other Matters.* Boston: Houghton Mifflin, 1946.

Writings from The New Yorker, *1927–1976*, edited by Rebecca M. Dale. New York: HarperCollins, 1990.

Other Sources

Adney, Tappan. "Milicete Indian natural history." *Abstract of the Proceedings of the Linnaean Society of New York* 5 (1892–93).

Anderson, A. J. E. *E. B. White: A Bibliography.* Metuchen, NJ: Scarecrow, 1978.

Angell, Roger. *Let Me Finish*. New York: Harcourt, 2006. See especially his essay "Andy."

Aron, Cindy S. *Working at Play: A History of Vacations in the United States*. New York: Oxford University Press, 1999.

Ashley, Sally. *F.P.A.: The Life and Times of Franklin Pierce Adams*. New York: Beaufort, 1986.

Batteiger, John. Marquis bibliographer and host of http://don marquis.com.

Bernstein, Burton. *Thurber: A Biography*. New York: Dodd, Mead, 1975.

Blother, Joseph. *Faulkner: A Biography*. University Press of Mississippi, 1974.

Blount, Margaret. *Animal Land: The Creatures of Children's Fiction*. New York: William Morrow, 1974.

Brunetta, Leslie, and Catherine L. Craig. *Spider Silk*. New Haven, CT: Yale University Press, 2010.

Burroughs, John. *Wake-Robin*. Boston: Houghton Mifflin, 1904.

———. "Real and Sham Natural History," *Atlantic Monthly*, March 1903.

———. *Time and Change*. Boston: Houghton Mifflin, 1912. See especially "The Gospel of Nature."

Comstock, John Henry. *The Spider Book: A Manual for the Study of the Spiders* . . . Revised and edited by W. J. Gertsch. Ithaca: Cornell University Press, 1948. (Originally published in 1912.) This was one of White's three major technical sources for information about spiders.

Davis, Linda H. *Onward and Upward: A Biography of Katharine S. White*. New York: Harper & Row, 1987.

Elledge, Scott. *E. B. White: A Biography.* New York: Norton, 1984.

Epstein, Joseph. "E. B. White, Dark and Lite." *Commentary,* April 1986. Reprinted in *Partial Payments: Essays on Writers and Their Lives.* New York: W. W. Norton, 1991.

Forbes, Peter. *The Gecko's Foot: Bio-Engineering New Materials from Nature.* New York: W. W. Norton, 2005.

Gannon, Susan R., Suzanne Rahn, and Ruth Anne Thompson. *St. Nicholas and Mary Mapes Dodge: The Legacy of a Children's Magazine.* Jefferson, NC: McFarland & Co., 2004.

Gertsch, Willis J. *American Spiders.* Princeton, NJ: Van Nostrand, 1949.

Gill, Brendan. *Here at* The New Yorker. New York: Random House, 1975.

Grant, Jane. *Ross,* The New Yorker *and Me.* New York: Reynal/William Morrow, 1968.

Hall, Katharine Romans. *E. B. White: A Bibliographic Catalogue of Printed Materials in the Department of Rare Books, Cornell University Library.* New York: Garland, 1979.

Hearn, Michael Patrick. *The Annotated Wizard of Oz.* New York: W. W. Norton, 2000.

Hillyard, Paul. *The Book of the Spider: From Arachnophobia to the Love of Spiders.* New York: Random House, 1994.

Holmes, Charles S. *The Clocks of Columbus: The Literary Career of James Thurber.* New York: Atheneum, 1972.

Kahn, E. J. *About* The New Yorker *and Me.* New York: Putnam, 1979.

Kammen, Michael G. *A Time to Every Purpose: The Four Seasons in American Culture.* University of North Carolina Press, 2004.

Kramer, Dale. *Ross and* The New Yorker. Garden City, NY: Doubleday, 1951.

Kunkel, Thomas. *Genius in Disguise: Harold Ross of* The New Yorker. New York: Random House, 1995.

Lerer, Seth. *Children's Literature: A Reader's History from Aesop to Harry Potter.* Chicago: University of Chicago Press, 2008.

Levin, Betty. "The Universe and Old Macdonald." In *Innocence and Experience: Essays and Conversations on Children's Literature,* edited by Barbara Harrison and Gregory Maguire. New York: Lothrop, Lee & Shepard, 1987.

Long, William J. *A Little Brother to the Bear.* Lexington, MA: Ginn and Company, 1903. Reprint, Chapel Hill, NC: Yesterday's Classics, 2006.

Long, William J. *Ways of Wood Folk.*

Lutts, Ralph H. "John Burroughs and the Honey Bee: Bridging Science and Emotion in Environmental Writing." *ISLE: Interdisciplinary Studies in Literature and Environment* 3, no. 2, pp. 85–100.

Lutts, Ralph H. *The Nature Fakers: Wildlife, Science, & Sentiment.* University Press of Virginia, 1990.

Maiken Peter T. *Night Trains: The Pullman System in the Golden Years of American Rail Travel.* Baltimore: Johns Hopkins, 1992.

Mankoff, Robert, editor. *The Complete Cartoons of* The New Yorker. New York: Black Dog & Leventhal, 2004.

Marcus, Leonard S. *Minders of Make-Believe: Idealists, Entrepreneurs, and the Shaping of American Children's Literature.* Boston: Houghton Mifflin, 2008.

Marquis, Don. *Archy and Mehitabel.* Garden City, NY: Doubleday, Page, 1927.

————. *Archy's Life of Mehitabel*. Garden City, NY: Doubleday, Doran, 1933.

————. *Archy Does His Part*. Garden City, NY: Doubleday, Doran, 1935.

————. *The Annotated Archy and Mehitabel*. Edited by Michael Sims. New York: Penguin Classics, 2006.

————. *Dreams and Dust*. New York: Harper & Brothers, 1915.

Maxwell, William. "The Whites." In *The Outermost Dream: Essays and Reviews*. New York: Knopf, 1989.

McCook, Henry C. *American Spiders and Their Spinningwork: A Natural History of the Orbweaving Spiders of the United States with Special Regard to Their Industry and Habits*. Published by the author, 1889.

McCord, David. "E. B. White." In *20th-Century Children's Writers*, edited by D. L. Kirkpatrick. New York: St. Martin's, 1978.

Neumeyer, Peter F. *The Annotated Charlotte's Web*. New York: HarperCollins, 1994.

Nordstrom, Ursula. *Dear Genius: The Letters of Ursula Nordstrom*. Edited by Leonard S. Marcus. New York: HarperCollins, 1998.

Ross, Harold. *Letters from the Editor*. Edited by Thomas Kunkel. New York: Modern Library, 2000.

Russell, Isabel. *Katharine and E. B. White: An Affectionate Memoir*. New York: Norton, 1984.

Sale, Roger. *Fairy Tales and After: From Snow White to E. B. White*. Cambridge, MA: Harvard University Press, 1978.

Schmitt, Peter J. *Back to Nature: The Arcadian Myth in Urban America*. New York: Oxford University Press, 1969.

Seton, Ernest Thompson. *Lives of the Hunted: Containing a True Account of the Doings of Five Quadrupeds and Three Birds and, in*

Elucidation of the Same, over 200 Drawings. New York: Charles Scribner's Sons, 1902.

————. *Wild Animals I Have Known.* New York: Scribner's 1899.

Silvey, Anita, editor. *Children's Books and Their Creators.* Boston: Houghton Mifflin, 1995.

Sims, Michael. "A View from the Under Side." Introduction to *The Annotated Archy and Mehitabel.* New York: Penguin Classics, 2006.

Stewart, Frank. *A Natural History of Nature Writing.* Washington, DC: Island Press, 1995.

St. Nicholas magazine. Various issues, 1873–1917.

Tatar, Maria. *Enchanted Hunters: The Power of Stories in Childhood.* New York: W. W. Norton, 2009.

Thorson, Robert M. *Beyond Walden: The Hidden History of America's Kettle Lakes and Ponds.* New York: Walker & Company, 2009.

Thurber, James. *The Years with Ross.* Boston: Atlantic Monthly/ Little Brown, 1959.

————. *Selected Letters of James Thurber.* Edited by Helen Thurber and Edward Weeks. Boston: Little, Brown, 1981.

————. *The Dog Department: James Thurber on Hounds, Scotties, and Talking Poodles.* Edited by Michael J. Rosen. New York: HarperCollins, 2001.

Wake, Lynn Overholt. "E. B. White's Paean to Life: The Environmental Imagination of *Charlotte's Web.*" In *Wild Things: Children's Culture and Ecocriticism*, edited by Sidney I. Dobrin and Kenneth B. Kidd. Detroit: Wayne State University Press, 2004.

————. "E. B. White's Environmental Web." Ph.D. dissertation, English Department, University of Nebraska–Lincoln, 2007.

White, Katharine S. *Onward and Upward in the Garden*. New York: Farrar, Straus, 1979.

Yagoda, Ben. *About Town:* The New Yorker *and the World It Made*. New York: Scribner, 2000.

INDEX

Acadia National Park, Maine, 121
Adams, Bob, 80
Adams, Bristow, 72
Adams, Franklin Pierce (F.P.A.):
 "The Conning Tower," 62, 76,
  158
 influence of, 72, 74, 84
 White's poems published by,
  76, 114
Addams, Charles, 223
Ade, George, 150
Aesop's fables, 4, 201
Alcott, Louisa May:
 An Old-Fashioned Girl, 50
 Little Women, 214–15
Algonquin Round Table, 84, 107
Allen, Frederick Lewis, 148
Allen Cove, Maine, 122–23
 barn in, 1–2, 129–31, 242–44
 Whites' farm in, 127–35, 141,
  147–49, 167
 Whites' permanent move to,
  238–39
American Museum of Natural
 History, 88–89, 183
Andrews, Dana, 232

Angell, Ernest, 109–13
Angell, Katharine, 106–23
 children's books reviewed by,
  143–45, 146, 231
 death of, 238
 first marriage of, 109–13
 and grandchildren, 227
 health concerns of, 227, 239
 marriage to White, 115, 116
 and *New Yorker*, 102, 108, 128,
  129, 141, 143, 149, 189–90,
  238, 239
 as object of White's affections,
  106, 108, 111, 112, 207
 *Onward and Upward in the
  Garden*, 239
 pregnancy of, 118–20
 retirement of, 238–39
 trip to Paris, 108–9, 112
 White's job interview with,
  82–83
 White's later thoughts of,
  239
 and White's writings, 111, 114,
  117–18, 119–20, 146, 147, 153,
  159, 167–68, 185, 206, 207

Angell, Nancy, 109, 113–14, 115,
    119, 189
Angell, Roger:
    birth of, 110
    childhood of, 113, 119
    family of, 189, 233, 235, 241
    and his parents' divorce, 113
    and White, 115–16, 129,
        242
animals:
    amorality of, 191
    as independent actors,
        17–18
    talking, 4, 214
    White's interest in, 3–4, 9,
        10–13, 75, 130–31, 134–35,
        160–61
    in White's writings, 117–18,
        120–21, 149–50, 185, 207
anthropomorphism, 3, 43
Arable, Avery (fict.), 197
Arable, Fern (fict.), 196, 197, 198,
    206, 218, 221
arachnids, use of term, 176–77
Aranea (spider), 206
Archy (cockroach), 63–64, 74–75,
    190, 201, 207
Armstrong, Louis, 240
Arno, Peter, 228
Atlantic Monthly, The, 46, 140, 171,
    232
Autola, 24
Averill, Esther, *Jenny's Adopted
    Brothers,* 230

Baby (canary), 97, 98–99
Baclanova, Olga, 81
Barrymore, Ethel, 107
Barton, Ralph, 108
Baum, L. Frank, *The Wizard of
    Oz,* 23

Belgrade, Maine:
    White family summers in,
        35–41, 167
    White's return visit to, 139
Bellamy, Edward, 27
Bellamy, Francis, 27
Benchley, Robert, 82, 84
Benét, Stephen Vincent, 73
Bentley, Wilson A., 53–54
Beppo (Irish setter), 54, 111–12
Bigelow, Edward F., 53
Bikini Atoll, 163
Boston Red Sox, 109
Botsford, Anna, 181
Brady, E. Barrett, 51
Briand, Aristide, 89
Bridges, Jimmy, 10
Bronx Zoo, 23, 87–88
Brooks, Walter R., *Freddy and
    Mr. Camphor,* 213–14
Broun, Heywood, "It Seems to
    Me," 74
Brown, Margaret Wise, 237
    Goodnight Moon, 211
    The Little Fur Family, 216
    The Runaway Bunny, 152
Brunhoff, Jean de, *The Travels of
    Babar,* 144
Burchfield, Alice "Burch," 73
Burroughs, John, 43
    "Real and Sham Natural
        History," 46
    Wake-Robin, 46
Byron, George Gordon, Lord, 112

Camp Otter, 117
Canfield, Cass, 169, 195, 229, 231
Cantwell, Robert, 231
Carroll, Lewis:
    Alice in Wonderland, 2
    Through the Looking-Glass, 92

Cavanah, Frances, *Boyhood Adventures of Our Presidents*, 144

Cerf, Bennett, 231

Chace, Lynnwood M., and Evelyn M. Chadwick, *Little Orphan Willie-Mouse*, 144

Charlotte (spider):
death of, 180, 183, 202, 205, 215
descendants of, 206, 224–25
name of, 1, 181–82, 193, 197
scientific data on, 180–82; *see also* spiders
spider traits of, 191, 200–201, 203, 207, 219–23
and Wilbur, 199, 207, 210, 221, 222
words in web of, 199–200, 223

Charlotte's Web (White):
author himself reflected in, 204–5
author's public letter about, 234–35
author's reading of, 243–44
barn in, 171–72, 192–93, 194, 203, 206, 207
characters in, 190–92, 196–97, 199–200, 202–3, 205; *see also specific characters*
closing of, 205–7, 208, 215
contract for, 211–12
dung as motif in, 194, 195
illustrations for, 208, 209, 214, 215–24, 238
mortality as theme in, 202–3
movie rights to, 232–33
popularity of, 5, 211, 224, 233–34, 236
publication of, 210, 215, 227, 229, 234
public response to, 229–35

research for, 173–74, 175–83, 185–88, 219
seasonal cycle in, 203, 205, 206
sources for, 2, 3, 160–61, 164–68, 185–86
writing of, 169–74, 175–88, 190–201, 205–7

Chekhov, Anton, *Uncle Vanya*, 118

children's literature, 2
animal stories in, 4, 50, 152
at Harper, 151–52, 236
for Katharine's review, 143–45, 146, 231
nature writers, 42–47
and Nordstrom's career, 151–53, 236–37
reviews of, 230
Williams's illustrations for, 156, 208–9, 215–16, 217, 237–38

Childs restaurant, New York, 80–81

Chrysler Building, New York, 232–33

cockroaches, 163

Cohan, George M., "Over There," 65

Comstock, John Henry, *The Spider Book*, 181, 182, 183, 185

Conan Doyle, Arthur, 62
"The Adventure of the Speckled Band," 88

Connelly, Marc, 84

Coolidge, Calvin, 78, 100

Copeland, Charles, 43

Cornell University:
Cornell Daily Sun, 72–73
military training in, 71
White in, 64, 66, 69–77

Crusade in Europe (TV), 226

Cushman, Howard, 196

Daisy (dog), 119, 120–21
Day, Clarence, 146
Dempsey, Jack, 97
Denman, Billy, 24, 29
Disney, Walt, 190
Dixie, Henry E., 152
Dodge, Mary Mapes, 49–50
Dodgson, Charles (Carroll), 2
Donald Duck, 190
Donovan, John, *I'll Get There*, 237
Doubleday and Company, 161–62,
    163

Eeyore (donkey), 2
Eighteenth Amendment, 75–76
Einstein, Albert, 91–92, 116
Eisenhower, Dwight D., 226
Elements of Style, The (Strunk &
    White), 5, 240
English sparrows, 93–95

Fadiman, Clifton, 3
Farm Cadet Corps, 65–66
Farrar, Straus & Giroux, 239
Faulkner, William, 51
Fields, Eugene, "Sharps and
    Flats," 84
Film Fun, 77
Fitzgerald, Scott, 51
Fitzhugh, Louise, *Long Secret*, 236
Forster, E. M., 234
Francis (movie), 214
Frank Seaman, Inc., 76–77, 85, 158
Frascino, Edward, 238
Fred (dachshund), 161
Freeman, Don, 153
Fry, Rosalie K., *Bumblebuzz*, 144

Galbreath, Mike, 80
Gallant, Mary and Robert, 1, 2,
    242–44

Gatti-Casazza, Giulio, 79
George VI, king of England,
    229
Gertsch, Willis J., 181, 183–84
    American Spiders, 183, 184, 185,
    186, 188, 219, 220
Gibbs, Wolcott, 141
Gilbert, Henry, 216
Gish, Lillian, 118
Golden Books, 209
Grahame, Kenneth, *The Wind in
    the Willows*, 154, 201–2
Grand Central Station, New
    York, 35, 77
Great Depression, 128, 140
Greenstein, Milton, 212
Griffith, Mary, 237, 240

Halley's Comet, 17
Harding, Warren G., 77–78, 110
Harper & Brothers:
    and *Charlotte's Web*, 169, 195,
    208, 215, 234, 236
    children's department of,
    151–52, 236
    and contracts, 211–12
    and *Is Sex Necessary?*, 104–5
    and *The Lady Is Cold*, 104
    and Nordstrom, 151–55,
    209–11, 236–37
    and *Stuart Little*, 147, 151, 153,
    208, 229
    and White's collected letters,
    240
Harper's, 112
    "One Man's Meat" in, 141, 142,
    148, 169, 204
    White's essays in, 140–41, 143,
    161, 163, 204
Harriman, William Karl, *The
    Story of Tea*, 144

Harris, Jed, 118
Hart, James McDougal, 20
Hart, William, 20–21
Harvey, Morton, 65
Here Is New York (documentary),
226–27, 232
Herriman, George, 162
Hesse, Mildred, 60–61, 65, 66
Hippodrome Theater, New York,
23
Hoban, Russell, 237
Horace Waters & Company,
19–20
Horn Book Magazine, 230
Houdini, Harry, 81
Hudson River School, 20
Hughes, Charles Evans, 63

Ingersoll, Ralph, 140, 232
Irvin, Rea, 103, 116

Jacoby, Lois, 226
Johnson, Crockett, *Harold and the
Purple Crayon*, 211
Joy (spider), 206

Kaufman, George S., 107
Keaton, Buster, 77
Kellogg, Frank B., 89–90
Kellogg-Briand Pact, 89
Kerr, M. E., *Dinky Hocker Shoots
Smack!*, 237
Kieran, M. F., 231–32
Kinkead, Katherine, 232,
233
Kipling, Rudyard,
"Rikki-Tikki-Tavi," 88
Kirkus, Virginia, 152
Kirkus Reviews, 152
Knopf, Alfred, 107
Kober, Arthur, 84

Krauss, Ruth, *A Hole Is to Dig*,
211
Krazy Kat, 162

Lardner, Ring, 73, 84
Lawson, Robert, 153–54
Leaf, Munro, *The Story of
Ferdinand*, 153
Lewis, Sinclair, *Babbitt*, 76
Liddell, Alice, 2
Lincoln, Abraham, 50
Linnaeus, Carolus, 181
Little, Stuart (human), 155
Lobrano, Gus, 80, 112, 170, 227
Lombardo, Guy, 158
London, Jack, 47
Longfellow, Henry Wadsworth,
62
Long, William J., 43–45
Beasts of the Field, 43
detractors of, 46, 47
Following the Deer, 43
Fowls of the Air, 43
influence of, 131, 135
A Little Brother to the Bear, 44,
52
Ways of Wood Folk, 43–44
Lurvy (fict.), 197, 220
Lustig, Elsie Louise, 52

Mac (collie), 11–12
Magdol, Rosanne, 97
Maine:
Allen Cove, 122–23, 127–35,
167
White family summers in,
34–41, 121–23
White's barn in, 1–2, 129–31
White's memoirs of, 48
Whites' permanent move to,
238–39

Marquis, Don:
  "The Almost Perfect State," 163
  Archy and Mehitabel, 63–64,
    162–64, 201
  Archyology, 238
  death of, 163
  Dreams & Dust, 75
  influence of, 72, 74–75, 84, 136,
    162–64, 198, 207
  "The Name," 75
  and the Old Soak, 75
  "The Sun Dial," 62–64
Marx, Julius H. "Groucho," 107
Marx Brothers, 107
McCarthy, Mary, 189
McCook, Henry C., *American
    Spiders and Their Spinning-
    work*, 175–77, 179–80, 181,
    219–20
McGuire, Kathryn, 77
McKinley, William, 13
Mehitabel (cat), 64, 75, 198, 201
Mendel, Kenny, 30
Millay, E. Vincent, 51
Milne, A. A., 144, 201–2
Montaigne, Michel Eyquem de, 5
Moore, Anne Carroll, 146, 147,
    153, 230–31
Morley, Christopher, 73, 76, 84,
    136
Mount Vernon, New York:
  egg collection in, 29, 131
  high school in, 55, 60, 61–62
  schools in, 26–28
  stable in, 10–11, 12–13, 14, 129,
    167
  White family homes in, 13–15,
    32, 40–41, 65
Mr. Ed, 214
Muir, John, 43
Mutt (dog), 73

Nabokov, Vladimir, 189–90
Nation, The, 74
nature:
  authors writing about, 42–47,
    50
  White's interest in, 3, 29, 42,
    87, 90
Nellie (spider), 206
New, Harry, 77
Newberry, Rosie and John, 115
Newmark, J. H., 85
Newsweek, 231
New Yorker, The:
  cartoons, 78–79, 100–102,
    116
  and *Charlotte's Web*, 232
  Christmas issue, 81–82
  critical views of, 140
  "Desk Calendar," 111
  first issue of, 78–79
  format of, 84
  growth of, 84, 127
  "Home Song," 149, 197
  "New Beauty of Tone in 1925
    Song Sparrow," 79
  "Notes & Comment," 84, 129,
    140, 147, 148, 150, 158, 162,
    167, 170
  "Of All Things," 79
  "Onward and Upward in the
    Garden," 238
  "Profiles," 79
  at quarter-century mark, 189
  "The Talk of the Town," 84
  "To the Bronze Bust of Holley
    in Washington Square,"
    96–97
  "Vermin," 149–50
  voice and style of, 107–8, 140
  White on staff of, 85, 86, 128
  White's job offer with, 82–85

White's submissions to, 79,
80–81, 89, 93–95, 108, 140,
141, 159–60, 169
New York Herald Tribune, 232
New York Post, 74, 76
New York Public Library, 146,
173, 219, 230, 231
New York Sun, 62–64, 74–75, 163
New York Times, 74, 77, 206
New York Times Book Review, 229
New York Tribune, 62, 76
New York World, 74, 76, 158
New York Zoological Park
(Bronx Zoo), 23, 87–88
Nordstrom, Ursula:
and *Charlotte's Web*, 196,
208–10, 213, 215, 219, 220–21,
223, 227, 230, 233, 234
and Harper, 151–55, 209–11,
236–37
in later years, 237
professional reputation of, 211,
236–37
The Secret Language, 236
and *Stuart Little*, 151, 153
Ursula Nordstrom Books, 237
and White's collected letters,
240

O'Connor, Donald, 214
O'Hara, John, 189
Oracle, The (Mount Vernon
High), 61–62
Osborn, Mary, 96–97, 99, 104

Paine, Albert Bigelow, *Hollow Tree
and Deep Woods Book*, 51
Parker, Dorothy, 73, 84
Penn, Irving, 159
Perkins, Osgood, 118
Pervear, Howard, 127

Peterson, Roger Tory, 141
Pledge of Allegiance, U.S., 27
Potter, Beatrix, 2
Presidential Medal of Freedom,
240
Prohibition, 75
Pulitzer Prize, 240
Punch, 78, 216, 228

Queensboro Bridge, 201

Ramsey, Doris H., 52
Raymond, Ida Louise, 152
Rey, H. A., *Curious George Rides a
Bike*, 230
Rey, Margret and H. A., *Curious
George*, 152
Roberts, Charles G. D., 47
Robert the Bruce, 212–13
Robin, Christopher (fict.), 2,
201–2
Rochemont, Richard de,
226, 232
Roosevelt, Theodore, 13, 47, 65
Roosevelt Hotel, New York,
157–58
Rose, Carl, 101
Ross, Harold:
death of, 227–28
health problems of, 170
and *New Yorker*, 84, 100–102,
103, 106–7, 108, 128, 149,
189, 227
personal traits of, 83, 107, 108
and *Stuart Little*, 154–55
White's job interview with,
82–84
White's work for, 84–85, 140,
149, 227–28
Runyon, Damon, *In Our Town*, 216
Rural New Yorker, The, 133

Sacco and Vanzetti, trial of, 89
Sackville-West, Vita, 51
Saint-Exupery, Antoine de, *The Little Prince*, 143
St. Nicholas, 49–54, 74, 76, 167
    St. Nicholas League, 50–52, 111
Salinger, J. D., 228
Saturday Review of Literature, The, 136
Saxton, Eugene, 147
Schuler, Freddie, 18, 29–30, 48
Scribner's, 140
Selden, George, *Cricket in Times Square*, 238
Sendak, Maurice, 211, 237
Sergeant, Katharine, 51
Seton, Ernest Thompson, 43, 45–46
    detractors of, 46, 47
    Lives of the Hunted, 45
    Wild Animals I Have Known, 45
Seuss, Dr., *The 500 Hats of Bartholomew Cubbins*, 145
Sewell, Anna, *Black Beauty*, 43
Sharp, Margery, *The Rescuers*, 237
Shawn, William, 228, 238
Shepard, Ernest, 154
Shirer, William, 100
Silverstein, Shel, 236
Simon & Schuster, 208
    Elves and Fairies, 216
Simpson, Kezzie, 20
Slaven, Nila, 121
sparrows:
    English, 93–95
    song, 79, 203
    white-throated, 141
Speaker, Tris, 109–10
spiders:
    anatomy of, 186–88
    as arachnids, 176–77, 188

Aranea cavatica, 181–82
    ballooning, 183–84
    in children's books, 212–13
    egg sacs of, 165–66, 180, 204
    killing and eating their prey, 185, 221
    life cycle of, 164–67, 173–74, 177–78, 180, 183, 215
    mating of, 186
    as metaphors, 167–68, 185
    "Natural History," 117–18, 167–68, 185, 207
    orb weavers and their webs, 178–79, 180, 184–86
    reclusiveness of, 176
    usefulness of, 179–80
    use of term, 177
    White's interest in, 1, 2, 13, 117, 164–68, 234–35
    White's research on, 173–74, 175–83, 185–88, 219
Stafford, Jean, 189
Stewart, A. T., 74
Strunk, William Jr., *The Elements of Style*, 5, 71–72, 240
Stuart Little (White):
    contract for, 212
    illustrations for, 153–54, 216, 217, 218, 219, 222
    and Nordstrom, 151, 153
    popularity of, 5, 155–56, 211, 229
    publication of, 154
    public response to, 153, 154–55, 208, 230
    writing of, 145–47, 150–51, 173, 196
Subtreasury of American Humor, A, 150, 151
Suzy (West Highland terrier), 239

Teale, Edwin Way, 196
  Near Horizons, 163
Templeton (rat):
  and Charlotte's words, 199, 200
  at the fair, 204
  name of, 197
  rodent traits of, 191, 198, 200,
    201, 202, 204, 218, 223
  sources for character of, 172
Thomas, Eileen, 58–60
Thomas, J. Parnell, 58
Thoreau, Henry David, 141, 155
Thurber, James, 163, 196
  drawings by, 102–3, 104–5, 186
  Is Sex Necessary? (with White),
    103–5
  at *New Yorker*, 100–105
  "The Thin Red Leash," 119
  The Thirteen Clocks, 170
Travers, P. L., *Mary Poppins*, 232
Tunney, Gene, 97
Twain, Mark, 17
  Tom Sawyer Abroad, 50

Updike, John, 238

Villa, Pancho, 63
Vogue, 159

Walden Pond, 141
Watson, Aldren, 153
Weigold, Hugo, 88
Welty, Eudora, 229–30
White, Albert (brother):
  childhood of, 15, 16
  at Cornell, 22, 23, 24
  in Maine, 37
  teen years of, 37, 39, 56
White, Andrew Dickson, 69
White, Clara (sister), 136, 137,
  138–39

White, E. B.:
  advertising agency work of,
    76–77, 85, 158
  and Angell, *see* Angell,
    Katharine
  as author, *see* White, E. B.,
    writings of
  awards and honors to, 158–59,
    240
  birth of, 15
  and boats, 38–40
  bookstore described by, 226
  childhood of, 9–18, 19–32,
    33–41, 47–54, 139
  and children's books, 144–47
  and Cornell, 64, 66, 69–77
  and dating, 55–61, 66, 73,
    96–97, 98–99, 105
  death of, 241–42
  and depression, 26, 114
  family background of, 15,
    20–22
  and farm life, 130–35, 141–42,
    147–49, 160–61, 195, 212, 234
  fears of, 25–26, 28, 30–31, 55,
    91, 98, 118, 242
  hay fever of, 33–34, 66, 121
  health concerns of, 71, 148–49,
    159
  imagination of, 4, 25, 40, 42,
    45, 49, 56, 167
  income of, 81, 84–85, 128
  injury to, 240–41
  interest in animals, 3–4, 9,
    10–13, 75, 130–31, 134–35,
    160–61
  interest in nature, 3, 29, 42, 87,
    90
  interest in weather, 25–26, 87,
    203
  in Manhattan, 73, 80, 127

White, E. B. (*continued*)
Meccano set of, 29, 131
and music, 24
name and nicknames of, 15, 18,
69
personal traits of, 3–4, 26, 70
reputation of, 136, 140, 159,
228–29
schooling of, 26–28, 64
solitude of, 32, 40, 48–49, 87, 131
summers in Maine, 34–41,
121–23
teen years of, 55–66
and writing style, 170–71, 206,
229
White, E. B., writings of:
Archy introduction, 162–64
*Charlotte's Web, see Charlotte's
Web*
in childhood, 47–54
chronicles of everyday life,
86–95
classical references in, 198
collected letters, 1, 240
"Compost," 163
contracts for, 211–12
diary, 48, 65
early published works, 76, 81
Elements of Style (Strunk), intro
to, 5, 240
essays, 5, 140–41, 142, 143, 161,
163, 169, 204, 240
Every Day Is Saturday, 140
for *Harper's*, 140–41, 142, 143,
161, 163
"Here Is New York," 226–27
"Home Song," 149, 197
Is Sex Necessary? (with
Thurber), 103–5
to Katharine, 111, 114, 117–18,
119–20

The Lady Is Cold, 104
"Natural History," 117–18,
167–68, 185, 207
"New Beauty of Tone in 1925
Song Sparrow," 79
One Man's Meat, 169, 212
The Points of My Compass, 240
popularity of, 5–6
"Portrait," 98
to preserve memories, 47–48, 54
"Rhyme for a Reasonable
Lady," 114
The Second Tree from the Corner,
240
Stuart Little, see Stuart Little
submissions to *New Yorker*, 79,
80–81, 89, 93–95, 108, 140,
141, 159–60, 169
"To the Bronze Bust of Holley
in Washington Square,"
96–97
The Trumpet of the Swan, 5, 238,
240
"Vermin," 149–50
White, Jessie Hart (mother),
21–22, 25, 131, 135–36, 137–39
White, Joel "Joe" (son):
birth of, 120–21
and *Charlotte's Web*, 242–44
childhood of, 132, 135, 141, 143
and farm life, 160
and his father's illness, 241
as teenager, 148, 149, 160, 189,
204
White, Katharine (wife),
see Angell, Katharine
White, Lillian (sister):
advice from, 70, 137
childhood of, 15, 22, 31
in Manhattan, 73
teen years of, 57–58

White, Marion (sister), 15, 61, 227
White, Samuel (father), 19–20, 21
    and cars, 56
    death of, 136, 137, 139
    and the family, 22–23, 25, 49
    and his son's writings, 105, 198
    travel to Maine, 34–40, 135–36
White, Stanley (brother), 149
    childhood of, 15, 16–17, 21
    and Maine, 37, 139
    teen years of, 37, 39
Whitman, Charles, 65
Wilbur (pig):
    in barn environment, 194
    birth of, 203
    and Charlotte, 199, 207, 210,
        221, 222
    and end of story, 205–6
    at the fair, 202, 204
    food trough of, 203–4
    influence of, 235
    name of, 193, 197
    piglike traits of, 193, 200, 220
    sources for character of, 2,
        160–61, 164, 171, 243
    and threat of execution, 198,
        202–3, 210

in White's imagination, 184,
    187, 188
Wilder, Laura Ingalls, 152, 236,
    237
Williams, Garth:
    and Charlotte's Web, 208, 209,
        212, 214, 215–24
    as children's book illustrator,
        156, 208–9, 215–16, 217,
        237–38
    early years of, 217
    in later years, 238
    The Rabbits' Wedding, 237
    and Stuart Little, 154, 155–56,
        216, 217, 218, 219, 222, 237
Wilson, Edmund, 154, 189
Wilson, Woodrow, 63, 64, 110
Woman's Home Companion, 49,
    150
Woollcott, Alexander, 73, 84
World War I, 64–66, 71, 141
World War II, 141–42, 147,
    157, 204

Youth's Companion, The, 27

Ziegfeld Follies, 90

A NOTE ON THE AUTHOR

MICHAEL SIMS is the author of the acclaimed *Apollo's Fire: A Day on Earth in Nature and Imagination* and *Adam's Navel: A Natural and Cultural History of the Human Form*, and editor of the recent *Dracula's Guest: A Connoisseur's Collection of Victorian Vampire Stories* and *The Penguin Book of Gaslight Crime*. He lives in western Pennsylvania.